To the memory of those Islanders for whom the
Pacific colonies were Home, and not a tour of duty

Preface

This is a book about the nature of Pacific Island politics under colonial rule. By the late nineteenth century and the partition of the Pacific among the European Powers, violence and conquest were established features of cultural contact. Colonialism was a dirty business, even to contemporaries who believed in the white man's burden. The Governor of German East Africa told the Reichstag candidly in 1905: '*Kolonialpolitik* has always been the politics of conquest, and nowhere in the world does the occupation of a land by a foreign people succeed without conflict'. Governor Albert Hahl in German New Guinea frequently took exception to press reports sensationalising acts of violence because, as he pointed out, they were simply part of the inevitable conflict between 'culture' and 'savagery'. Colonial settlers in general worked and lived on the assumption that 'the natives' were constantly waiting for the opportunity to murder the white people and seize their treasures. Many believed that Pacific Islanders would not accept foreign domination, that when a foreign flag went up over their islands the people would be ready to rise up against it and must be stopped from doing so, if necessary by force.

In this book I have endeavoured to correct these assumptions, which have found their way down even to fairly recent histories of the Pacific Islands. The study deals with a whole range of political and economic activities which were characterised as resistance by fearful administrators and settlers. It sets out to show that, for the German Pacific empire, violence was not automatic nor always the prerogative of the Islander, and that resistance to Germans and their policies, when it did occur, was a great deal more subtle and limited than contemporary German colonists, and indeed a long line of later historians, were prepared to accept. Over all it demonstrates the power and ability of Pacific Islanders to make their own adjustments—of interest and of ideology—to the demands of a foreign regime and to the social changes that followed.

While the Islanders play the leading roles in these pages, I have tried also to provide a wider and deeper understanding of colonisation as it was perceived and practised by the German rulers of the islands. Consequently, there is much in the book that relates to German colonial attitudes and policy, to their methods of administration and control. This by no means amounts to an exhaustive analysis of German administration in the Pacific. My main interest was in the demands that the Germans made on the Pacific Islanders and the way in which German officials handled conflicts between the two communities.

The book is divided into two parts. The first consists of 'case studies' of Germany's three colonial areas in the Pacific, Samoa (now Western Samoa), New Guinea, and Ponape in Micronesia. If the treatment of Ponape, an island only some 334 square kilometres in area, seems to exaggerate its importance within the Pacific empire, that is because its people became the most serious threat to imperial domination within Micronesia, perhaps within the whole Pacific. For this reason it is also a convenient basis for comparison with Samoa: both were the scenes of large-scale, open opposition to German policy which required a massive response from the Reich in order to overcome. There are other reasons for comparison: both presented similar problems of scale to the German administrations, with relatively small, homogeneous populations enjoying comparable economic standards; both had superficially similar cultures; both could boast of well-developed political systems which had a long history of familiarity with European civilisation. The small size and isolation of Ponape and Samoa from metropolitan centres meant also that the character of German rule on both islands bore very much the imprint of their individual chief administrators.

German New Guinea provides a special case study. In its geographic size, in its diversity of population groups, of cultures and languages, New Guinea represented a different sort of colony from the comparatively small islands of Samoa and Ponape, indeed from any other colony in Africa or the Far East. The history of contact here is of a unique quality, for the German period was one largely of discovery and exploration, and much of the contact with local inhabitants was desultory and fleeting. The records on German New Guinea are impressionistic, of whole populations rather than of individual people, except in the areas of dense white settlement. To avoid too uneven a treatment, therefore, I have concentrated on three areas within the protectorate for which there was an abundance of evidence about the changing pattern of colonial rule. These are the Gazelle Peninsula in New Britain, Madang and the Astrolabe coast on the mainland, and the Huon Peninsula, also on the mainland, south of Madang. As an area of subsidiary interest the Admiralty Islands, Manus especially, have been touched upon because they afford a special insight into changes in traditional leadership structures brought about by German rule.

The seven chapters of Part I are intended to be analytical as well as descriptive, providing genuine histories of change and resistance in the islands. Part II of the book is an attempt to draw the three studies together in order to define what Pacific Island opposition was all about. I have not attempted to construct an abstract model about social relationships which would have universal validity whatever the historical context. Models are useful research tools and they do have explanatory value but, at least in history, they do not have a life of their own which will reduce human actions through time and over several societies to a predictive formula. Instead, I have used the case studies as a framework for interpreting and explaining 'resistance' in all its manifestations in the German Pacific, proceeding on the assumption that research on the Pacific has reached the stage where a comparative approach would help to underline cross-cultural regularities and enlarge our understanding of island societies under varying conditions of political and social stress. History may deal in the vagaries of human behaviour and the so-called uniqueness of events, but this behaviour and these events contain common elements which make them amenable to generalisation. There are sufficient similarities and differences between Samoa, Ponape and German New Guinea to provide the raw material for a serious comparison of the experience of Pacific Islanders under German rule.

Having laid out the ground plan, let me enter a caution about the book's pretensions where the history of German New Guinea is concerned. The problems of field research, of interpretation for the entire range of New Guinean societies under German rule, or even for the three areas chosen, were in the end so overwhelming that I have relied mainly on European documents (as wide a range as possible) supplemented by a large body of anthropological research, both latter-day and contemporary, in which German New Guinea is fairly well served.

However, I am aware that these sources alone fail to do justice to the whole history of Papua New Guineans. Many events, conflicts and interpretations which Papua New Guineans themselves consider important have been neglected, while the bald account of colonial rule over large areas of German New Guinea lacks the sense of regional identity which helps to stamp and explain the relations of one group of New Guineans with another and with European governments. Nonetheless I have been persuaded to publish the account of New Guinea under German rule with all its deficiencies, because basic information about the German period is still very incomplete. It is imperative to present Papua New Guineans, indeed Pacific Islanders in general, with as much information about those early times as possible so that they may refine and balance the interpretations from their own store of social knowledge and oral tradition. The work is offered in this spirit: that it may serve as a useful building block in the construction of a proper, Islands-written history of the Pacific. In the final analysis, only the Pacific Islanders can capture the full dimension which they give to their own past, and to time and change.

Acknowledgments

There are a host of people around the world without whose generous assistance this project could never have been undertaken. The book is a revised and updated version of a doctoral thesis for the University of Oxford, and I am grateful to the Rhodes Trustees, the Board of Management of the Beit Fund, the officials of the Deutscher Akademischer Austauschdienst and the Fellows of Magdalen College for unstinting financial aid throughout my research in Europe. Sincere thanks go also to the staffs of the Bundesarchiv Koblenz, the Bundesarchiv/Militararchiv Freiburg, the Hamburg Staatsarchiv, the Berlin Staatsarchiv, the Hamburger Weltwirtschaftsarchiv and members of Hamburg University for their time and patience in pointing out and providing source material. I particularly appreciate the dedication and co-operation of the Zentrales Staatsarchiv of the German Democratic Republic. I am also grateful to the authorities of the Neuendettelsau Mission, the Rheinsische Missions-Gesellschaft (now the Vereinigte Rheinische Mission), the Herz Jesu Mission and the Kapuziner Missionsprokur, the *Anthropos* Institut, the Liebenzeller Mission and the London Missionary Society for kindness and hospitality over and above that which is the due of an importunate researcher. In Australia both the staffs of the Australian Archives, Canberra, and the Mitchell Library, Sydney were indefatigable in providing material. The Government of Western Samoa was very generous in giving me use of papers on the German period in its possession.

I am most deeply indebted to several individuals: to Dr John Moses who gave the initial impetus and direction to my work; to Dr Colin Newbury, supervisor of the original thesis, whose constant encouragement, criticisms and close interest stimulated me beyond words; to Dr Stewart Firth who cheerfully shared the results of his prodigious research and in large measure made this study possible. Dr Peter Sack was generous in providing sources and criticism which never went unheeded.

In the islands I gained both friendship and assistance from Kilifoti Eteauti and his family. They took me under their roof and taught me more than the records ever revealed. Paul M. Ehrlich in Ponape acted as guide, interpreter and raconteur, tutoring me unselfishly in the results of his own extensive fieldwork. I owe him special thanks for permission to quote from his paper, 'The Sokehs Rebellion 1910-1911', presented to a conference of the Association for Social Anthropology in Oceania, Florida, March 1975. Others in the islands to whom I am indebted for information and insights were Ersin Santos, Nansau Ririn en Kiti, Carlos Etscheit and Fr McGarry S. J., all of Ponape; and Tupuola Efi in Western Samoa. Ms Robyn Gay typed the manuscript with care and infinite patience. Finally, to my wife, who had to live so long with the project and still managed to keep us both sane, I owe the deepest debt of all.

Contents

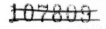

Maps

Maps drawn in the Cartographic Office, Department of
Human Geography, Australian National University

Plates

A History
of the German Pacific

Introduction

The Islands

The Pacific colonies of Germany were a far-flung post of empire in more ways than one. They were a long way from Europe, by sail three to four months away. They were small; all except for New Guinea, mere dots in an endless sea. And they were separated from each other by thousands of miles of blue, unrelenting ocean: German New Guinea and Micronesia were each composed of a myriad of islands scattered over hundreds of miles. To begin with, let us look at Samoa, a perfect example of isolation and economy of scale.

The Samoan group is a chain of islands stretching west to east about 480 kilometres north-east of Tonga and forming the northern apex of a triangle with Tonga and Fiji, further to the west. It consists of three main islands, Savai'i in the west, with an area of 1800 square kilometres; Upolu across the straits of Apolima, about seventy-six kilometres long and 1036 square kilometres in area; and, 111 kilometres to the east, Tutuila, a steep, densely-forested island of 140 square kilometres, nearly cut in two by the magnificent harbour of Pago Pago. Savai'i and Upolu, with the smaller islands of Manono and Apolima lying between them, form what was the former colony of German Samoa and is today the independent state of Western Samoa. Tutuila is the principal island of American Samoa, which includes the Manu'a group and Rose atoll further eastwards.

Savai'i is the largest island in the Samoan group. It has no good harbours, is rocky and mountainous, rising to over 1829 metres, and has been susceptible to volcanic eruptions, the last from 1905 to 1911. Most of the relatively sparse population lives in the extreme east, on a low, flat, fertile strip of coast across the straits from Upolu.

Upolu has always been the social and commercial centre of Samoa. It is densely populated, the people living in open, airy and well-organised villages along the shorelines, predominantly in the north-west. A mountain ridge topped by the cones of extinct volcanoes runs the length of Upolu like a backbone, but the coast, at least in the north-west, is flat and sandy, gradually becoming rocky and mountainous in the east beyond Saluafata. Western Samoa's major port and only large town is Apia, roughly in the middle of the north coast. Today it lies about thirty-nine kilometres from the pleasant airport of Faleolo, which lies in Mulifanua district at the western end of Upolu, along a road which follows the coastline and gives uninterrupted vistas of sea, reef and mountain. The well-surfaced road passes through innumerable villages with their neat oval houses, high roofs of thatch or corrugated iron supported by an open cluster of stout poles, with no walls and surrounded by hibiscus, frangipani and greenery of all kinds. The local church, perhaps paint peeling in the tropical sun, is a landmark in the village, along with the *fale*, the round house for ceremonial meetings.

Apia is a sudden departure from this colour and order. An old port town with dusty roads and patched weatherboard buildings, it fringes the shoreline along Beach Road. The harbour itself provides little inspiration to lift the setting. It is a reef harbour in an open bay, roughly semicircular, and about one and one-half kilometres across. It has no special virtues and can be quite dangerous in the hurricane season with winds from the north-west quarter, a feature which was demonstrated dramatically in 1889 when three German and three American warships were driven onto the shore in a hurricane, with the loss of 210 lives. To the west of the town lies the peninsula of Mulinu'u. For over a hundred years it has served as ceremonial seat of government and figured in all the major political disputes. Today the round, *fale*-inspired House of Assembly occupies a prominent position on the peninsula.

Presently there are over 100,000 citizens of Western Samoa, a threefold increase in the population which helped to glorify the German Empire before 1914.

The social structure of Samoa is founded on a number of ranked lineages, within which lesser chiefs and groups must defer to greater, on the basis of inherent societal rank.[1] The descent groups consist of people born or adopted into localised households, as well as their descendants outside the village, all adult members having a network of relations throughout Samoa with whom they have frequent communication in a variety of ceremonial and social activities.

At the local level, the unit of social and political control is the village, consisting of several extended families joined together to deal with common problems. A chief, or *matai*, is at the head of each household, controlling the domestic tasks of its members and taking part in village organisation. Decisions affecting the latter are taken in the formal village council, the *fono fa'alenu'u*. Only *matai* possess a seat and a

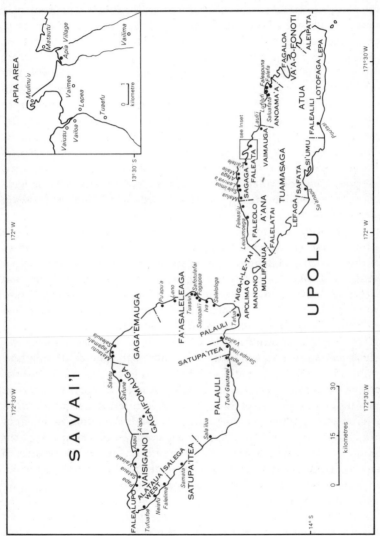

Map 2 Samoa

5

voice in its proceedings and their authority and influence relate directly to their seniority of position within the village hierarchy. Decision-making is not based on majority votes; the authority of one or of several high-ranking *matai* is the crucial factor. Family heads possess a quasi-consultative vote in discussing a problem prior to an assembly, but during council proceedings a heavy emphasis is placed on at least a public show of unanimity.

Above the village units there was no centralised political institution with control over all Samoans in the nineteenth and early twentieth centuries. The problem of maintaining order in the complex of cross-cutting associations fell to the village, which jealously guarded its independence, and acted vigorously against transgressors of its residence rules. Though villages were linked in loose, ascending grades of political association, and sub-districts did develop in former times, based on common village locality and lineage affiliation, these were generally less stable than the village system itself, and were always susceptible to factionalism and disintegration.

Villages were also loosely linked together in wider district organisations. These were rarely distinct and permanent groupings, depending for their shape and definition upon allegiances to one or other 'royal' lineage and support for senior chiefly titles. The most important districts exhibiting this cohesion in the nineteenth century and thus enjoying relatively fixed boundaries were Atua, Tuamasaga and A'ana in Upolu; the combination of Manono, Apolima and Mulifanua; and Fa'asaleleaga in eastern Savai'i.

Districts were not administrative units but spheres of influence grounded in kinship, traditional history and policy. Their politics revolved around questions of family prestige, important marriage alliances and the pursuit of the highest chiefly titles, at the apex of which lay a claim to paramount chieftaincy, and with it nominal ascendancy throughout Samoa. Contention for the paramountcy was to Europeans the most disruptive feature of Samoan political life in the nineteenth century. To understand why, it is necessary to sketch in the structure of chiefly politics and examine the complexities of traditional group alliances in Samoa.

Chiefs with high titles are the elites in Samoa and they are divided into two categories, the *ali'i* and the *tulafale*. The *tulafale* or 'orator chief' was originally a kind of personal assistant to the *ali'i*, who possessed a particular sanctity in Samoan tradition and enjoyed exclusive privileges and the right to special deference. On public occasions it was the duty of the *tulafale* to proclaim the will of the *ali'i*, and to supervise the ceremonial exchange of food and other goods.

As 'speaker' and as skilful orator, the *tulafale* was in a position to involve himself in all sorts of political affairs, and to exercise influence in areas where he had no formal rights. A shrewd and energetic talking chief might thus arrogate virtually independent power to himself. His most influential role lay in the distribution of fine mats, an event which possessed special ceremonial and ritual value for Samoans and represented a means of payment. Such distributions took place on various family and public occasions, but the most important was the bestowal of titles on a chief, particularly the award of the *Tafa'ifa* titles, the four highest in the land—*Tui Atua, Tui A'ana, Gatoaitele* and *Tamasoali'i*. The candidate awarded all four titles was designated the paramount chief of the group. Control of these titles was vested in groups of orator chiefs representing confederations of districts; they were, in a very real sense, the 'kingmakers' of Samoa.

The first confederation was composed of Atua and A'ana, whose orators controlled the first two titles, together with the politically influential villages of Tuamasaga district in Upolu, which awarded the other two. The second confederation comprised the *tulafale* of six Savai'i districts, the island of Manono and parts of Tuamasaga, which participated in the award of the titles. To the first configuration of districts the term *Tumua* was applied, while those based on the Savai'i districts were called *Pule*. To *Pule* was linked a subsidiary confederation called *A'iga*, which was based on Manono and Apolima.

The historic battle for political supremacy in Samoa revolved, at one level, around the mutual opposition of these two power cartels. But it was complicated by a further level of alliances, those of different districts to two major 'royal' lines which were the focus of political intrigue for the paramountcy. These lines, actually patrilineal lineages, were the *Tuia'ana* or *Sā Tupuā*, and the *Sā Malietoā*, each of which traditionally looked to support from combinations of orator groups in various districts, A'ana and Atua on the side of *Sā Tupuā*, and Tuamasaga, Savai'i and Manono on the side of *Sā Malietoā*. It is little wonder that the representatives of various European Powers in Samoa have been consistently bewildered and exasperated by the intricacies of Samoan politics.

This was especially the case in the nineteenth century when the wars which inevitably resulted from the multi-layered intrigues never resolved the issues along lines that appealed to European conceptions

Map 3 Ponape

of victory and authority. For victory by one or other of the major lineages never guaranteed a new level of stability in Samoa. The government of the victorious group (*Malo*) was only an alliance of convenience, with no commitment to principle or 'party' government. Its dissolution after a victory was usually rapid and complete since it interfered constantly in the local affairs of its members; moreover the practice of harassing the vanquished groups at every opportunity, demanding ever more goods and labour, soon led to new alliances and rebellion. Such was the prestige of the *Tafa'ifa* titles that eventual peace only inaugurated fresh disputes and intrigues by chiefs competing to secure them for their various candidates.

Paradoxically, this structured chaos probably saved Samoa from the straitjacket of early annexation by a European Power. With a strong, continuous central government in Samoa, Europeans undoubtedly would have gained quicker and tighter control over Samoans by funnelling the political and economic forces at their disposal through the 'head of state' or the government. The Powers tried desperately to impose a centralised system of authority on Samoa in the late nineteenth century, but failed; the partition of the islands between Germany and America followed from that failure. Even then Samoans refused to surrender their freedom of action and their political creativity.

By contrast with Samoa, Ponapean social and political structure is more regular and authoritarian, though the political possibilities in some areas are more flexible than in Samoa. Ponape is the largest island of the Carolines group in Micronesia, an island world which is still a Trust Territory of the United States. Ponape lies roughly north-east of the Bismarck Archipelago at longitude 158° east and 6° north of the equator, and, like most of the islands of Micronesia, is isolated, her largest island neighbour being Kusaie, 494 kilometres away to the south-east. Truk is 708 kilometres to the west; to the north-west, Saipan is over 1600 kilometres, Manila 3803 kilometres. In the east only the Marshall Islands lie between Ponape and Hawaii. The distance to San Francisco is 7469 kilometres.

Ponape is a towering volcanic dome, roughly hexagonal in shape, about 23 kilometres from north to south and 26 kilometres from east to west. Mangrove swamps fringe the inner reef around the island and a narrow belt of alluvial land lies between them and the foothills. The interior is extremely mountainous, with eleven peaks rising above 610 metres; overland travel is thus very difficult. Most Ponapeans use shallow canoes for transport around the island, though low tide on the inner reef can restrict movement in many places. There are three main harbours: Langar in the north where the Spanish built the first European settlement, Kolonia; Madolenihmw in the east; and Ron Kiti in the south. The Japanese built a second large town on the eastern edge of Ponape, but during the Spanish and German periods Kolonia was the only centre of foreign occupation outside mission stations. To the west of Kolonia, across a narrow channel, lies the island of Sokehs with the most dominating feature of Ponape's dominating landscape: the enormous Sokehs scarp, which falls away sheer from a height of 274 metres to the sea at the island's northern end. A modern causeway now replaces the rickety wooden bridge which connected Sokehs to the mainland in German times. The effect of the Sokehs scarp, together with the rugged interior, where the air lies thick and heavy, where dark clouds obscure the matted tops of mountains and thunder rolls uneasily across the valleys, is to give Ponape a sinister and brooding quality which contrasts markedly with that of the low, open and vulnerable atolls of Micronesia.

At the time of German rule, the native inhabitants of Ponape, like most of the Caroline Islanders, were divided into eighteen matrilineal clans which were further divided into sub-clans ranked by seniority.[2] Political power at district level was based on these sub-clans and their senior individuals rather than on the clans. The clans were distributed throughout the five districts or states into which Ponape was divided during German times: Madolenihmw, Uh, Kiti, Sokehs and Net. Each was territorially distinct from the others and acted independently in every aspect of social and economic life, yet it would be misleading to call them tribes since they all had a series of cross-cutting kinship ties with one another. Ponapean legends refer to a time when the whole island was united under a single ruler (the Saudeleurs), but that era ended with the conquest by the culture hero Isokelokel, when the separate districts of Ponape were founded.

The districts themselves were, in turn, subdivided into a number of geographical sections composed of several farmsteads. These were not villages in the ordinary sense of the word. Households belonging to each section were scattered along the shore and separated from one another by the land holdings of each farmstead. Sections were the units of local political control and were supervised by section chiefs, who were appointed by the principal chiefs of the district and required to keep an eye on the productivity of the various farmsteads as well as regulate tributary offerings to the High Chief.

One's position within a district and section was fixed originally by strict heredity and succession rules. Each district had a theoretically identical series of ranked titleholders in two chiefly lines. Below these were the commoners, bound to a particular section chief by ties of obedience, tributary labour and war service. There is an obvious, though rather loose, analogy here with the medieval European system of royalty, nobility and the common people. Within the district, the ultimate repository of power and authority was the High Chief, or Nahnmwarki, who originally decided what was right and wrong without any distinction between civil and criminal law. Failure to observe proper etiquette, to respond to a call for service, or a deliberate disregard of one's place in the scheme of things could be punished by the confiscation of land, by the removal of titles, or banishment. In theory, chiefs, especially highly-ranked chiefs, had an unconditional right to appropriate or confiscate the goods and property of commoners.

Land was the most valuable commodity vulnerable to confiscation. The common people did not possess a right to the land where they dwelt and farmed. Ultimately they held it at the will of the High Chief of the district. According to the first German Governor of Ponape, the land of a tenant farmer went back to the High Chief after his death, the Chief reissuing it as he pleased.[3] Recent findings by anthropologists however suggest that this is a statement of the ideal rather than what usually happened. Commoners were dispossessed in olden times, even during their period of tenancy, but only in a minority of cases did this occur and then for some unforgivable misdeed. Generally, matrilineal rules of inheritance operated and there was fairly automatic confirmation of the heirs to a plot of land. Ponapean land will play a large part in our story for it lay at the centre of the conflict between the Islanders and their Spanish and German rulers.

Like land inheritance, succession to chiefly titles was also automatic, according to matrilineal seniority in the sub-clan. But, again, this was the theory rather than the practice. In fact, the inheritance principle was modified by several considerations which made the structure of authority more flexible than its hierarchical nature would suggest. Personality, relative age, physical disability, martial exploits, industry and obedience to the Nahnmwarki could all produce differential rates of promotion, while institutionalised forms of tribute and respect to High Chiefs were exploited by aspirants to titles in a form of competition for prestige. The result was a degree of social and political mobility which was certainly greater than the more socially-conservative Samoan system.

Another comparison with Samoa can be made in the relationship between the Nahnmwarki and the Nahnken, the principal chief of the second line of titles in each district. The Nahnken has been likened to the talking chief or *tulafale* of Samoa because he enjoyed frequent, direct communication with the ordinary people of his district. Unlike his Samoan counterpart, however, the Nahnken played a much more consistent role in the administration of daily affairs, since the Nahnmwarki was regarded as holy and remote in a way that the Samoan *ali'i* never was. This did not mean that the Nahnken was the real autocrat of a Ponapean district. Traditionally there was a very close relationship between the Nahnmwarki and the Nahnken, and a state of delicate balance which seldom erupted into open discord. Throughout Ponape great social pressures operated in favour of political conformity, and in public affairs the Nahnmwarki and Nahnken presented one face to the world.

Ponapean political life centred round the pursuit of enhanced status, the capture of titles, and personal competition. The major cause of conflict was the inherent contradiction between theory and practice, in particular between the rules of matrilineal seniority and the effects of personal performance on the promotions system. Between districts, political vainglory played a large role in the frequent collisions. Each district guarded its independence and power fiercely and worked to have them acknowledged by other districts. A balance of power had gradually crystallised, so that by the time of German rule hostilities had been fixed for some years: the northern districts of Sokehs and Net against the rest. Clan members of different districts enjoyed much less contact than in Samoa. For a commoner, travel into another district was always dangerous unless a message had been sent ahead by the Nahnmwarki. High Chiefs themselves never travelled unless accompanied by displays of men and equipment sufficient to maintain the frail peace. It was this situation, fraught with instabilities and worsened by the Ponapean experience of Spanish colonisation, that Germany inherited in 1899.

As for New Guinea, it would be impossible here, as well as pointless, to describe fully the area's physical and cultural characteristics. It will suffice, first, to establish the scale of the colonial enterprise in which New Guineans and Germans were involved and, second, to give a broad and superficial description of those social features which most influenced relations between the two communities.

The protectorate of German New Guinea consisted of the north-east quadrant of the mainland of New Guinea together with about 600 islands stretching east through the Bismarck Archipelago to the western fringes of Polynesia. With its most northerly point less than 80 kilometres from the equator, the protectorate ran south to the border with Papua and the British Solomon Islands protectorate, and from the Dutch border in the west to Nukumanu in the Tasman Islands—740 kilometres from the northern extremes to the southern, and 1770 kilometres from west to east.

The mainland is 181 299 square kilometres in area and extremely mountainous, a feature it shares with most other parts of the protec-

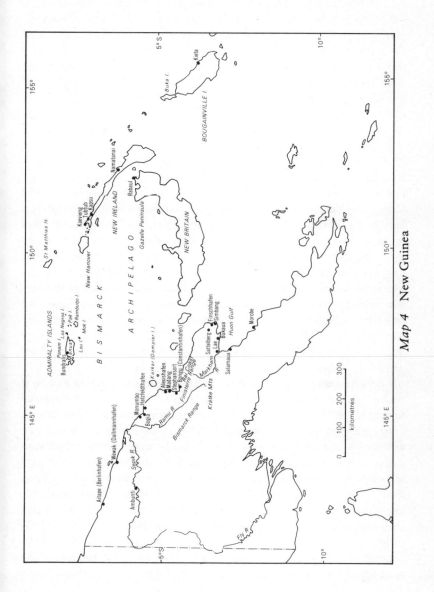

Map 4 New Guinea

torate. The Bismarck, Kratke and Finisterre ranges rise to over 3048 metres, forming a massive cordillera covered with thick tropical jungle lying between the thin coastal belt and the western Highlands. Extensive plains on the coast are few, concentrated around the lower reaches of the Sepik and the Ramu rivers, on the Astrolabe/Maclay coasts and in the lower Markham River valley. As for rivers, only the Sepik and Ramu were navigable during German times. Nearly a quarter of the total population of the old protectorate lived in the Sepik area. The rest of the coast was populated only in patches. The Germans never reached the western Highlands where almost a million people dwelled.

Of the archipelago's islands, New Britain is the largest, with an area of 33 670 square kilometres. Still-active volcanoes exist around Willaumez Peninsula in the west and at Blanche Bay on the east coast of the Gazelle Peninsula, where over half of the island's people live. The largest population group in the Peninsula are the Tolai, a comparatively light-skinned Melanesian people inhabiting the coasts and hinterland in the north and east. In the north-west lie the Baining Mountains where there dwells a racially distinct group of the same name, perhaps the original coastal dwellers who were driven into the mountains by the Melanesians who emigrated from New Ireland. During German times the Baining lived in small, dispersed hamlets in the mountains and practised a backward, shift-and-burn type of agriculture. The other large islands to which the Germans devoted their attention were New Ireland and Bougainville, but they will only briefly concern us in this work.

The social and political scale of population groups in German New Guinea was the most obvious difference from those in Micronesia and in Samoa. In New Guinea, the Germans rarely came into contact with corporate groups whose immediate range of authority was more than 100 people. Local kinship-residential groups were common, and consisted of a small village or a cluster of hamlets which were roughly equal in political terms and were tied to each other economically. Within these, New Guineans enjoyed a variety of political forms, including matrilineal and patrilineal descent groups, cognatic groups, men's clubhouses, secret societies, or a combination of these.

Social and political authority in these societies did not reside permanently or institutionally with one person or body. On those societies with which the Germans had most dealings there is little ethnographic work that dates to the time of earliest contact; and German sources, both official and unofficial, are silent or unreliable about the authority structures that were in operation when the Germans first made contact with the New Guineans. Nonetheless, from the records of travellers, administrators, scholars and Papua-New Guineans themselves over a hundred years we can make a number of general observations about leadership which hold true for the range of groups with which the Germans came in contact. There did exist individuals in each group who were recognised as wielding greater powers of initiation and organisation than others. They were men who, through martial renown and/or economic enterprise were able to attract a personal following, which they then manipulated to aggrandise power and resources for themselves and for their group. By paying bride price for younger men, by debt collecting, or by cultivating new land and dependants, such men were able to establish a coterie of followers and mobilise their productiveness for prestige-building through public distribution of resources; they became the 'big men' of their societies, though the social range of their influence remained limited. Their primary social roles seemed to be as the focal distributors of wealth, as initiators of large-scale economic activities, and as spokesmen in inter-village affairs.

Tolai leaders were perhaps the nearest thing to an indigenous elite with which the Germans came in contact.[4] Traditional leadership was based on the *lualua*, the senior male member of a lineage or clan in a particular district, and successful Tolai leaders during German times tended to be natural products of the social system, controlling at least the landholdings of their lineage or clan. Yet sources of power other than seniority also operated. Personal initiative was important, perhaps through prowess as a warrior, and a dynamic personality or special entrepreneurial abilities were requisites for someone aspiring to be *a ngala* or a 'big man'. In the end, quality of performance determined one's continued influence.

With the coming of the Europeans, individual 'big men' were able to arrogate increased power to themselves, selling land on behalf of the descent group, cultivating support from one or other mission, and promoting inter-district solidarity through war alliances and monopolies on white people's goods. But this new, expanded position never became institutionalised, even after the Germans introduced a system of government appointees.

Leadership is one of the most rewarding areas of study in the story of Pacific Island adjustment to government by Germany. It will become plain that changes were rung on the character of Island leadership which are perhaps some of the more enduring results of Germany's thirty-year reign in the Pacific.

The Germans: Commerce, Colonies and Control

The beginnings of European enterprise in the Pacific are obscure. Precious stones, metals and whales were the object of the earliest voyages. The harvesting of tropical products began relatively late; German participation in it even later. The Hamburg firm of J. C. Godeffroy und Sohn had been trading in Latin America since the 1830s, and by the 1850s operated a network of commercial agencies around the rim of the Pacific: in Chile, California, South-East Asia and Australia. In 1855 the company's agent in Valparaiso, August Unshelm, was sent out into the South Pacific to capture for Godeffroys a share in the rapidly-expanding coconut oil trade. Unshelm chose Apia in Samoa as the base for his operations, and, with the firm's wide variety of ships plying the Pacific, Godeffroys very soon succeeded in seizing the bulk of the trade in the south-west. By the time of Unshelm's death in 1864, forty-six stations had been established throughout the islands, as far north as the Marshall and the Caroline islands.

But the real expansion took place under Unshelm's successor, Theodor Weber, merchant, innovator and empire-builder extra-ordinaire. Weber is credited with discovering that it was more efficient and profitable to export copra in sacks, and then to refine it in Europe, than to carry coconut oil in leaky barrels, and in 1865 he established the first large-scale plantations in Samoa. Under him the company tightened its grip on trade in the Marshalls and Carolines and moved into the New Guinea islands with a trading post at Matupit in 1874. Here they were joined by Robertson and Hernsheim, a small trading firm with its headquarters in the islands north of New Guinea.

Such was the extent and strength of German trade by 1875 that German warships were thereafter regularly dispatched to the Pacific to provide official support for the growing commercial empire. Treaties of friendship and commerce were concluded between 1876 and 1879 with various island groups—Tonga, the Gilbert, Ellice and Marshall islands, parts of the Society Islands, and Samoa. In 1878 the harbours of Makada and Mioko in New Britain were purchased on the initiative of a German warship captain, von Werner, in order to reinforce the claims of Germany's traders in the area. By 1879 official sources claimed that German business houses were currently exporting over six million marks worth of products from the South Seas.[5]

During these years, agitation was growing in Germany from economists and publicists in favour of overseas expansion for the Reich, and a number of associations were founded to promote the idea of colonies. Their hardest task was to win over the Iron Chancellor, Bismarck, who regarded colonies as a waste of time and a danger to the new nation's resources. With strains on the economy from rapid industrialisation, Bismarck was keen to secure overseas markets, but his vision was of a free-trade empire, with no formal territorial attachments. That he reversed this 'no colonies' policy is now well-known and it is not necessary to detail his reasons here: that is a continuing debate. Suffice it to say that, from 1884 on, Bismarck sponsored colonial annexations which expanded the Reich to Africa, the Pacific and the Far East, and that commercial interests in the Pacific provided a great deal of the pressure on the Chancellor to change his mind.

Despite the image of prosperity which German Pacific business conveyed in the late 1870s, there were a number of seeming threats to its position. Already in 1874 the Spanish had tried to obstruct German traders in the Philippines and the Carolines by demanding customs duties, and in the same year Germans in Fiji had most of their land confiscated when the British government annexed that group. The following year the United States obtained a privileged position over German commerce in the Hawaiian Islands, and in 1881 the French annexed the Society Islands where a subsidiary of Godeffroys, the Société Commerciale de l'Océanie, had been enjoying a large share of trade. Then, in 1879, Godeffroy's European investments deteriorated and new capital could not be raised for a company to take over the Samoan interests. Bismarck, with an eye to the potential of the Pacific trade, came forward to support the idea of a guaranteed government dividend for a new firm, the *Deutsche Handels-und Plantagen-Gesellschaft der Südsee Inseln zu Hamburg* (DHPG), to replace the projected successor to Godeffroys. But, in a celebrated confrontation between the Government and its enemies in the Reichstag, the Samoan subsidy bill was defeated. The DHPG was rescued only when Berlin and Hamburg financiers agreed to reconstruct it with private capital.

As successor to Godeffroys, the DHPG dominated trade in Samoa. In spite of increased financial backing its difficulties did not disappear after 1880. Its plantations in Samoa suffered from constant civil wars over the paramountcy question, while increased competition added a new threat to its sources of Pacific Island labour. Furthermore, the Germans had to face strong agitation from New Zealand interests for annexation of the group, and the reigning chief, Malietoa Laupepa, made clear his preference for things English.

The DHPG faced the same situation in New Guinea, its main centre for labour recruitment and an increasingly important trade and plantation area. Here there was pressure on Britain, from the Australian colonies, to annex the entire eastern half of the island as a bulwark for their defence. All these dangers led German companies in the area, and imperial representatives in Australia and the islands, to inundate Bismarck with information about the extent of German enterprise and to urge annexation of Samoa, New Guinea and parts of Micronesia.

They had their reward. A promise of State protection for a Chartered Company to colonise north-east New Guinea was one of Bismarck's first decisions in favour of colonial expansion. Annexation of the mainland and the offshore islands took place in November 1884. In early 1885 the Marshall Islands were annexed. The Carolines group was to be next on the list, but Spain protested on the grounds that western Micronesia was already part of an overseas Spanish empire dating back to the sixteenth century. The question was submitted, at Bismarck's request, to Pope Leo XIII as international arbiter, and he ruled in favour of Spain's claim.

As for Samoa, during the 1880s Bismarck entertained the hope that he could acquire the group by negotiations with Britain. But he was thwarted here too. Continual diplomatic gaucheries by his consuls in Apia turned opinion against the idea of German sovereignty in Samoa, and the United States adamantly resisted all attempts to negotiate a partition of interests.[6] In the end Bismarck had to be satisfied with a co-protectorate over the group, in which all three Powers were involved. It was not until 1899, with the complete breakdown of European control and the effects of a particularly ferocious civil war, that the three Powers were able to agree on a realistic solution to the imbroglio: the western islands were then delivered into German hands, the eastern into America's. When, the same year, Germany purchased the Caroline, Palau and Mariana islands from Spain in the wake of the Spanish-American war, the German trade and plantation empire in the Pacific was complete.

Bismarck had not pursued an offensive *Kolonialpolitik* in the Pacific in the sense of staking out new spheres of influence for Germany. The colonial empire was based on already-existing trade and plantation holdings in whose administration Bismarck wished to engage the government as little as possible. He looked to the Hansa cities to promote material and political development overseas, through *Frei-briefen* or Charters for private enterprise on the model of the British North Borneo Company, and he even tried, unsuccessfully, to enlist Hamburg merchants as colonial directors in a new Imperial Bureau which would remove responsibility from the Foreign Office.

Bismarck's hopes did become reality in the Pacific when the New Guinea Company, founded by Adolf von Hansemann in 1884, was awarded a far-reaching Charter on 17 May 1885 to administer the new protectorate of north-east New Guinea. On condition that it erect a governing apparatus at its own cost, the Company was given the exclusive right to regulate the internal administration of the colony, to levy taxes and duties, to take possession of all unowned land and to conclude contracts for land and labour with the local inhabitants. Only four years later the Company surrendered the reins of government to the Reich, though it continued to pay the costs of administration. It resumed control in September 1892, but was never able to overcome the conflict of interest between its public and private policies. Company expenditure increased steadily without any proportional return as a number of subsidiary companies rose and fell on the New Guinea mainland. In 1895-96 the New Guinea Company entered into nego-tiations for the permanent transfer of control to the Reich, and this finally took place, after some domestic opposition to the terms of the treaty, in April 1899. Up to that time the Company had lost a total of nine million marks in New Guinea.[7]

In only one area of the Pacific was Bismarck's model of Charter Government successful—the island sphere north of New Guinea. The DHPG and the firm of Robertson and Hernsheim, both of which controlled trade in the Marshalls (as well as in the Carolines under Spanish rule), founded a joint company in late 1887, the Jaluit Gesellschaft, which was given an Imperial Charter on 21 January 1888. The treaty gave the firm the right to take possession of all unowned land in the Marshall, Brown and Providence islands and to extract their guano deposits, while the actual administration remained in the hands of an Imperial Commissioner whose costs were borne by the Jaluit Gesellschaft. After the Carolines became part of the empire, the Company was granted a trading and plantation monopoly there also. The smallest of the privileged firms in Germany's colonies, the Jaluit Gesellschaft was also the longest lived and the most successful. In 1906, when the Company became a purely private business, it was already paying a dividend of twenty per cent. In that year the separate status of the Marshalls protectorate was abolished and it was united with the Carolines, Palau and Mariana islands, which had been administratively a part of the New Guinea protectorate since their incorporation into the empire.

As these events were occurring, changes were taking place in the machinery of colonial administration at home, changes that affected directly the policies adopted in the Pacific. In the early years, Bismarck's open dislike of government involvement in the colonies meant that decisions about them were taken within the political section of the Foreign Office. Bismarck was determined that colonies would not become a new avenue of growth for the all-enveloping Imperial Civil Service; the activities of officials like the Samoan consuls only reinforced his conviction that inflated bureaucracies and petty despotism were the real fruits of overseas empire. But the concerns of the colonies grew rapidly after 1885, and, though he was disenchanted with the whole enterprise, Bismarck was forced in 1889 to ask for help in administering them.[8] A year later, after he had already been replaced as Chancellor, a special Colonial Department was created within the Foreign Office.

Independence in policy making did not come with this arrangement. The new Department remained the responsibility of the Foreign Office and under the jurisdiction of the Chancellor. More importantly, the Department in its policy deliberations always had to reckon with articulate public discussion of colonial issues, and with pressure from the Reichstag. Unlike colonial organisation in most countries (Britain, for example, where the House of Commons had no direct authority over basic administration in the colonies), the German Reichstag was empowered to review each year the budget submitted by the Colonial Department. As an important weapon in its struggle to strengthen parliamentary control over Germany's political life, the Reichstag guarded this right jealously, examining every aspect of colonial affairs rigorously, both in the House and in its Budget Commission. Because the various parties represented large-scale pressure groups, those interests with the most patronage in the colonies or in Berlin exerted a great deal of influence on colonial politics, especially after the so-called Hottentot elections of 1907.

Though criticism of the Colonial Department and its ways built up steadily after 1890, no major structural changes were made, except to incorporate the administration of colonial troops, post office and treasury affairs into the system and set up a Colonial Council (*Kolonialrat*) of 'experts' to advise on matters of trade, shipping, settlement, etc. Charges of excessive legalism and incompetence, of brutality and criminal misbehaviour by officers in the African colonies culminated in the Herero-Nama war of 1904 in South-West Africa and the Maji Maji rebellion in East Africa the following year. These produced a great crisis in Germany's domestic politics. In the elections of 1907 the parties of the Right—Conservatives, National Liberals and *Freisinnige*—gained power, and hence the interests of right-wing pressure groups, virtually identical with commercial interests in the colonies, commanded even greater authority in colonial policy making.

The reform of colonial administration in 1907 and the elevation of the Department to the status of a Ministerial Office did not diminish the influence of the Right. If anything, the trend was reinforced. Bernhard Dernburg, the new State Secretary for Colonies, was a Berlin banker, hand-picked by Chancellor Bülow to bring a new broom to the Wilhelmstrasse. In a matter of months, Dernburg rose from political obscurity to the centre of public attention. In the elections of 1907 he took upon himself the colonial cause and proved an untiring and inspiring advocate. He brought immense energy, imagination and decisiveness to his task of cleaning up the system, and the reforms he engineered were real and far-reaching. A purge of the ranks of Berlin officials was Dernburg's first move. Then he turned to the tasks of arranging more coherent planning for the long-range development of Africa and the Pacific; of streamlining financial practices; of revising colonial law to incorporate local custom; of encouraging private investment.[9]

This last was the crux of the matter. Dernburg was at heart a mercantilist. His vision was a materialist one: the colonies were chiefly sources of raw materials and outlets for investment capital. True, he envisaged a reciprocal program in which Germany would bring civilisation and technology to the colonised peoples, and he attempted a number of liberal reforms aimed at improving relations between the colonies' native peoples and their German masters, such as eliminating forced labour and the use of the whip. But his efforts were curtailed in extent and depth by the opposition of large, colonial, settler interests which would not accept radical interference with their commercial objectives and put pressure on Dernburg through the Reichstag. Dernburg initiated an economic take-off in Germany's colonial empire, but the consequent material growth and the intensified pressures on the native populations posed enormous difficulties for those responsible for a humane native policy.[10]

These last were the men out in the field, the bureaucrats, civilians and soldiers who organised the day-to-day communication of German policy to Africans and Pacific Islanders. In the Pacific, the isolation of island colonies one from another and from the mother country, their insignificance in the larger German empire, and the relatively moderate level of investment at stake all resulted in a minimum of supervision from home and more freedom of action for local administrators. Unlike the older British, Spanish and French empires, the Germans followed no 'system' of colonial rule in the Pacific in the sense of a standard pattern of administrative attitudes and actions based on abstract theory or predetermined by long experience. There is in the records a striking absence of instructions from the Colonial Department to the Governor of Samoa; the Governor of New Guinea, too, was generally left a free hand to determine the way he would handle things, though the presence of powerful settler groups and large corporations meant that he had to proceed more cautiously.

Within the colonies themselves, isolation threw decisive responsibilities onto individual station officers, and often dictated the pattern of racial relationships. On mountainous, forested Ponape, small boats were the chief means of transport around the island. It took up to seven hours to reach the southern district of Kiti from the European settlement on the northern shores. It could take five hours to sail from Upolu to Savai'i in Samoa: the isolation of Savai'i proved a major factor in the problems the Germans encountered in Samoa. In New Guinea, district stations such as Aitape, Morobe, the Admiralties and Kieta were often isolated from the main planting and trading communities, and communication was dependent on desultory visits by the one government steamer or an occasional recruiting ship. District officers were thus left very much to their own devices. They were not required to seek approval from headquarters before opening up new country or taking action against local villages, and the tendency to one-man rule was reinforced by the absence of European subordinates, the personal loyalty of coloured police troops, and the New Guinean preference for social relationships of a personal and reciprocal nature.

These practices were to prove more arbitrary and militaristic in Africa, where soldiers seconded from the metropolitan army provided the bulk of field officers for the colonial service into the 1900s. The Pacific colonies were staffed mainly by civilian personnel, both at higher executive levels and out in the field. This did not mean that the relations between rulers and ruled in the Pacific were free of all violence, but the civilian tone of German rule, particularly in Samoa and early Ponape, did make for more flexible responses in the face of island opposition.

Unlike Africa, too, the regimes in the Pacific were not supported by large military forces. None of the colonies had a special colonial troop (*Schutztruppe*), and only New Guinea boasted a considerable police force, over 800 men by 1914, which was also used to open up new territory. Ponape got by with fifty Melanesian·and Malay police, Samoa with a mere thirty young Samoans. Compared with the size of the security forces in Africa, these numbers were trifling. German East Africa, for example, could call upon a troop of 230 white and 2500 African soldiers; the Cameroons on 175 whites and 1550 Africans. The largest force of all was in South-West Africa, where there was an all-white force of 2500, and 500 African police late in the German period. During the Herero wars some 21 000 soldiers had been stationed in the colony.[11] Only France among the Powers in Africa possessed a colonial army larger than that of the German Reich.

Since, in an island empire the size of the German Pacific, land-based security forces were too expensive and inefficient to maintain, the Pacific administrations leaned heavily on the German navy for support. This created a special set of difficulties, for so jealously did each side guard its prerogatives of authority, that the exact function of the navy within the framework of colonial rule was the subject of frequent disagreement between administrators and ships' captains; the impotence of the navy in land exercises and the infrequency of naval visits added to these difficulties. Nonetheless, because of chronic lack of finance, and the extensive perimeters of the island colonies, the navy remained the most important sanction of the Pacific administrations right up to 1914.

But the nub of the German navy's activities lay elsewhere. When, in 1914, war was declared, none of the three colonies could count on naval protection against the invasion of enemy forces. In the event, Samoa and Ponape fell into Allied hands without resistance; New Guinea fell after a token encounter between German settlers and Australian troops. It was not just that the Reich's two small Pacific cruisers, even with Graf Spee's Far-East Cruiser Squadron, were hopelessly outnumbered by the range of battle craft which Britain and her dominions could deploy. The reason was more that Berlin's priorities lay closer to home. Well before 1914, Admiral Tirpitz's strategy for a battlefleet to counteract the

British in the north Atlantic demanded that the colonies be abandoned in the event of war.[12]

Such were the instruments of imperial policy in the colonies. This book aims to add a further dimension to the story—that of the Pacific Islanders and their reception of German rule—and to show how the conflict between Berlin's objectives, the local administrative possibilities, and the aspirations of Islanders was handled in the colonies themselves.

1

German Samoa:
Early Disquiet

When the Imperial German flag was raised in Mulinu'u on 15 March 1900, Europeans and Samoans had been engaged for more than two decades in a constantly-fluctuating struggle over the right to control the Samoan group's political and economic destiny. Samoan affairs had dissipated a disproportionate amount of diplomatic energy in the capitals of the Western Powers as the islands became a focus of imperial rivalry in the late nineteenth century.

European familiarity with Samoa dates back to 1722 when the Dutchman, Jacob Roggeween, first sighted the island. He described the inhabitants as 'a harmless, good sort of people, and very brisk and likely, for they treated each other with visible marks of civility and had nothing in their behaviour that was wild or savage . . .' Subsequent visitors were to rue the words of Roggeween.

A series of sporadic and largely disastrous contacts took place over the years[1] until 1830, when John Williams and Charles Barff of the London Missionary Society arrived off Savai'i. Malietoa Vai'inupo had just triumphed decisively over a rival for the paramountcy, and this fortuitous circumstance, together with the practical and polytheistic leanings of the people, served the missionaries well, for the Samoans readily took to the formal structure of religious observances and the new education.[2] Already by 1860 over 5000 adherents were contributing £1200 each year to the upkeep of the mission, and upwards of a thousand individuals had been influenced directly by the teaching seminary established at Malua in 1844. In following decades the Samoans voluntarily adopted compulsory schooling, to the extent that, by 1905, twenty-five per cent of the population could claim an education from the London Missionary Society alone.[3]

The Christian revolution was, however, neither wholehearted nor complete. Samoans were not necessarily prepared to accept all the Western religious sanctions which missionaries attempted to superimpose on indigenous life, and, in the absence of a monopoly of foreign influence, the missionaries were forced to acquiesce in what amounted to an exchange of religious cultures as the Samoans institutionalised

25

their own interpretations of Christian doctrine. Without recourse to Western military power, the growing community of beachcombers and itinerant traders also had to accept traditional authority, for the Samoans refused to compromise either their standards of propriety regarding the behaviour of foreigners or the sanctions imposed for transgressions of the social and political code.

With the growth of Samoa as an entrepôt and as a centre for plantations, the balance of physical power tended to swing in favour of the European community. Expectations of Western support and intervention accompanied the advent of consular representatives, and European navies now provided the means to intimidate the local populations. Island chiefs gradually found themselves competing with the consuls and the navies for the loyalty of beach residents. It was only a short step to a situation where Europeans began treating the Samoans as a second-class race, a hindrance to the development of commerce, and an exploitable commodity.

European interests soon began to attempt to dictate the outcome of Samoan district rivalries in a way most favourable to themselves. In 1869 the London Missionary Society and the foreign consuls interfered in the *Tafa'ifa* titles dispute between Malietoa Talavou and Malietoa Laupepa. Inter-district war followed inevitably until 1873, when, by mission entreaties and consular intervention, once again an uneasy peace was secured. But Samoan allegiances were now deeply divided between the two Sā Malietoā parties. In quick succession there followed an abortive republican experiment under an American premier and, from 1876 to 1881, a new war between Malietoa Laupepa and Malietoa Talavou.

The exigencies of warfare led to the growth of a vigorous arms trade operated by the planters and land speculators now crowding into Apia. Ridiculously large amounts of land were alienated from the Samoans for guns and ammunition, and fraudulent practices were the order of the day on both sides. By 1880 American and British interests laid claim to 185 000 hectares of land throughout the group; Godeffroys, the old German firm under Theodor Weber, claimed 61 500 hectares on Upolu alone. Only a quarter of this had been purchased with cash—largely with debased Chilean dollars—the rest was acquired in guns and kind at enormously inflated prices. Weber was no more scrupulous than his competitors, but he was a far more methodical man. Careful to reinforce title by effective occupation, he founded large copra and cotton plantations in north-western Upolu, and imported native labour from the Gilberts and Melanesia to work them since the Samoans could not be induced to do plantation labour at an 'economic' wage rate.

By the 1880s, Germany was the power least trusted by the Samoans, as German merchants were ruthless in seeking conditions favourable to the development of their lands and business. Godeffroy's strict occupation of land, the use of German gunboats to overcome resistance to occupation, the dependence of the Islanders on Company credit, and the importation of Melanesian labour were all objects of Samoan resentment. Germany's political capital was not improved when it appropriated two harbours in 1879 in order to extract a 'treaty of friendship and commerce' from the Samoans. Britain had already secured a similar treaty voluntarily. There had always been a historical and perhaps temperamental preference for the English, and Apia was all but a British colony in appearance, composition and manner. The Germans, despite their commercial preponderance, gave the impression of being outsiders. Very few considered Apia their home; most were employees of 'the Firm' and intended to leave Samoa as soon as they had made some money.

Two distinct centres of power had by now crystallised in Samoa: the chiefs in their districts, and the Municipality in Apia. The Municipality was formed in 1879 to protect the infrastructure of trade built up by foreigners, and to regulate relations between the Samoans and the Europeans. Interactions between these two groups were determined thereafter largely by the conflict of interests within each. Rivalries among the consuls who now assumed command in the Municipality evenly matched Samoan intrigues in the districts: the governing ability of this European oligarchy was regularly impeded by mutually incompatible instructions from Home Offices, and by the tendency of incumbents to take matters into their own hands when any problems arose bearing in any way on national interests.[4]

The major problem was, of course, the continual political disturbances among the Samoans themselves. Throughout the 1880s, settlers and consuls threw their weight behind whichever Samoan party seemed most capable of creating a semblance of European-style order. Misconstruing the essentially delicate balance between the paramountcy and the powers of chiefly groups in the various districts, the Europeans contrived to establish a centralised monarchical regime which would be able to control all Samoans. To strengthen one of the parties sufficiently to hold the others in order, arms were constantly dispensed to the warring factions by different national interests. For their part, the

Samoan district factions encouraged such European interference where it aided their candidates in the competition for the *Tafa'ifa* titles. It is impossible to determine the exact numbers of firearms in the possession of Samoans during these years, but the DHPG admitted in 1886 that it had supplied 467 rifles to the Islanders between January and October, declaring that it could have been thousands more had the company not had the peace of the group at heart. The same year, non-German firms were rumoured to have sold 700 rifles in full view of the Municipality, while many more were smuggled in through outlying harbours.[5] None of the attempts made in the 1880s and 1890s to regulate the flow of arms into Samoa worked because of the mutual suspicions of the three Powers.

In November 1884, the German Consul, Stuebel, forced upon Malietoa Laupepa a treaty designed to give Germany overriding influence in the conduct of native affairs. When the chief ignored the treaty, as was Samoan custom with agreements which hedged their fundamental political freedoms, Stuebel used it as a pretext to drive him from the seat of Samoan government at Mulinu'u and raise the flag of the German Empire. His coup, however, was repudiated by Bismarck who was hopeful of obtaining Samoa through negotiations with the other two Powers. A firm negative stand by America thwarted Bismarck's hope however, and, together with continuing damage to German interests through Samoan fighting, this provoked Berlin into approving unilateral action by her local representatives. War was declared on Malietoa Laupepa and he was deported on a German warship. In his place the Germans installed Tamesese Tupua, who accepted alignment with Germany as an effective means of checking the aspirations of a new contender for the *Tafa'ifa* titles, Mata'afa Josefo, also of the *Sā Tupuā* lineage.

Tamasese Tupua's regime, under the tutelage of a former employee of the DHPG, Eugen Brandeis, was very soon discredited in the eyes of Samoans and non-German Europeans by the methods it used to eliminate political opposition and to impose the demands of a centralised government on the decentralised Islanders. A revolt, with Mata'afa Josefo at its head, broke out in 1888, and the German navy found itself hard pressed to cope. In an attempt by German marines in December 1888 to disarm a party of rebels near Vailele plantation, sixteen Germans were killed and over thirty wounded in a well-executed ambush by Mata'afa Josefo's forces.

This event rather upset all the previous European assumptions about

Samoan powers of resistance. Bewildered German officers and other eye-witnesses commented on the apparently 'un-Samoan' action of firing on Germans. The ferocity of Mata'afa Josefo's attack was rationalised by blaming 'a white American' at the head of the Samoan troops for firing the first shot and encouraging others to do likewise.[6] The German set-back contributed greatly to the growing movement towards resolution of the international conflict by negotiation. The final result was the Berlin Conference of 1889. A diplomatic rather than a realistic solution to the ethnic and political confusion in Samoa, this whole exercise simply converted the dangerous imperialist rivalries of the three Powers into a delicate balance of interests. The fiction of an autonomous Samoan kingship was preserved, and the tribunal of consuls was replaced by a tribunal of specially-created international officials. The arrangement was meant to function as a tridominium, but the retention of a monarchical concept for which Samoa was not well suited only perpetuated the political confusion and provided the leverage by which the various Samoan factions continued to exploit European power in their own interests.

The sequence of Samoan initiative and European response continued when Mata'afa Josefo was deported in 1893 for rebellion against the established regime of Malietoa Laupepa. His adherents, the real 'kingmakers', carried on the struggle in his name, skilfully manipulating the shifts of power and alliance within the European community, and growing stronger and more uncontrolled. While the navies of the Powers in conjunction probably prevented the disquiet from boiling over into a general conflagration, the measure of their control was strictly limited, extending little further than the range of their deck artillery. The Germans, in particular, acknowledged that if the Samoans withdrew to the bush, where they could live off the land and move with a facility that eluded European troops, the naval forces' tenuous control would vanish completely.[7]

It was brought home vividly in 1898 when, after the death of Malietoa Laupepa, Malietoa Tanumafili I and the newly-returned Mata'afa Josefo contested the *Tafa'ifa* titles. The weight of Samoan preference clearly lay with Mata'afa Josefo, but, in a surprise move, the European Chief Justice of the tripartite administration declared his opponent 'king'. At this point all European pretension to control of the situation broke down. Mata'afa Josefo's huge body of supporters, which included the districts of Atua, A'ana and half of Savai'i, rose up against the party of Malietoa Tanumafili I in a civil war of unequalled ferocity, for Mata'afa Josefo, spurned by the very powers that claimed to be preserving Samoan autonomy, was fighting for a decade of lost rights. His ability to marshal a large force behind him was due in great measure to the support of the leading orator chief of Safotulafai, and thus the virtual spokesman for Savai'i, Lauaki Namulau'ulu Mamoe.[8] Lauaki traditionally supported the *Sā Malietoā* lineage, but he despaired at the indecisiveness of Britain in refusing, time and time again, to give a watertight guarantee to the Malietoa regimes despite their English sympathies. In 1898 he decided to give his allegiance to Mata'afa Josefo as the only hope for uniting and stabilising Samoa in the face of foreign intervention. In so doing he demonstrated a power to mobilise sentiment and a political flexibility which, ten years later, made him the scourge of the German government.

The American navy led the operations on behalf of the legally-constituted monarch, Malietoa Tanumafili I, while Germany, in a defensive bid to arrest the decline of her influence in the group, threw her weight behind Mata'afa Josefo. Open engagements with the Anglo-American forces were studiously avoided. However, when the Americans pounded Mata'afa Josefo's villages with artillery fire, the rebels attacked the European lines in Apia itself and killed three sailors. In addition, they ambushed a party of troops which attempted to pursue them into the interior in April 1899, forcing the soldiers into a hasty and disorganised retreat and leaving three officers and several men killed and decapitated. It was an indication of what might be expected if the campaign deteriorated into guerrilla warfare. Mission societies provided a refuge for non-combatants and dispensed medical care to the wounded of both sides. Though both major missions, the London Missionary Society and the Marists, officially maintained a discreet neutrality, Samoan pastors of the London Missionary Society did appeal to Lauaki in early 1899 to use his considerable influence in the cause of peace. Lauaki refused. 'We have not been a party to war with the Powers', he responded. 'We do not wish to resist. But we have the right to claim the privilege of free men and ask to be told plainly what is to be our future status.'[9]

A move in this direction was made when a Three-Power Commission was despatched to Samoa the same year. It brought about a temporary cease-fire, and both Malietoa Tanumafili I and Mata'afa Josefo were persuaded to renounce permanently future claims to the 'kingship', though their acquiescence was more a gesture of goodwill than a renunciation of traditional political ambitions. Meanwhile Britain and

Germany were conducting negotiations concerned with tidying up loose ends of empire. Influenced by a recent naval assessment as to the greater strategic importance of Tonga, Britain agreed to waive her claims to Samoa in favour of Germany. Subsequently America agreed to the German annexation of Upolu, Savai'i and Manono, with Tutuila becoming an American dependency. The solution was greeted with great joy in the Reich, where Samoa had been elevated to the status of a test case of the new *Weltpolitik*: Samoa had come to be considered an indispensable jewel in the crown of German prestige.

The solution to the international destiny of Samoa did not exorcise the difficulties that Germany faced in Samoa itself. The Islanders had at first shown signs of resenting the partition of the islands. A High Chief of the Malietoa line sent a petition of protest to the Kaiser, and the chiefs of Safotulafai—significantly enough, Lauaki's political base—refused to hold a *fono* to greet the news, in the mistaken belief that the United States was about to veto the agreement.[10] By early 1900, however, these initial reservations had been overcome and the parties of both great lineages declared their acceptance of German dominion before the flag was raised.

On the part of Mata'afa Josefo and his adherents there was a great deal of sympathy for Germany in 1899-1900, but it was rooted in gratitude for support in the recent civil war rather than in an inherent predilection for German culture and hegemony. Mata'afa Josefo's supporters reasoned that Germany's capacity to help during the war had been restricted by the provisions of the Berlin Conference of 1889. Now that Samoa was German, there was nothing to stop her from recognising Mata'afa Josefo as *Tupu Sili*, or supreme chief, and his faithful band of chiefs and speakers as the *Malo*, the government of Samoa.

There was no doubt that Mata'afa Josefo was the Chosen One of the majority of Samoans. Since the late 1880s he had been the focus and inspiration of a purely Samoan movement in opposition to the candidates favoured by the Powers. Despite his own renunciation of the 'monarchy', his chiefs and speakers had never relinquished their right to choose, or more exactly to create, a 'King of Samoa' according to recent tradition, and to have their creation installed in Mulinu'u. Accordingly, before the German flag was raised, Mata'afa Josefo, under the tutelage of Lauaki, called an assembly of the Tanu people to effect a reconciliation, and a government was set up with Mata'afa Josefo and thirteen chiefs claiming widespread executive powers. Residing in Mulinu'u and styling themselves 'the rulers of Samoa', this band proceeded to collect taxes and issue regulations concerning Samoans and Europeans alike.

There was little Germany could do. In 1900 Mata'afa Josefo's party still represented the strongest military force in the Samoan islands. It numbered some 2500 and was in a state of perpetual mobilisation, armed to the teeth with Western firearms. The Germans possessed one small cruiser which occasionally visited the islands, and two decades of erratic naval intervention had diminished considerably any deterrent effect such a warship could hope to have on the local population; there were no colonial troops beyond a largely-decorative force of thirty Samoan police (*Fitafita*) designed to keep order within the Municipality. Drawn from the young men of the more important families, the *Fitafita* was employed to do mechanical tasks for the administration, such as sentry duty and dispatch-carrying. Later on, the corps came to be regarded as a symbol of the interdependent relationship between Samoa and Germany, but in 1900 it offered no guarantee of security against sectarian violence.

Half a century of European penetration had not cowed the Samoans, nor had the traditional culture and its reinforcing values undergone any radical dislocation. At village and district level, established power elites were still very much in control of social and political activities, and they were extremely jealous of their prerogatives. Germany was faced with the problem of establishing a colonial relationship with a people who had never really accepted the premise of subjection as Europeans conceived it. As Herr Meyer-Delius, local head of the DHPG advised, it was a situation requiring freedom for the Samoans in their own administration and a governor who was not only purposeful in his methods but experienced in handling the Islanders.[11]

The man whom the Colonial Department chose for the task was Wilhelm Solf, then head of the provisional government instituted by the three Powers in 1899. Solf was a distinct departure from the usual German colonial official. Better educated than the majority of his service colleagues, a man of the world familiar with British colonial policy from his experience in India, Solf felt altogether superior to the more middle-class, nationalistic, somewhat pettifogging German administrator. He brought to Samoa a natural respect for the intrinsic value of exotic cultures and a readiness to deal with the Samoans on their own terms. Above all, he renounced force as a means of implementing policy. 'All radical measures are evil. Time and goodness and justice are the best means of governing in Samoa', was his firm conviction.[12] Together with the qualities which Samoans associated with leadership—an imposing presence, paternal interest, and the power of rhetoric—Solf's attitude was well suited to the social and political conceptions of the inhabitants.

Solf was convinced, as had been the International Commission before him, that nothing short of a major transformation of the traditional political system would guarantee peaceful development. If the customary system of factional rivalries continued to operate independently of the German government, then a constant state of uneasy peace would degenerate into civil war at Mata'afa Josefo's death, with disastrous results to plantation agriculture and trade, which was already at a low ebb after two decades of unrest. Solf set himself three immediate objectives: to reconcile the opposing parties, to abolish the 'kingship', and to break the power of the chiefs and speakers presuming to speak as the government of Samoa. A longer-term aim was gradually to shift the concentration of indigenous political interest from national to local level and in this way undermine the durability of political parties. Solf possessed a conception of an ancient Samoan 'parish' organisation and political system which he believed would eliminate the unstable influence of the Samoan districts. He envisaged a return to a Golden Age which had no interest in national politics.[13]

In the early months of 1900, however, Solf was powerless to implement his plans in the face of the superior power and influence of Mata'afa Josefo and his thirteen chiefs in Mulinu'u. In the weeks following the flag-raising, they badgered Solf with questions about the date and formation of a new government, and, led by Lauaki, pressed for a one-party administration that acknowledged Mata'afa Josefo's sovereign position. Mata'afa Josefo himself warned Solf that a failure to recognise him as *Tupu Sili* would be construed by his followers as 'disregard of a long-established right' and could endanger the peace.[14] It was clear that 'the thirteen' considered Germany simply to be assuming the former functions of the tripartite regime, and that the Governor was obviously a High Chief sent out by the Kaiser to complete, together with Mata'afa Josefo and his chiefs, the governing power, *Malo o Samoa*.

Solf waited for instructions from Berlin, though he knew it was futile to expect his resources to be increased substantially. In the Wilhelmstrasse, Samoa was regarded as a windfall colony: a ready-made, productive, going concern on the periphery of the overseas empire. Since the Director of the Colonial Department was responsible to a Reichstag which guarded jealously its right to examine the colonial budget, Berlin's first concern was for economy of administration in the colonies. There was a particular reluctance to underwrite expansion in the Pacific where the empire seemed so insignificant and potentially unrewarding in comparison with Africa and China. Consequently Solf, like his colleagues in New Guinea and Micronesia, had little but moral authority on which to fall back in trying to sustain his regime. When instructions had not arrived by April, Solf took matters into his own hands, in the manner of the consuls before him. But, unlike them, he could act with comparative freedom as the sole, legitimate, foreign authority in western Samoa. Unlike most of them, too, Solf was capable of creating virtue out of political necessity and of organising a system which served his ends while seeming to serve those of the Samoan high chiefs.

Accordingly, on 11 April 1900 he announced the institution of a new Samoan government with the Kaiser as *Tupu Sili*, Solf as his principal delegate in Samoa and Mata'afa Josefo as *Ali'i Sili*, or paramount chief, 'the channel through which the wishes and orders of the government are conveyed to the Samoans'.[15] As an auxiliary to this office, and to disarm those chiefs who regarded themselves as the true *Malo*, a bipartisan council of advisers to Mata'afa Josefo was set up—the *Faipule*—which was to contain chiefs of both royal lineages together with district representatives. Finally, the existing Samoan judicial establishment was retained, and provision was made for indigenous administrative officers ranking from district chiefs to village policemen. Lauaki Namulau'ulu Mamoe was prominent among the appointees to the *Faipule*. Indeed the London Missionary Society complained that 'all the old rowdies' had obtained high positions in the new government.[16]

The position of *Ali'i Sili* and a central government in Mulinu'u were not part of Solf's ideal plan for Samoan politics; nor, for that matter, was a local administration based on the districts, the historic centres of mobilisation for political intrigue. Solf harboured plans to abolish all of these institutions when the time was right. He anticipated difficulties, especially from 'that body of indolent intriguers' as he called the *Tumua* and *Pule* chiefs who were constantly scheming over the *Tafa'ifa* titles issue,[17] and they did not disappoint him as they became aware of his real political intentions. In the meantime, Solf was able to consolidate his administration by capitalising on the first flush of co-operation that followed his apparent submission to the desires of Mata'afa Josefo's party, and on widespread satisfaction that peace finally prevailed in the islands. In May 1900 the Colonial Department accorded him a great deal of freedom 'to determine the manner in which the question of native administration will be best solved while maintaining peace and order'.[18]

The most urgent problem was the disarmament of the population. None of the attempts made by the three Powers to control the number of arms in the possession of the Samoans had been successful until the International Commission in 1899 recommended the principle of financial compensation, the cost to be met by the Three Powers. The first experiment took place the same year and netted 3410 firearms. No-one doubted that the Islanders still retained considerable quantities of guns and ammunition, nor that a complete restructuring of the customs system was necessary if shipments of arms were to be prevented from reaching the Samoans in the future. The promised compensation money for 1899 (about US$41 000) finally arrived in 1900, but Solf delayed its distribution until December, by which time he had carried through the necessary reforms and had the arms trade under control. Shortly afterwards, he announced that all further arms and ammunition were to be surrendered against payment by 31 January 1901. It was a discerning move, designed to exploit the momentary euphoria of the Samoans at receiving the promised cash after so long. By mid-February the people had delivered up most of the remaining hoard, some 1500 guns.[19]

A number of other elements of colonial control and development were introduced without resistance in the first two years of German rule. In August 1900 Solf promulgated an ordinance directing every Samoan 'landowner' (the *matai*) to plant fifty coconuts annually on unused land, in order to offset the decline in production over the preceding years. Samoan 'plantation inspectors' were appointed to supervise the process. Samoans were also obligated to maintain public roads in their localities with tools supplied by the government, and the customary right of eviction of the defeated party in a district by the victorious was outlawed.

The final link in the chain of regulations was a poll tax, levied from late January 1901. Adult males were required to pay four marks annually, later raised to twelve, then to twenty-four marks for *matai*, and the tax yield rose each year: from 40 000 marks in 1901 to 211 000 marks in 1912.[20] The head tax was the only one of these early regulations to encounter some resistance, for Samoans openly distrusted the whites where money was concerned. Solf was able to obtain the chiefs' agreement only after conceding to their demand that it be used solely for the upkeep of the Samoan administràtion and not for the white community. Until 1905, at least, the Samoan administrative system was tied closely to the head tax revenue, and the size of official salaries was made dependent upon the amount collected. Then, in 1908, resentment over the poll tax and the Governor's use of the revenue played a prominent role in the great confrontation between Solf and the old chiefs, which had been threatening from the early years of German rule.

The political complications which Solf predicted in 1900 did not take long to emerge. For a start, there were substantial practical difficulties in the operation of his 'self-governing' local administration. Despite the appointment of functionaries who already possessed local authority, and the protection of *matai* from pressures to support intrigues beyond their villages, the fact was that Samoan officials were expected to pursue European objectives which were governed by German colonial policy and legal practice. They had to collect taxes, supervise road maintenance and coconut planting, and maintain German conceptions of law and order. These actions often clashed with Samoan ideas of law and order, and with their habit of discussing and debating demands on community resources. Moreover, in judging criminal acts, Western law, unlike Samoan custom, made no allowance for the respective social position of offender and offended, nor did it recognise the civil wrong suffered by the relatives of the victim. The contradictions with which individuals were faced were reflected in the high turnover of Samoan officers between 1900 and 1905, either through dismissal or rotation. Dismissals most often followed instances of dictatorial behaviour by village 'mayors' (*pulenu'u*) and district magistrates (*faamasino*).

Threats to the new system came also from established chiefs in Mulinu'u and in individual districts, who assumed authority over newly-appointed officials on the grounds that they—the chiefs—were the true representatives of traditional custom, prestige and influence (*fa'a Samoa*). From the beginning Solf had been forced to create the post of district chief (*Taitai Itu*) to placate a number of dissatisfied elites. His final objective, however, was to abolish these positions, and several others, so as to have as few 'middle men' as possible between himself and his European district officers.[21]

A more serious threat to the Governor's entire juggling act occurred after 1900-01 as the chiefs of the Mulinu'u *Malo* began to recognise the divergence between the form of political power conceded to them and the real intentions of the German government. Shortly after the new Samoan administration had been founded, a house of *Taimua* was created at Mulinu'u, consisting of the principal contenders for high Samoan titles from both of the leading families. Seemingly it was meant to encourage, in the minds of Samoans, the idea that competition for the great titles of the land now had no meaning, and that government service should thenceforward be the highest aspiration of the prominent families. This did not at all accord with the expectations of the *Malo*: the *Taimua* was a body quite foreign to Samoan custom.

The *Malo*'s conviction that it was being stripped of its powers was strengthened by Mata'afa Josefo's obvious subjection to Solf. Though the Governor was careful to protect Mata'afa Josefo's dignity and always to use him as the official mouthpiece of the administration, Mata'afa Josefo's image was sullied more and more by his identification with measures which were new to the chiefs and contrary to custom. The most radical of these included the removal of Samoan responsibility for the financial affairs of the *Malo*, and Solf's division of several traditional districts into independent administrative units, thus splitting the political support which 'royal' candidates could normally expect.[22]

Dissatisfaction was aggravated by the presence within Mata'afa Josefo's party of traditional, non-Mata'afan elements, especially Safotulafai of Fa'asaleleaga in Savai'i. Safotulafai was the spiritual centre of *Pule* and usually pro-Malietoan. But in 1898, under Lauaki's influence, and in order to increase the chances of Samoan unity, Safotulafai had opted for Mata'afa Josefo. The chiefs of Safotulafai were well aware that the support of their district had given Mata'afa Josefo his overwhelming strength in 1898-99, and that they held a virtual balance of power in the new coalition of parties under Solf.

Lauaki was one of the first to read Solf's design. Outwardly he was a Samoan who manifested a confident acceptance of European civilisation. A devout adherent of the London Missionary Society and deacon of the local church, Lauaki moved easily among Europeans. He recognised and accepted the benefits of the European economy; he even named his son Tivoli after a hotel in Apia.[23] Internally, however, Lauaki's life was guided by tradition. He had made and broken high chiefs in the era of the Three Powers, and skilfully exploited the latter's rivalries to gain benefits for his party and candidate. More than any other *tulafale*, Lauaki embodied the highest values of Samoa in his knowledge of custom and his skill in politics, and he remained committed to the cause of *Sā Malietoā* and to the prerogatives of the *Tumua* and *Pule* chiefs.

Mata'afa Josefo's alliance was therefore an uneasy one, with Lauaki and his district acting as power brokers. Increasingly, confrontations between the *Malo* and Solf became confrontations between Lauaki and Solf, though the ultimate crisis was still some seven years away. But in 1903 it was already whispered around that Lauaki had issued a warning against the Governor and his subtle ways. He acknowledged that Solf was a good man, but added that he was 'too tricky' for Samoans:

> At first he cuts up all the different districts so as to weaken them, and takes away gradually the power from the *Taitai Itu*, and lastly, he deprives the Samoans of the high position of *Faamasino Sili* [Chief Samoan Magistrate]. After this the Governor will even take away the position of *Le Ali'i Sili*, so that no higher office remains for the Samoan people.[24]

At this stage Solf did not dare move against Lauaki because of the chief's power and Solf's own obvious lack of it. Fear of passive, if not active, resistance made the Germans very cautious in their early relations with the *Malo*, despite provocation. During Solf's absence in 1902, Lauaki and the *Faipule* organised a strike by Samoan road workers for better pay and food, with the apparent purpose of intimidating Solf's deputy Heinrich Schnee into granting the *Faipule* a salary; they hoped thus to legitimise their occupation of Mulinu'u as imperial officials. Schnee stood his ground, knowing the Governor's desire to see the *Malo* dispersed, but he made no move to punish anyone for the disturbance, in fear of disaffecting the most powerful chiefs and speakers.[25] It was not until 1903 that Solf risked his first major confrontation with the *Malo*, when he exiled two orator chiefs to Herbertshöhe, one for preaching the hope of British annexation, the other for inciting his people to murder. The threat of deportation had always been a powerful argument in tripartite times, and Germany had early established a reputation for quick and determined action in such circumstances.

A new threat to Solf arose from a different quarter in 1902. In that year the white population of Samoa increased dramatically as a number of immigrants with very limited capital arrived from Germany to try their hand at plantation agriculture, several retired military officers among them. They had been influenced directly by one Richard Deeken, a young artillery officer in the German Reserve, who visited Samoa briefly in 1901 and proceeded to write an extravagant and superficial account of the opportunities that awaited the small settler with moderate capital.[26] The impact his fertile imagination had on people was reinforced by mounting propaganda in Germany in favour of occupying the colonies with small capital holdings. Deeken founded a plantation company, the Deutsche Samoa Gesellschaft (DSG), to compete with the DHPG, and in August 1902 he returned to Samoa as its director.

The new settlers were quickly disillusioned. They had been led to expect abundant land ideal for growing cocoa. The reality was far less hopeful. At Solf's invitation, an agricultural scientist, Dr F. Wohltmann, came out to Samoa in 1902-03 to assess its proper agricultural potential. Wohltmann concluded that Samoan soil was already considerably worked out and that only four per cent of it was suitable for cocoa cultivation, of which half was already being used by the Samoans for their own crops. A prospective settler would need at least 50 000 marks, he estimated, and must still cope with high land prices and labour costs. In addition, settlers had to confront the formidable competition of the DHPG, which in 1900 already possessed 82 hectares of cocoa besides its lucrative thousands of hectares of mature coconut plants dating from the 1880s. The old firm's most telling advantage lay in its privileged access to cheap Melanesian labour from the Bismarck Archipelago. As if this were not enough, the first settlers had to endure a drought in 1902, and try to acquire leasehold land from the Samoans who were withholding leases in the hope of inflated prices. It is little wonder that in 1903 Wohltmann found twenty-five of forty-six small planters urgently in need of government aid.[27]

They received scant sympathy from the Governor, who had done his best to correct the fanciful impressions of a colonial planting life in Samoa. As their early expectations were disappointed and their capital depleted, the small settlers became increasingly militant and chauvinistic, and at last turned on the government. Deeken, who was also discovering that the land and labour monopoly of the DHPG was virtually impregnable, gathered the dissidents around him in a Planters' Society (*Pflanzerverein*) which was founded in January 1903.

Deeken found a constant source of provocation in the intimate collaboration between Solf and the DHPG. 'The Firm' was the heir to the oldest German company in Samoa, Godeffroys, and had operated an extensive trade and plantation business throughout two decades of civil war. Its metropolitan directors were all old 'Samoa hands', familiar with the people, their customs, and their limits of tolerance. By 1900 the major conflicts between the company's exploitation of Samoa and its social concern had been resolved, and a relationship quickly developed with Solf which was characterised by mutual respect and support. Solf was careful to uphold the firm's monopoly of land, labour and trade, not only against local enemies but also against the attacks of Governor Hahl in New Guinea, who was pressuring Berlin to curtail the DHPG's recruiting privileges in the Bismarck Archipelago. In return, Solf could count on the company's support for his protective native policy, and there is no doubt that the pattern of his rule was strengthened by the friendship of men who had spent decades trying to establish orderly community relations in the Samoan islands.

In 1903-04 the Governor was in very real need of the DHPG's influence in Berlin, for Deeken used his position as president of the *Pflanzerverein* to launch a campaign against Solf's administration. Deeken was able to mobilise considerable influence in Germany through close contacts in the Catholic Centre Party (*Zentrumspartei*), and a press attack was orchestrated, alleging that Solf had done nothing for the small planters since the flag-raising, that he was pandering to the political whims of the Samoans, and that the administration was extravagant in its expenditure. There was even talk of a plan by Solf to deport twelve colonists and their families from Samoa. Deeken's proposed solution was to replace Solf's regime with a military one which would be more attentive to the 'demands' of colonial development.[28]

It did not take long for the unrest in the white community to percolate through to the Samoans. In the *Pflanzerverein* Deeken had inspired a resolution that the Samoans be compelled to work for Europeans at least eight months of the year. In June 1903 the chiefs of the *Malo* petitioned Solf to save them from its implications since it was Samoan custom 'that no one on these islands should perform servile labour'.[29]

The Governor had no intention of dragooning Samoans into plantation labour for the likes of Deeken, knowing as he did that the people were quite capable of effective counter-action: at the very best, copra cutting would cease, white traders would be boycotted, and the people would revert to subsistence agriculture. Since the export/import economy depended on Samoan production and consumption, the financial ruin of European business would inevitably follow. At worst the Samoans might rise in armed rebellion.

Solf was fortunate in having the support of the DHPG on this question. With privileged access to the recruiting grounds of Melanesia, the company's interest lay in the Samoans as trading partners, not as a labour force.[30] Nevertheless, there was a definite increase in inter-communal tensions, and Solf predicted that 1904 would bring further discontent in view of the projected poor copra harvest and sinking world prices. This would be grist to Deeken's mill.

By now Solf was a bitter enemy of Deeken and his clique of small planters. His liberal, cosmopolitan paternalism and Deeken's pan-German philosophy of colonial exploitation were irreconcilable. Deeken conceived of colonies simply as economic appendages to the fatherland, and considered that colonial resources and manpower were meant to benefit industrious settlers. Solf, while he did not despise the economic ethic, hated its apotheosis. Colonial development was, to him, a process in which the economic prosperity of European settlers should be balanced by the preservation and encouragement of the local Islanders. Solf therefore refused to treat the Samoans as an exploitable commodity, considering their cultural achievements worthy of parti-cular respect. There was a more practical reason too. A reading of Samoan history persuaded the Governor that the Islanders would not be bullied into subjection, and that foolishness, irresolution or excess on the part of the German regime would lead to passive resistance and general anti-white hostility. Before Deeken arrived, Solf had been working to convince the Colonial Department that he could guide the Samoans in the desired direction by a non-militant policy of close contact with them at village level.

Deeken presented a direct threat to the Governor's image in Berlin, and to the patriarchal authority which he was assiduously building up with the Samoans. In late 1903, Solf warned the Colonial Department of the dangers which an opposition of 'Catholics, pan-Germans, the disillusioned and the dissatisfied' presented in the young colony, and in desperation pleaded with the Department to put pressure on the Deutsche Samoa Gesellschaft to have Deeken removed. He even declared himself prepared to resort to deportation if the occasion warranted.

But neither entreaties nor threats moved Berlin, which remained very cautious of Deeken's influence in the Reichstag, and the Governor had to wait until early 1904 for a chance to rid himself of his *bete noire*. The chance came when Deeken was involved in suspicions of fraud con-cerning his company's first shipment of Chinese coolies to arrive in Samoa as plantation labour; Solf immediately revoked the company's recruiting permission. Provoked, Deeken insinuated that the Governor had been inciting his workers against him, after several of the coolies complained of maltreatment. Solf responded with a libel action and in addition charged Deeken with brutality to his employees. There followed a series of legal manoeuvres, smear attacks, calumnies and intimidations as Deeken attempted to wriggle out of the charge but he was finally brought to trial, and, in June 1904, convicted on two counts of assault and one of slander. The court sentenced him to two months' imprisonment.

It was during this period that contacts between the settler opposition and certain sections of the Samoan community came to light. In June the British and American consuls reported several rumours: that the Samoans were demanding that Mata'afa Josefo should countersign all ordinances; that the *Malo* be paid a monthly salary; and that it have the right to scrutinise quarterly balance sheets showing the details of government revenue. Both consuls were convinced that the demands could be inspired only by whites. The local newspaper even printed a rumour that the Islanders had refused to pay the head tax.[31]

Solf tried to calm everybody. He admitted the existence of a letter from the *Faipule* in Mulinu'u making imperious demands, and he agreed that it was inspired by whites, more specifically by Deeken who wished to discomfort the government. In a rare moment of discernment, Deeken replied that the Samoans 'follow proceedings among the whites with the closest attention and use them for their own purposes'.[32] For Solf had failed to consider the possibility that, as the local native bureaucracy consolidated its influence, the central government in Mulinu'u might seek to exploit dissatisfaction in the white community in an effort to offset its increasing loss of influence with the mass of Samoans. In this sense, the petition was an attempt to reassert the *Faipule*'s position, and it is possible that the Mulinu'u chiefs encouraged the rumours of unrest in order to wring concessions from the administration.

Solf would not be bluffed. As far as he was concerned, only a few of the *Faipule*—Lauaki at their head—would dare to go so far; Mata'afa Josefo and the majority, he knew, had no heart for the matter. The Governor demanded an apology from the body or they would be dismissed. He got his apology.[33] He was then able to dissuade the foreign consuls from reporting trouble to their governments, particularly as it was obvious that the general populace had remained completely unaffected by the *Malo*'s conduct. The captain of a German cruiser visiting Samoa in September 1904 endorsed Solf's view. 'I gained the impression anew', he wrote,

> that loyalty, confidence in the government, and attachment to the present representatives of the government are deeply rooted in the hearts of the Samoans; that they are contented with their lot and that they will not hear of rebellion and disturbance unless they are misguided and led on.[34]

The Deeken saga was far from finished with his conviction, for he was released immediately on appeal and the old intrigues began again. His appeal may well have been upheld thanks to the good offices of Deputy Trimborn, his uncle in the Reichstag, but, at the last moment, when it seemed that a full pardon might be granted, the Kaiser himself intervened on Solf's behalf and refused to sanction one. Instead Deeken's sentence was commuted to two months' confinement, and, at Solf's insistence, he was made to serve it in Germany, at the fortress above Koblenz-Ehrenbreitstein. The young reserve officer managed to alienate most of the fortress personnel during this stay there in 1905. In June 1907 he was back in Samoa to take up the reins of his company, and to continue his campaign to discredit the 'Solf system'.

The Oloa Movement

In the last months of 1904, it became evident that reports suggesting the Samoans were generally content with life under the Germans were premature. The activities of the settler opposition had significantly altered the equilibrium of relations between the two racial communities. New rumours were already circulating in September that Solf was in disgrace and about to be recalled, while Deeken came to be regarded as a powerful figure because he continued to go free in spite of his calumnies.

On top of this came the deterioration of the Islanders' economic prospects, as Solf had predicted in 1903. Copra produced by the Samoans was the backbone of the export trade, and through it the people were able to satisfy their demands for European consumer goods, as well as pay the administration's head tax. The Islanders produced well over half the 7614 tonnes of copra exported from the colony in 1903-04, but a slump in the world market price of copra in those years reduced their copra income from eight or nine pfennigs a pound to five pfennigs.[35]   The Samoan community was disgruntled at the drop, and Solf only fanned the discontent when he rejected an application by the chiefs at Mulinu'u to stabilise the price of copra in Samoa at nine pfennigs a pound. Thus, with the chiefs in Mulinu'u mortified at the loss of their power, the stage was set for a major challenge to the white community. This came when Pullack, a young half-caste son of a German customs officer, mooted the idea of a copra-marketing company to be run by Samoans themselves, with its own shipping facilities and guaranteeing a high, stable price for copra.[36] The Mulinu'u chiefs seized on the idea. They believed that not only would it solve the present copra crisis and help to update the industry, but also that it was an opportunity to acquire the economic power which, from their observations of European commercial enterprise and colonial practice, they perceived to be a prerequisite of political power. The *Malo* immediately began spreading propaganda in favour of the idea and ordered that every male Samoan was to contribute between four and eight marks (*Lafoga Oloa*) to the project, which ran under the name of the *Cumpani* or *Oloa*. To mobilise the widest possible amount of sentiment, the *Cumpani* was launched as a patriotic venture which would emancipate the Samoans from their 'slavery' to the white copra traders. Since manifold abuses and deceptions were practised on the Samoans by European traders, this approach was calculated to bring results.[37]

The government became fully aware of the significance of the scheme by about December when there was a drastic drop in copra cutting by the Samoans. For several reasons, Solf determined to put a stop to the *Oloa*. First, in common with most other Europeans in the colony, he was convinced that the Samoans did not possess the commercial knowledge or expertise to make the scheme viable. Second, it was a challenge to one of the platforms of colonisation—the white trader and the European monopoly of commerce—to which the Governor at heart was committed. Third, Solf recognised that it also was a bid by the chiefs and speakers in Mulinu'u to make a resolute stand against his projected native policy. They had never failed to assert that they were the 'kingmakers' of Samoa, with a mandate to carry out the affairs of the Samoan administration under the direction of Mata'afa Josefo. By institutionalising its power in the co-operative, the central government might have succeeded in regaining influence over the activities of the Samoan districts and thus restoring the traditional system of politics to which Solf was adamantly opposed. From this perspective the *Lafoga* looked very much like a form of direct taxation, to be used as a lever against the German administration.

Solf reacted quickly, and in early December he journeyed round the districts with his officials trying to persuade the people that the venture was hopelessly utopian. Pullack, who was suspected of preparing a major swindle for his own benefit, was deported. However, the *Malo* remained defiant, and the district *fonos* revealed that the idea of a co-operative had a broad appeal to most Samoans, including Mata'afa Josefo. Solf did not dare to risk a frontal assault. He did strictly prohibit the payment of any *Lafoga*; and he attempted to break the united front of the Mulinu'u chiefs by forbidding all native officials of the administration to participate in any way, under the threat of dismissal. Lauaki was even pressured into a promise to 'assist the government in keeping peace and tranquillity' by using his influence to turn the movement into more amenable channels.[38] By the end of December 1904, these dividing tactics had succeeded in discouraging many officials and their localities and slowing the flow of funds to the movement. Solf, confident that the affair would soon become a laughing stock as district rivalries asserted themselves, embarked on a voyage to New Zealand.

His departure was the signal for the revival of the movement. The *Oloa* had not been forced out of existence at all, merely pushed out of sight of the Europeans. Suddenly Solf was in danger of becoming a laughing stock himself. Rumours began circulating that Solf was involved in a conspiracy with the white traders against Samoan copra growers, and, in disgrace, had been recalled by the Kaiser. The pent-up frustration of the Mulinu'u chiefs at Solf's obstructionist tactics finally came into the open. Inspired by a recent petition of the Tutuila natives against the American administration, the chiefs addressed a petition to the Kaiser himself, complaining that Solf was discriminating against a legal Samoan venture and reiterating their demands for recognition as the official organ of native government.[39] A new campaign to solicit funds for the *Cumpani* was led by Lauaki's brother Namulau'ulu Pulali who claimed that the Governor and his deputy were in favour of the scheme. At a large *fono* in Fa'asaleleaga on 5 January 1905, one of Solf's appointed village mayors, Malaeulu, went so far as to threaten that if Solf did not consent to the *Oloa*, the Samoans 'must scrape his body with pipi shells', and the decision was taken to restart the *Cumpani*.[40]

The situation looked desperate to Erich Schultz, the Imperial Magistrate and Lands Commissioner who was Solf's deputy in his absence. Aware that he could not risk forceful suppression of the movement because of the danger of Samoan resistance, he was equally afraid that, unless he made an example of the ringleaders, the authority of the German administration would effectively be subverted by the *Malo*. Schultz decided to arrest Malaeulu and Namulau'ulu Pulali. On 26 January they were put in Vaimea prison on charges of disturbing the peace, spreading false reports and insulting the Governor, charges which were, Schultz was careful to emphasise, *fa'a Samoa* liable to punishment.

The *Faipule* in Mulinu'u presumed that the two chiefs had been imprisoned for being members of the *Oloa*, and Schultz's action was construed as an unfair belittlement of *Pule*, to which both chiefs belonged. Custom demanded that the chiefs' adherents come to their aid. Mata'afa Josefo sent a letter requesting the release of the two men since they were only doing the will of the *Malo*. 'When a white man has been sentenced for any violation of the law', he protested, 'his sentence is not executed'[41]—an obvious reference to Deeken's case. Before Schultz could reply, several chiefs broke into Vaimea prison on 31 January and freed the prisoners, as a gesture of the independence of the Samoan government and in an attempt to reinforce a sense of solidarity.[42]

In actual fact the unity of the *Oloa* movement had been dissolving under internal stresses. The non-Mata'afan members among the *Faipule* suspected that the adherents of Mata'afa Josefo were seeking to establish the superiority of their party through the *Cumpani*, and they made it clear that any attempt to raise taxes for it by force would be met with resistance. The Vaimea incident only had the effect of increasing the tensions between the two rival parties, and Schultz began to receive declarations of support from the non-Mata'afans. Mata'afa Josefo and the majority of the chiefs immediately regretted their action, and, in a meeting with Schultz the day after, agreed to return Malaeulu and Namulau'ulu Pulali to prison, which they promptly did. With the solidarity of the whole movement breaking down around them and the rumour of Solf's recall proving untrue, the chiefs feared for the consequences of their actions and hoped, by their repentance, to appease Solf on his return. Pleading that 'all is due to ignorance on our part', they pressed Schultz for a full pardon for the two chiefs.[43] Schultz refused, recognising from his knowledge of *fa'a Samoa*, that from this entire debacle, Solf could extract the grounds he had been seeking to remove the Mulinu'u government permanently.

By the time Solf returned in mid-March, the *Cumpani* virtually had shipwrecked itself and the 'patriotism' of the movement was a dead issue. Solf set about trying to restore his own authority and break permanently the influence of the chiefs and speakers in Mulinu'u. In this he was assisted by the eagerness of Mata'afa Josefo and the chiefs to salvage some of their prestige. First they prepared a lavish welcome festival for his return, and then they performed the traditional cere-monial act of atonement and self-humiliation (*Ifoga*) before his house: Solf ostentatiously rejected both. Accompanied by the captain and officers of SMS *Condor*, Solf then made a speech in Lufilufi, one of the two great political centres of *Tumua*, in which he ridiculed the actions of the chiefs in fables transparent to every Samoan. He confronted Mata'afa Josefo with his 'deceit' in encouraging the events connected with Vaimea and styled the guilty chiefs 'treacherous rebels' who were fit only for deportation.

It was a shrewd strategy of intimidation entirely in accord with Samoan custom in such circumstances. Ridicule and loss of face, particularly before the public in a hallowed place like Lufilufi, were powerful sanctions among Samoan elites, so that in June, when Solf issued an order that Mulinu'u be vacated, the chiefs complied; they had expected much worse.

Solf followed up with an assembly on 14 August in which he explained the necessity to dissolve the central government of chiefs and speakers because 'they had proceeded against the decrees of the regime whose allies they had been'.[44] He also imposed a series of punishments for individual misdemeanours: Moefaauo and Lauaki, as chief representatives of the *Tumua* and *Pule* were to be deported, though Lauaki was later placed on probation for fear of making him a martyr to the Samoan people; those responsible for the Vaimea incident were dismissed from their government posts and fined 1000 marks; Malaeulu lost his position as village mayor while Namulau'ulu Pulali was imprisoned for two months. These individual penalties were accompanied by a purge of the Samoan judiciary and of certain native commissions.

Solf also took the opportunity to make changes to the Samoan administration, changes which would place it entirely in his hands. The house of *Taimua* was abolished and a new salaried council of *Faipule* established, consisting of twenty-seven deputies who were to reside in their districts and assemble in Mulinu'u twice a year. Only loyalists and those too influential to dismiss were considered for the appointments, but Solf was careful to select members of both major parties and to establish a parity between Protestant and Catholic officials. By limiting the number of orator chiefs in the new council to a maximum of seven, Solf was able to restrict their influence at the national level. By 'promoting' district governors (*Taitai Itu*) to deputies and making appointments to sub-districts which traditionally did not hold power, he was also able to achieve his original objective of reducing the institutional importance of the districts, as well as to create a nucleus of supporters dependent on him for their positions.

The new system destroyed completely the fiction of a Samoan 'self administration' which Solf had cultivated in 1900, using Mata'afa Josefo as mouthpiece. From now on all appointments emanated from the Governor himself and were to be terminated at his discretion, while the *Faipule* were now directly responsible for conveying his orders to the *pulenu'u* of the villages.

The seeds of a new Samoan reaction were sown in these changes of 1905, for it was clear to the chiefs and speakers that they had lost all semblance of independence. Solf made it explicit when, in his speech announcing the alterations, he excluded the power cartel of *Tumua* and *Pule* from any further say in Samoa's official future:

> ... there is no room in that Government for *Tumua* and *Pule*. The old *fa'alupenga* or formal traditional salutation of Samoa which was made use of by the former Council to arrogate power to themselves is no longer in existence, and I shall make a law forbidding use of that salutation in any meeting.[45]

But not all initiative had been removed from the chiefs. Solf's one big error of judgment was to allow Lauaki to remain in the islands. Lauaki's colleague, Moefaauo, on the eve of his deportation, had warned Solf to get rid of the Savai'i orator while he could. He claimed vehemently that Lauaki was 'the root of all evil' in Samoa: 'He has a sweet tongue and [is] a slippery man at that—the *palagi* don't understand him as well as the Samoans do'.[46] Solf would soon rue Moefaao's words, for Lauaki's presence was a pledge of continuing resistance to the Governor's politics.

Lauaki had championed consistently the conservative cause against Solf. During the *Oloa* movement he figured prominently, notably in restarting agitation after Solf's departure and in joining the petition to the Kaiser. Some confusion exists about his role in the Vaimea incident, but since Namulau'ulu Pulali was his brother, it is more than likely that Lauaki supported, if he did not directly encourage, the freeing of the prisoners.[47] When retribution seemed near, with the return of the supposedly-disgraced Solf, Lauaki was very deft in retracing his steps and working against the co-operative idea, so successfully that he weaned his entire district away from it. It was undoubtedly Lauaki's about-face which increased the confusion in the Samoan camp and contributed to the rapid disintegration of *Oloa* solidarity before Solf's return. His final triumph was in convincing Solf and Richard Williams, district administrator on Savai'i, that his repentance was genuine, his loyalty unimpaired. Over the protests of Mata'afa Josefo, and with the unanimous disapproval of the other *Faipule*, this 'crafty and perceptive man', as Solf described him,[48] was given a place on the new council.

Though Mata'afa Josefo was highly implicated in the train of events, Solf refused to sacrifice him to the reaction from the white community which followed the affair. Solf blamed Deeken for leading Mata'afa Josefo astray. He also blamed the settler clique for the original rumour of his disgrace, as well as for the *Malo*'s petition to the Kaiser and the subsequent Vaimea incident. Nothing could be proven against Deeken, but there was ample evidence of contacts between his group and the leading chiefs in Mulinu'u. Direct contacts between Lauaki and Deeken could not be traced, but Schultz at least was convinced that Lauaki was clever enough to use the planter for his own purposes, which perhaps was corroborated by the fact that Deeken was regarded by the majority of the *Malo* as prospective manager of the *Cumpani* in succession to Pullack.[49] This ploy was obviously both a business manoeuvre to exploit Deeken's expertise, and a contingency measure against the future: if Deeken proved more powerful than Solf and the Governor really were disgraced, it obviously made sense to support Deeken and commit him to the future of the co-operative. At no time, however, did the Samoans openly engage themselves in Deeken's cause. In fact, they had strenuously opposed from the start his campaign to force them onto the European plantations, and considered it an affront that he should retain his freedom in Samoa after his conviction.

Deeken's group of disaffected small planters led the white reaction to the Vaimea incident. In a petition to the Chancellor, purporting to represent the majority of business opinion in Apia, the opposition presented the affair as evidence of the complete shipwreck of Solf's control policy. They argued that the European population was now 'completely at the mercy of the Samoans' and that it was essential to act with a mailed fist—to send naval cruisers, to deport chiefs and to establish a garrison of colonial troops.[50] The petition received short shrift from the Colonial Department which had no intention of increasing administrative, let alone military involvement in the Pacific, in the face of the demands made by the recent Herero rebellion in South-West Africa. Solf's success, not only in maintaining peace and security, but also in breaking the power of the corporation of chiefs and speakers in Mulinu'u without the use of force of any kind, was the strongest possible vindication of his policy. And in Samoa itself, Deeken's panic patently was not shared by all. The DHPG newspaper, the *Samoanische Zeitung*, declared confidently, if predictably, in Solf's favour. It concluded there were now better grounds 'for anticipating a lasting peace for Samoa than have previously existed within the memory of living men' (26 August 1905).

2

Lauki versus the Solf System

The three years 1905 to 1908 were a period of relatively peaceful development. Trade and agriculture took an upward turn, and in 1906 Samoa achieved a favourable balance of trade for the first time. From 1908 onwards, the administration was able to prepare its annual budgets without relying on a Reich subsidy. For their part, the Samoans were enjoying an increase in purchasing power as copra prices began to rise once more in 1905. With the regulation of Samoan copra production following the ordinance of 1900 and the administration's struggle to improve its quality through legislation and closer supervision, the Samoan community was able to maintain its high degree of participation in the export economy: between 1905 and 1908 it produced on average two-thirds of all the copra exported from Samoa. Moreover, encouraged by the example of several new plantation companies in these years, Samoans had planted 1362 hectares of the new cash crop, cocoa, by 1906. They also continued to meet the fiscal demands made on them by the head tax, but were showing a greater interest in the way the taxes were being employed.

In the wake of the political changes of 1905, the Samoans were now being governed by an unrestrained, patriarchal regime founded squarely on Solf's authority and his conviction that 'a tactful Governor can rule the natives without laws'. Understanding better than most Europeans the limits to which Samoans would allow themselves to be pushed, Solf used only indirect methods to bring the Samoans within the colonial economy. The regular planting of young coconuts, which the Governor enforced through plantation inspectors, together with the head tax levy, helped to stimulate use of village land and increase productivity; legislation against false weights and measures protected the Samoan grower against the unscrupulous copra buyer; while at the village level salaried Samoan officials were the levers of government. Solf interfered in this *'fa'a Samoa* hinterland'[1] only when a breakdown in law and order was imminent, or when Samoan economic aspirations clashed with the vital interests of European commerce, as the co-operative movement had.

Solf was determined that his rule should provide a preferable alternative to the 'para-administrative' organisation which the various mission societies had come to represent to the Samoans through their long history of contact. The Governor had maintained consistently good relations with the missions since 1900. There had been a number of controversies—for instance, with the London Missionary Society over the extent of their annual district collections (*Me*) and the puritan regulation of Sunday activity, and over the Marists' privileged influence with Mata'afa Josefo—but these had been only temporary irritations. Solf was realistic enough to concede that the Samoans could not be expected automatically to transfer their primary allegiance from the one form of Western discipline they had accepted for fifty years to a still largely unfamiliar secular regime.

With the conversion of the Samoans virtually complete by 1905, the missions were now concentrating on meeting the educational demands of the community. In 1906 the London Missionary Society could count 24 808 Samoan adherents, or two-thirds of the population; 6022 Samoans were Catholics while the remainder spread themselves among a number of smaller Christian societies. An elementary school functioned in every one of the London Missionary Society's villages, and there were a series of district high schools as well as the Malua seminary. In all, 299 schools of various denominations existed in Samoa in 1906, with 470 teachers and nearly 10 000 pupils. The government began its own public school in 1907.[2]

It was the Samoans' avidity for education, as well as their economic activity, which moved Solf to respond to their appeals for a permanent prohibition on the further sale or leasing of Samoan land to whites. Samoans rarely seem to have been losers in the rush by Europeans for land holdings before 1900. There were more cases of Samoans defrauding Europeans in land deals during the 1880s than the reverse, and successful local wars had been financed from the profits. In 1889 the Berlin Conference had established the principle of prohibiting the sale of Samoan land to foreigners and of restricting leaseholds, while the land commission set up by the three Powers in the following years confirmed only a small percentage of past European purchases.[3] Most claims were rejected on the grounds that the sale had not been made by the rightful owner, an ironic indication of Samoan accomplishments in land transactions.

But the advent of new plantation companies after 1900 brought widespread pressure to bear on the German government to reintroduce freehold sales or at least to permit long-term leases. Prominent Samoans countered with the argument that Europeans had long overestimated the area of cultivable land in the group, an argument supported by Dr Wohltmann's analysis in 1902-03. Wohltmann found that only half of Upolu's land area was suitable for cultivation, and only one-fifth of the area of Savai'i. Whites had already alienated more land than was safe in the circumstances, and Wohltmann advised that 50 000 hectares be reserved to the Samoans for their own needs.

Solf and the *Faipule* discussed the question at length in the August 1907 meeting of the Mulinu'u council. The result was an ordinance of 26 November, providing that land could be transferred by sale or lease only in the 'plantation district' around Apia. Outside this limit the government might lease land to foreigners provided that Samoan cultivable lands were not diminished to less than 1.29 hectares per head of population.[4] It was a solution which patently favoured the DHPG, since it possessed the only considerable land holdings outside Apia already in the hands of Europeans.

Predictably, Solf had to withstand a new storm of criticism from small planters. Their opposition to the Governor was reinforced during these years by the return of Richard Deeken. Deeken arrived this time with instructions from his company to keep out of Solf's way, but it was not long before the two men clashed openly over an attempt by Deeken to inveigle his way into the advisory council for settlers which Solf had set up early in his administration.

Solf's critics in the colony and abroad did not waver in their opposition to his 'system'. The Governor's self-conscious independence, and his reliance on personal authority in dealing with the Samoan community were a continual affront to the Deeken faction. They wanted to see more direct mobilisation of Samoan manpower to ease the shortage of labour for small plantations, and advocated the use of 'positive' force should the Islanders resist. Solf reacted to all this badgering with occasional petulance and self-righteousness, but he stubbornly refused to abandon his Samoan policies: 'I will not be the grave digger of the colony which I have helped to baptise', was one of his favourite retorts.[5]

Wilhelm Solf (like his deputy Erich Schultz-Ewerth) was a man sensitive to the ethics and history of Samoan society, and outspokenly determined to preserve its integrity. His administrative strategy of defending Samoans, their land and their labour had its roots in a well-reasoned analysis of Germany's role in Samoa, which he articulated in a series of reports to the Colonial Office in 1906 and 1907.[6] Sent in response to a general request for ideas about the future of Germany's colonies, Solf's 'program' was much more than a survey of past achievements and a list of developmental priorities. With his cosmopolitan background and outlook, and his small 'l' liberalism, Solf found it necessary to offer some form of ideological rationale for his involvement in Germany's *Kolonialpolitik*, with its blatantly economic ends and occasionally brutal consequences. The result was a conception which comes closer to a philosophy of colonialism than any other official collection of ideas in the German Pacific.

The Governor made it clear from the beginning that his plan for Samoa revolved primarily around the Samoan people: they would be the focus of his energies rather than the small community of German and English colonists. He argued that with the raising of the imperial flag in 1900, Germany had accepted the legal and moral obligation to create for the island people 'better and more rational conditions of life than they themselves in the narrowness of their hearts and minds could create'. To do so required not force but patient and sensitive leadership. The Samoan people were only 'wild, truculent, superstitious children', susceptible to cajolery, and capable of reaching a higher ideal of civilisation if led by guides and mentors who, like Solf, were prepared to ground themselves in the emotions and thought processes of the island people. Solf's ideal was development with and through the Samoans, not in spite of them.

To suggest that these ideas represent a liberal humanism years ahead of its time in Germany would be an exaggeration. Solf may not have subscribed to the crude rhetoric of Social Darwinism, but his sympathy for Samoans was based on a subtle variation of the same theme, namely, that Germany, as the foremost *Kulturstaat*, possessed the duty to civilise a society which had achieved as much as had Samoa in the pursuit of the West's educational values; in other words, that the Samoan people should continue to prosper as deserving servants of the colonising intelligence. It was also impractical politics to exploit the people ruthlessly, since, in his scheme of things, they were to provide the engines of Samoa's future development within the Reich. As Solf saw it, he was merely preparing a seedbed in Samoa for other generations of colonists. They would reap the benefits of his cultivation. Wilhelm Solf's ideas thus occupy a place firmly within the intellectual traditions of Wilhelmine Germany. If further evidence were needed, it might be seen in his approval of the English disdain for 'over-familiarity' with the coloured races of their colonies. Solf, in the final analysis, believed firmly that, to achieve anything in the colonies, Germany must maintain strict standards of racial pride and purity.[7]

Towards the end of 1908, the focus of attention swung back dramatically to indigenous politics. Mata'afa Josefo, at seventy-six years of age, was fast becoming senile, and a series of illnesses he suffered in 1908 raised in the minds of Samoans the question of succession to the paramount chieftaincy. There were four candidates for the position—Malietoa Tanu, Tamasese, Fa'alata and Tuimalealiifano (two from each of the royal lineages)—and efforts were being made by the influential chiefs to have Mata'afa Josefo prepare a political testament in which he would designate his successor.

Alongside this purely Samoan movement sprang up another in opposition to Solf's government. Solf was convinced the next challenge to his authority would be the occasion of Mata'afa Josefo's death, at which time he planned to abolish the post of *Ali'i Sili*. But he reckoned without the orator chief from Savai'i. Lauaki, whose whole life had revolved around political activity, was not prepared to accept the role of spectator forced on him by Solf in 1905. The official suppression of *Tumua* and *Pule*, and the dispersal from the sacred seat of government of those chiefs who came to power in 1899 had lifted the veil from the Governor's real intentions. Lauaki was already convinced of Solf's deviousness; the recent events inevitably confirmed it, and, despite an outward show of conformity, Lauaki resented Solf deeply.[8]

In addition he was, at heart, a *Sā Malietoā* man because of the traditional affiliations of Safotulafai district. His expedient support for Mata'afa Josefo in 1898-99 did not, in Samoan eyes, impose the obligation of unqualified loyalty, and Lauaki looked to the day when a Malietoan should succeed to the apex of Samoan politics, with Lauaki at his side. Mata'afa Josefo's deteriorating condition, plus the fact that Solf went on leave in mid-1908, presented the chief with a perfect opportunity to take up the fight for *Tumua* and *Pule*, as well as for a reconstructed central government over which his candidate, Malietoa Tanu, would preside.

Lauaki, now over sixty years old, began a propaganda campaign in August 1908, after the close of the *fono* of *Faipule* in Mulinu'u. Realising that he must create a united front amongst Samoans if he was to have an efficient lever against Solf, he planned to organise a mass demonstration of thousands to greet the Governor on his return in

November, and, after the welcoming ceremonies, to present Solf with a list of petitions. These were to urge four main reforms: that the upper house, *Taimua*, together with the *Faipule*, be reinstated permanently in Mulinu'u as salaried advisers to the government; that the four contending 'princes' be appointed as salaried officials at Mulinu'u; that the Samoans be furnished with records of administrative revenue and expenditure; and that the head tax be eased.[9]

The first demand was designed to achieve the restoration of a 'national' political structure which Solf had toiled so hard to dismantle, even though the *Taimua* and *Faipule* would not represent a traditional *Malo*. The second would safeguard the principle of continuity to the paramountcy by the presence of the 'royal' candidates at the seat of government. By ostensibly supporting everybody's candidate for the succession, Lauaki was able to recruit chiefly support throughout Upolu districts as well as in Savai'i; no doubt he was assisted by some general resentment at Solf's high-handed action of dispersing the *Malo* in 1905. There can be also little doubt about the orator chief's real objective: to prevent Mata'afa Josefo from declaring unilaterally whom his successor should be until Lauaki had secured Malietoa Tanu's prospects; then the question of the re-establishment of the role of *Tumua* and *Pule* would be introduced. The remaining petitions were calculated to strike a responsive chord among the people, for they played on the prevailing Samoan suspicion of money matters where Europeans were concerned. In particular it was suggested that the head tax made Samoans into slaves of the whites.

The parallels with the *Oloa* movement are obvious. In fact, in its conservative aspects, Lauaki's campaign was simply an extension of the *Oloa*: a rearguard action by a minority which longed for the days when it was the strongest power in the land and could manipulate Samoa's political fortunes at will. This time it was 'diplomacy by intimidation',[10] a ploy which had a respectable antiquity dating back to the period of Three-Power rule. As to what would happen after the Apia demonstration, Lauaki was probably unclear. The visit in August 1908 of sixteen ships of the United States battlefleet may have induced him to believe that the Powers would once more come to the Samoans' aid.

It was not until November, on the eve of Solf's return, that Deputy Governor Schultz learned of the movement. By that time Lauaki had managed to mobilise the most important political districts of Samoa by capitalising on the traditional elite status of chiefs and orators as 'kingmakers', and on his own standing as high priest of the political citadel. Saleaula and Safotulafai in Savai'i, along with Leulumoega and Lufilufi in Upolu, accepted Lauaki's appeal to the old ways and corporate political issues. Their support, representing the power of *Tumua* and *Pule*, theoretically put him in a formidable position.

Schultz could not afford to let the demonstration take place. He realised at once the meaning of the petitions, and knew that Solf's response must be negative. Not only might the presence of so many Samoans create difficulties for the government, but a refusal could provoke the spread of passive resistance to subsequent administrative demands. Schultz immediately sent letters round the Upolu and Savai'i districts forbidding all but those officially connected with the welcome for Solf to congregate in Apia, while the administration's most trusted local officials journeyed round the islands to argue against the Apia demonstration. Lauaki, however, maintained his determined stance and, with twenty-two boats of Savai'i supporters, he moved to Manono and the district of A'ana in Upolu, seeking some excuse to go to Apia 'to bring forward their opinions'.[11]

At this point Mata'afa Josefo, who originally had been brought on side by the promise of suitable honours for his high position, left the movement. He was not prepared to risk a confrontation with the government, and instead began to apply his considerable weight as *Ali'i Sili* in support of Schultz's efforts to keep the people in their districts. In the face of this pressure Lauaki finally submitted to Schultz's injunction and remained absent from Apia on 19 November, when Solf arrived with his newly-wedded wife. The demonstration failed to take place.

Solf now took the reins in his own hands and embarked on a tour of Upolu and Savai'i to remind the chiefs of their duties and warn them against disloyalty. Lauaki he confronted in Safotulafai, but in the presence of so many followers of the orator chief Solf was powerless to do more than warn Lauaki of 'the vengeance of the German eagle'. Lauaki retorted that there was no rebellious intent among the chiefs of the *Pule* and, declaring that he was appointed by the people to guard 'the sons of old Samoan Kings and the darlings of the Nation', he beseeched Solf to allow again the *'Faipule Kaiserlike'* to assemble in Mulinu'u.[12]

Despite the fact that, as a result of Solf's tour, the local press was prepared to consign the rumours of unrest to the realm of fable, it was just at this stage, in late December, that the movement got under way with renewed vigour and began to take on rebellious overtones.

Schultz's original refusal had had serious repercussions for Lauaki. In the failure of his demonstration he had lost face *fa'a Samoa* and exposed himself to Samoan ridicule. He would not see his plans so easily thwarted. After Solf's departure from Savai'i, the rumour spread that Lauaki had humbled the Governor in their encounter. Then Lauaki took an action which effectively cut him off from any hope of clemency by the German government: he sent his aide, the chief I'iga Pisa, to seek the support of the United States regime in Tutuila in case Lauaki found himself in difficulties. Clearly Lauaki was directing the movement, which now acquired the names *mau e pule* (opposition movement of Savai'i) or *o le mau*, against the German grip on Samoan powers of decision-making. *Pule* was 'on the march' again, as one of Solf's more trusted *Faipule* put it.[13] The *Faipule* of the Governor's council were themselves caught up in the movement. Some chose to wait and see if Lauaki would be successful. Others, as well as many ordinary Samoans, followed Lauaki because of his authority as a traditional leader and because of his oratorical powers, though the evidence suggests they were unsure of his ends.

Solf was in an unenviable position, faced with a developing opposition front of *Tumua* and *Pule*, with the masses at their heels, while he lacked any sort of military support with which to assert his authority. As in the early stages of the *Oloa*, Solf could not simply break the movement by imprisoning its leader. Lauaki had been careful to organise *o le mau* along the lines of a legitimate, *fa'a Samoa* form of protest and opposition. Direct suppression would have been construed by the majority of Samoans as tyranny and injustice.

However, cracks were already appearing in the alliance which Lauaki had constructed. Upolu chiefs were always suspicious of political initiatives which did not originate in their own districts, and the relationship between *Tumua* and *Pule* was often attended by covert distrust. Lauaki found that even his base of support in Savai'i was not firm: some of the Fa'asaleleaga villages would not join him, while one of the most powerful chiefs of Safotulafai was his committed opponent.[14] Perhaps most importantly, Lauaki found that among ordinary Samoans he could not count on any general movement aspiring to change the state of society. Since 1900 village Samoans had experienced a minimum of deprivation under Solf's low-key administrative policies. German rule had brought a peace the Samoans had not known for decades: their lands were secure and they were protected from the labour demands of planters; regulated copra production ensured a steadily rising standard of living; and they were governed by local officials who were also familiar village chiefs. None of this had been changed by the abolition of the *Malo* in 1905; indeed there had followed three years of peace. Under these conditions, the intrigues of orator chiefs did not have the appeal they once had.

Solf's close rapport with *fa'a Samoa*, developed sensitively over the years through study, through consulting, through touring and feasting from village to village, enabled him to recognise the signs of instability in Lauaki's relationships. He decided to play Lauaki at his own game—in the circumstances his only recourse. At a *fono* of Upolu chiefs and speakers in mid-January, the Governor baited his audience, carefully and sarcastically painting a picture of Lauaki installing himself in Mulinu'u with his Savai'i adherents at the cost of Lufilufi and Leulumoega, the districts which represented the majority of *Tumua*. 'Your glory is gone', he taunted them,

> for Lauaki is the maker of kings. He confers the high honours, not you. He anointed Mata'afa. He will anoint himself—as *Tafa'ifa* he will go with his queen Sialata'ua to Mulinu'u and will be lord over you fools.[15]

So successful was he in persuading the chiefs that Lauaki's plans did not include them in the final victory (which was not altogether devoid of truth), that most of A'ana and Atua deserted the alliance immediately and, with parts of Tuamasaga, began making preparations for war against Lauaki and his district Fa'asaleleaga.

Solf summoned Lauaki to Apia for a private interview on 16 January. When Lauaki landed in Upolu and became aware of *Tumua*'s attitude, he instructed his Savai'i followers to accompany him, and, as he made his way to Apia, a thousand of his men lodged themselves in Vaiusu and in sympathetic parts of Tuamasaga district. Solf now refused to negotiate with Lauaki until his 'army' had dispersed. The chief answered that they were simply supporters who wished to farewell him in case he was apprehended and hanged.[16] A few boatloads of Lauaki's supporters left Vaiusu in the next few days, but they went only as far as Manono on the pretext of bad weather. Lauaki himself remained in Vaiusu.

Throughout the different confederations of districts preparations were now being made for a full-scale war, a prospect which in no way consoled Solf. A Samoan war meant not only the plunder of Apia and the German plantations, and the possible ruin of the cash-cropping industry, but also probably acts of violence against Europeans. It would signify a return to the confusion and bitterness of the last century and make illusory any gains which the administration had made since 1900. To forestall an outbreak Solf sent his most trusted and influential Samoan officials, the secretary Saga and the chief Taumei, to dissuade *Tumua* from taking up arms.

Meanwhile, on 18 January, two letters arrived in Solf's office. One was what Solf termed 'an open declaration of war' from Lauaki, in which the chief declared that if he were forced to take a 'holiday' to Tonga and Fiji as the Governor had requested in their recent interview, 'on that day when I set foot upon the steamer, the Samoans will fight'. It confirmed what he had already told the chief Taumei: 'I fight for the liberty of Fa'asaleleaga and for *Pule*. Whether I die or be banished is the same to me'.[17] The other letter came from the corporation of chiefs representing Savai'i and Manono, *Pule* and *A'iga*, and reiterated the demand that Samoans be given responsibility for their own monies. Other information reaching Solf from loyal chiefs warned that Lauaki had assembled his forces in Vaiusu. From the DHPG in Vaitele came a report that Samoans, painted for war and armed, were headed for Apia. The situation looked more and more desperate, and, after a hasty consultation with his deputies, Solf decided that he must confront Lauaki in Vaiusu and try to dissuade him from violence.

The Vaiusu meeting stayed vividly in Solf's memory, and he later admitted to being genuinely afraid at the size and temper of Lauaki's gathering. He had chosen not to take an armed escort for fear of provoking Lauaki's supporters, and it was well that he had, for crowds of blackened warriors, well-armed and chanting for war, surrounded the meeting house. The scene had about it the air of a confrontation between the leading warriors of opposing sides — which traditionally took place in Samoan wars before the commencement of hostilities. Both the Governor and his European aide were convinced that they stood on the knife-edge of a rebellion similar to that of the South-West African Herero in 1904.[18]

In reality, it was an object lesson in the political skills which had preserved Lauaki throughout his long career. After Solf refused to give Lauaki his hand, the 'silver-tongued' orator chief launched into an impassioned speech which lasted more than an hour, begging the Governor's pardon for his obstinate conduct and swearing on the Bible that the 'evil genius' behind all the Samoan disturbances since 1904 was really Mata'afa Josefo. The speech transferred the moral onus squarely to Solf's shoulders. By accusing Mata'afa Josefo, Lauaki had answered the accusations of conspiracy upon which the governor had built the basis of inquiry against him. Since Mata'afa Josefo in his reply to the speech, made no attempt to repudiate Lauaki's allegations, Solf was faced with the possibility that there were now two guilty chiefs. To punish one and free the other would not have accorded with the Samoan concept of justice; to raise the question of Mata'afa Josefo's disloyalty at the time might only have hastened the prospect of civil war. At the same time it was clearly impossible to take Lauaki from his followers and examine him in court. Solf's only alternative was to grant Lauaki the pardon which he had requested. But he did so reluctantly, and it was only a conditional pardon. He insisted that Lauaki retire immediately with his supporters to Savai'i and cease all agitation. He also made it clear to Lauaki that the pardon would not apply if Lauaki was found to be guilty of treason by sending political ambassadors to Tutuila for American aid.

The next day, 19 January, found Lauaki on Manono where, again using the weather as a pretext, he remained. The conflict was obviously unresolved, particularly so when Solf's investigation revealed that attempts had been made to draw the United States in to aid the dissidents. Tension between the Samoan parties and between the Samoans and the European community increased steadily. The first reports of unrest since late December now appeared in the local press; rumours of war and general animosity to German rule flooded in and out of Apia; Solf was continually beseeched by *Tumua* chiefs to supply them with weapons to capture Lauaki and defeat his followers. At a *fono* of *Faipule* at the end of January there was strong pressure on Solf to begin military action against Lauaki, and only four chiefs spoke against dismissing Lauaki from the assembly and deporting him from the islands.[19]

Solf managed to withstand the pressure of the Upolu chiefs while he worked to prevent a panic among the whites. While the government's more loyal collaborators, the chiefs Saga, Taumei and a few of their colleagues canvassed the districts, testing the attitudes of their people and arguing in the councils against taking up arms, Solf hid the colony's explosives, and immobilised the weapons in the magazine. He gave strict instructions to the Europeans not to resist any attempt by *Tumua* forces to seize the weapons lest this provoke them to an attack on the European quarter. 'In all cases we must try to keep the peace', he urged, 'even on the condition that Lauaki restores peace in Savai'i'.[20]

61

It was a hollow hope: Lauaki seemed to have no intention of restoring the peace anywhere in the islands. Though by this time he had returned to Savai'i, his agitation continued unabated. A new crop of rumours maintained that Solf had sworn on the Bible against Lauaki's deportation and that the Governor had agreed in principle to all the orator's original demands. From Lauaki's allies in Manono came the particularly ominous threat that every German in Samoa would be killed if Lauaki were deported.[21] In the face of these mounting events, Solf finally lost hope that he alone could stabilise the situation. Reluctantly, with a sense of defeat of his hard-won policies, he telegraphed Berlin on 5 February 1909 for the urgent dispatch of military support.

Six weeks of anxious waiting followed, during which Solf was reduced to inaction against Lauaki. His energies were concentrated on restraining the Upolu chiefs from taking action on their own initiative and on calming the Europeans. On 18 March a German cruiser, SMS *Leipzig*, arrived from the East Asian Squadron in Kiautschou, under the command of Rear Admiral Coerper. By 26 March it had been joined by a further two cruisers and a supply ship, bringing some 680 sailors and marines to Samoa's undefended shores.[22]

Solf now dropped his pretence and returned to the initiative. His plan was still to avoid military action at all costs and to rely on the mere presence of the largest German naval detachment Samoa had seen since the civil war of 1898-99. Resort to physical force would provoke Lauaki to take to the bush where, as history had shown, European forces were at a serious disadvantage; only a long, bloody and costly guerrilla war would then dislodge the rebels. There was the added danger that eventually the loyal Samoans would make common cause with Lauaki and his supporters in a liberation crusade against colonial rule. Solf found a staunch ally for his caution in Coerper, who deferred completely to the Governor's discretion.

On 22 March Solf sent an ultimatum to Savai'i ordering Lauaki to report for deportation by 29 March along with eight other ringleaders: Letasi Tuilagi, Namulau'ulu Pulali, Malaeulu, Tagaloa, Tevaga Matafa, Asiata Taetoloa, Asiata Ma'agaolo and I'iga Pisa. It was accompanied by a letter from Mata'afa Josefo urging obedience for the sake of peace. When these messages reached Lauaki the confrontation entered its most critical phase. Lauaki and his two deputies, Letasi Tuilagi and Namulau'ulu Pulali, replied the following day, protesting that *Pule* and *A'iga* had been pardoned and declaring that they would rather fight and die than be deported.[23] As Lauaki's supporters on

Savai'i began conveying their goods into the bush and stockpiling provisions, the navy moved in to blockade the island and confine any revolt to Savai'i alone. Rumours that the Melanesian police-soldiers accompanying the vessels were to be released 'like dogs' on the Samoans and that the 'rebels' were to be hanged from the yard-arms, only hardened resistance in Lauaki's villages and made loyal Samoans uneasy. Coerper immediately repudiated all these stories, and at a *fono* on 27 March he made a personal appeal to the movement's leaders to surrender, promising that no force would be used if Solf's directions were obeyed. There was no response. At this juncture, Reverend John Newell of the London Missionary Society, partly motivated by accusations from the settler community that he had been sending letters of encouragement to the disaffected districts, offered his services to try and persuade Lauaki to surrender without violence. When Newell reached Savai'i on 27 March, he found that the whole west of Savai'i, as well as Palauli, Sapapalii, Saleaula and Matautu were in fact opposed to Lauaki, and he was greeted as the harbinger of peace.[24] However, feelings of defiant solidarity were still strong in Lauaki's own villages, and, in a last-ditch effort to retrieve the situation, Lauaki appealed to the British Vice-Consul in Apia, Thomas Trood, to call in the Three Powers to the protection of Samoa. On 28 March Trood replied shortly that Samoa was now under German rule and there could be no redress from the other Great Powers.[25]

The first break in Lauaki's immediate circle of support came when Reverend E. G. Neil, of the Methodist Mission, persuaded one of the ringleaders, Asiata Taetoloa of Satupaitea, to surrender.[26] This virtually defused the rebellious situation from Satupaitea to the west coast, and left Fa'asaleleaga isolated in the east. Other chiefs followed Asiata Taetoloa's example when they realised that the Germans were not extracting a brutal revenge from their colleague. In a public meeting in Safotulafai, presided over by Newell, Lauaki's brother, Namulau'ulu Pulali, declared that he was prepared to surrender if it meant avoiding war for Samoa.[27] A further round of discussions finally led Lauaki to send Newell a message on 29 March, promising that he and the Safotulafai chiefs would give themselves up on 1 April. In response, Coerper and Solf agreed to extend the deadline of the ultimatum. Lauaki and his men arranged their affairs and took leave of their friends. As the ships *Leipzig* and *Arcona* steamed towards Savai'i to take up positions for a military assault, they received a message that Lauaki and five chiefs had presented themselves punctually on board SMS

Jaguar. On the same day the chiefs, numbering nine in all, together with their families, left Apia on board the *Jaguar,* bound for Saipan in the Mariana Islands where they were to live in exile.

Solf later remarked privately that there had been a moral onus on Lauaki to accept his fate ever since the first chiefs had surrendered, for the respectful treatment accorded them by the Germans had done a great deal to legitimise German authority in the eyes of ordinary Samoans.[28] Imponderabilia like the people's ethical expectations and notions of duty and reciprocity no doubt played a part in Lauaki's decision. However, as a devout Christian and deacon of the local church, Lauaki had been convinced finally by Newell's arguments that rebellion would only lead to Samoan fighting Samoan and to 'the opening of the flood gates of misery that might last for years and years'.

His surrender was no doubt also made easier by the fact that Solf, too, with the Admiral's support, was anxious to avoid bloodshed. No actual charges were laid against Lauaki in a court of law. If the German code had been employed, the movement's leaders would have been guilty of rebellion and treason, which presumably would have led to their execution. Deportation was, in the circumstances, a restrained course of action. Solf continued to act temperately in punishing the errant districts, studiously avoiding any impression of a witch-hunt or a wholesale purge of Samoan officials. The Lauaki affair had shown that fears of the Samoans taking to the bush if pushed too far were well founded, and there seemed even greater need now for adhering to the existing lines of Solf's native policy. The Governor dismissed for twelve months all officials in the districts of Manono, Fa'asaleleaga, Saleaula and Satupaitea; land was confiscated at Tuasivi in Fa'asaleleaga for government purposes; in the guilty districts every *matai* was fined thirty marks and all shotguns on issue for hunting purposes were withdrawn.[29]

For the rest, Solf vented his righteous anger on Richard Deeken's planter clique, which, he tried to convince himself, had stirred up the entire hornets' nest. Rumours were rife during the critical period that, once again, Europeans were mixed up in the movement and the local press argued that the Samoan petitions relating to public money could only have been inspired by whites.

In fact, the settler opposition had been guilty only of spreading false rumours about the Governor, in particular that he had sworn on the Bible in Vaiusu to pardon Lauaki and meet all his demands. The American planter and trader, H. J. Moors, was known to be

Plate I *Above right:* Mata'afa Josefo,
Paramount Chief of German Samoa
(from Krämer, *Die Samoan Inseln*,
Stuttgart, 1962)

Plate II *Below left:* Richard Deeken
(from *The Cyclopedia of Samoa, Tonga,
Tahiti and the Cook Islands*, 1907)

Plate III *Below right:* Lauaki
Namulauulu, Orator Chief of
Safotulafai with his wife Sialatana
awaiting deportation, 1909 (from New
Zealand National Archives)

Plate IV   *Above:* Solf's Faipule meeting at Mulinu'u (from *The Cyclopedia of Samoa, Tonga, Tahiti and the Cook Islands*, 1907)

Plate V   *Left:* Wilhelm Solf (from E. von Vietsch, *Wilhelm Solf*, R. Wunderlich, Tübingen, 1961)

sympathetic to the chief's claims, and he had leaked news of unrest and rebellion to the New Zealand press long before most Europeans in Apia were aware of what was going on. But he was acquitted in court of any attempt to assist Lauaki in his cause, or of encouraging the use of force. No concrete evidence existed to suggest that Deeken and his friends were deliberately inciting Lauaki. The truth was, as Deeken had suggested at the time of the *Oloa* movement and as Reverend Newell now perceptively agreed, that the Samoans were quite capable of twisting anything the whites said or did independently to buttress their own demands.[30]

The Lauaki affair inspired the *Pflanzerverein* to rear its head in a new attack on Solf's policies. It was linked closely to the government's failure to settle the still-pressing labour question, for the Chinese government was making difficulties over the conditions for further shipments of coolies to Samoa. The small planters blamed Solf's native policy for these difficulties, and they regarded his forbearance of the Samoans as a direct encouragement to the Chinese to be obdurate and unreasonable in their demands about conditions of employment.[31]

Yet another campaign was initiated in Germany to prove the inadequacy of Solf's administration. This time Solf was accused of moving too fast to destroy indigenous organs of government and strip old and experienced chiefs of their powers. In a petition in June 1909 addressed to the Kaiser, Deeken argued that the establishment of a garrison of colonial troops after the *Oloa* movement in 1904-05 would have forestalled the recent unrest, and he submitted that the only guarantee of peace for Samoa was 'a consistent policy to some extent based on the customs and traditions of the Samoans, but with force at hand'. His uncle in the Reichstag, Deputy Trimborn, was influenced to urge the Colonial Office for a permanent military presence in Samoa, while the Deutsche Samoa Gesellschaft harassed it with petition after petition in 1909 and early 1910 demanding that, together with a garrison of Melanesian troops, a naval vessel be stationed constantly in Samoa.

The Colonial Office remained unimpressed, and made no secret of its disinclination to alter the existing line of policy on Samoa or to put restrictions on Solf's security decisions. An article in the semi-official *Norddeutsche Allgemeine* in mid-1909 dismissed the question of militarisation as far too expensive and dangerous. Not only was Samoa not worth the two million marks which would be needed to maintain a battalion in the islands, it claimed, but a garrison would also be a constant source of disturbance for whites and the native people. Pressure for a military establishment came from whites who had little knowledge of the Samoans themselves, it argued, and from whites who saw themselves as absolute masters and saw 'natives' as subjects without rights. The piece concluded:

> Such a people (as the Samoans) can not be ruled with the mailed fist, but only with benevolence, justice and considerable attention to their laws and customs.[32]

The argument could only have come from an old Samoa hand, probably Heinrich Schnee, who believed, like most Europeans in Samoa, that military mobilisation would only incite the Islanders. As early as 1899, the wider European community in Samoa had rejected the proposal of the German Consul and naval representative that a volunteer European corps be established to protect the settlers, for it was convinced that the best guarantee of security lay in the fact that the European residents were not armed for war.[33] Fear of the Samoans as formidable enemies if provoked, was, in the following years, a central *leit-motiv* running through Berlin's decision to maintain a non-militant posture in the islands. Despite the constant battle by the pan-German settler clique to have the Samoan *Fitafita* replaced by a more effectual garrison of Melanesian troops, Berlin refused to capitulate. Staffed with men of Samoan experience for much of the period, the Colonial Office shared Solf's opinion that to substitute Melanesians for the *Fitafita* would be considered an unforgivable affront by the Samoan community because of the special tie between Germany and Samoa which the *Fitafita* symbolised. The resentment which followed the rumour that the Melanesians were to be released 'like dogs' on Lauaki and his followers tended to corroborate their view.

So, in 1909, Colonial Secretary Dernburg himself took up the cudgel in Samoa's defence to tell Deputy Trimborn that the Reich must 'come to terms' with the Samoans since only at great expense could they ever be tamed by colonial troops. And at the same time the Deutsche Samoa Gesellschaft was informed flatly that troops were not 'absolutely necessary' since a second cruiser had just been approved for the Pacific station.[34]

In Samoa itself the majority of the European community gave Solf its vote of confidence. One of its oldest and most eminent residents, the former British Vice-Consul, Thomas Trood, paid the Governor his highest compliment when he remarked that even England could never have guaranteed nine years of peace in the group without the employment of 'humane repression'. And Lauaki's chiefly enemies had already celebrated Solf in biblical terms, likening him to Moses who had freed his people from bondage to the old ways.[35]

So, in the end, the Lauaki affair proved not a defeat but a victory for the Governor's non-military style of administration. In August 1909 Solf was able to affirm that he would continue to govern the Samoans 'with love and peace and no tyranny will be exercised'.

There was one political issue, however, which still faced Solf, the issue which originally inspired Lauaki's movement and which, until solved, would continue to thwart the German Governor's control policy: the position of paramount chief and the question of succession after Mata'afa Josefo's death.

It took Solf the next eighteen months to devise a formula which would complete this control over the Samoan political structure. 'If . . . the German Government [showed] power, together with goodwill in respecting the holy traditions of the Samoans'—proven ingredients in Solf's Samoa—then the Governor guaranteed to preserve peace among the Islanders.[36] His idea was for a proclamation from the Kaiser as *Tupu Sili*, declaring his will that no more *Ali'i Sili* be appointed after Mata'afa Josefo's death because of the implied slight to the just claims of both 'royal' families. Instead, Solf suggested the naming of two advisers to the Governor (*Fautua*), one from each 'royal' lineage.

Paradoxically, Solf's solution, and the Colonial Office's acceptance of it, was a considerable achievement for the Samoan people. It reveals the extent to which the Samoans and their actions had purchased respect in the formulation of colonial policy. Berlin acknowledged this respect by allocating some 40 000 marks to be used by the Governor as compensation for Samoan leaders who showed themselves dissatisfied with the solution.[37]

In the end the Samoans denied Solf any final, personal triumph over the islands' politics. For Mata'afa Josefo was still very much alive late in 1910, when the Governor departed for Berlin the last time. His old enemy, Richard Deeken, had already gone in February.

The Governor's final directive to his officials was entirely in keeping with his concerns of the past ten years as chief executive:

> While not losing sight of the natural desire of our Government to have some advantage from its colonies, never forget that they are the homelands of human people who have been promised our protection and for whom we must provide. Remember too that one

does not achieve success merely from the legal relationships between people, and that even a Christian attitude towards life is not enough. Unless one has lived for years among a people and shares their joys and sorrows, unless one's heart beats with theirs, unless one feels Christian charity for these people of different thoughts and feelings, one will never understand the delight and enthusiasm with which the inspired coloniser and missionary attack their work.[38]

This was no mere statement of an unattainable ideal nor a simple admonition to fair-mindedness. It was a plea for cultural sensitivity and for a breadth of vision which saw beyond national goals. Tinged though he may have been with the conviction of Germany's world mission, Solf had shown that his vision could work. He had made a covenant with the Samoan people that they should not be destroyed by colonial rule, but prosper. They, with few exceptions, remained loyal, if not to the German eagle then to Solf himself.

And they continued to remain loyal, though Solf never returned to Samoa. In December 1911 Solf became State Secretary for Colonies in succession to Friedrich von Lindequist, who had resigned suddenly in protest at a treaty which, without consultation, the Foreign Office negotiated with France over the Cameroons. The period after the First World War brought Solf to Japan as German Ambassador. There, in September 1923, in the aftermath of the earthquake which destroyed Tokyo and Yokohama, Solf received a telegram from 'the Samoan people', asking him to return as Governor once more.[39]

His successor in Samoa had been the man who had held the posts of Native Secretary, Chief Judge and Deputy Governor successively since 1902, Erich Schultz-Ewerth. Schultz was an ardent supporter of Solf's way of government, and he openly sympathised with the problems Samoans had to face in conditions of intensifying contact with Western civilisation. By a meticulous observance of their ethical and ceremonial values, he had already achieved understanding with the Islanders, and they accepted easily the mantle of patriarchal authority which Solf bequeathed to Schultz.

It was Schultz who was left to deal with the contentious issue of Mata'afa Josefo's death and succession. As the old chief became ever more bed-ridden, Schultz had to contend with increasing pressure from a variety of Samoan groups all seeking a definitive expression of Mata'afa Josefo's political testament. Schultz resisted them all, gently insisting on the prerogatives of the *Tupu Sili* in Berlin, and attending the ailing High Chief regularly. His harshest act was to banish, reluctantly, two chiefs from Falefa who had aroused public excitement by extracting from Mata'afa Josefo a declaration in favour of Tui-malealiifano. Mata'afa Josefo, for his part, approached death stoically, knowing he was the last of his kind. Practically his last thoughts were for the exiles in Saipan, for whose forgiveness and return he petitioned the Kaiser.[40] Finally, on 6 February 1912, the High Chief died, amid great demonstrations of grief from the people whose political fortune he had embodied for more than two decades.

Schultz's low-key approach and his deterrence of political agitation seemed to have had the desired effect. He encountered no excited indignation when he proclaimed at Mata'afa Josefo's funeral: 'the clouds have burst asunder, the titles have fallen to pieces'.[41] In fact, explicit assurances were received from some of the chiefs that, in order to observe the Government's wishes, they would not carry through the customary practices associated with a great chief's death. There would be no *fono*, no funeral feasts, no fine mats or gift offerings (*mea alofa*); the bereaved family would be left in peace. This boosted Schultz's optimism, and he made no move against the office of *Ali'i Sili* during the time of mourning. So confident was he of the security of Samoa that he risked a trip to Germany at the end of 1912 to work out with colonial officials the final details for a public abolition of the paramountcy. The event took place on 12 June 1913, at a *fono* in honour of the Kaiser's twenty-fifth anniversary as Head of State. Malietoa Tanu and Tamasese were appointed as the *Fautua* and, in the shadow of SMS *Cormoran*, the occasion passed off in harmony. The navy had been unable to send the East Asian Cruiser Squadron for the occasion, but a visit was planned for August, to drive home the appropriate impression.

Schultz dared to look to the future with cautious hope. The new political system had still to be tested: although the term *Fautua* carefully avoided any connotation of independent powers of decision, no-one could say how the new advisory positions would develop. But the Governor had no doubt about the 'undeniable administrative gifts' of the Samoans, and he put great faith in the people's essential vitality (*Lebenskraft*), which, he felt, would enable them to make a significant contribution to the future prosperity of the colony.[42]

In economic terms the Samoans were already showing the way. The Islanders returned quickly to copra and cocoa production after the Lauaki episode, and throughout the last five years of German rule they still supplied the overwhelming proportion (three-fifths) of export copra for the colony. In 1909-10 experts put the number of coconut palms belonging to Samoans at 800 000, with an annual rate of increase of 25 000-30 000 trees; Samoan stands of coconuts covered three times the area of European copra plantations. Moreover, because of the labour shortage, Samoans were able to earn the very high wage of three marks a day plus food working casually on European plantations.

European industry also prospered, though not uniformly. None of the small German plantations was a success. Deeken's own firm lost 253 000 marks on cocoa in 1913 alone, and never paid a dividend. The DHPG remained pre-eminent, protected by its land and labour monopoly. It acquired forty-nine per cent of all copra produced by Samoans between 1902 and 1913, and its annual turnover in copra alone amounted to two million marks. Furthermore, the company's extensive plantations enabled it to maintain consistently higher profits over smaller firms which relied on trade copra. The general base of European industry expanded with the development of cocoa and rubber plantations, and by 1914 these represented forty-five per cent of all cultivated European-owned land. German exports quadrupled between 1900 and 1912, though copra remained the staple. There was even a pineapple canning industry by 1914.[43]

Samoa was, on the surface, a prosperous and peaceful corner of the empire. But the prosperity was brittle and the peace hollow. It is easy to say with history's hindsight that Samoa would never have been the same for the Germans had they returned in 1918, for Germany's reign since 1900 had been Wilhelm Solf's reign and there could have been no guarantee of continued peace and stability once he and Schultz had left. Pressure from white settlers to acquire greater autonomy and a more influential role in the running of the community was mounting in all the colonies in 1914, and there were signs that Berlin would have granted these wishes if the war had not intervened.[44] Moreover, by 1918 Germany would have inherited a colonial world in which tropical produce was at a discount and economic depression rampant. Such developments, coupled with the first faint stirrings of colonial nationalism, would have been bound to affect adversely relations between Samoans and Germans, as they did between Samoans and New Zealanders.

But, in 1914, there were also more immediate signs of coming trouble, which tarnished Samoa's external image of well-being. Socially, the colonial relationship was undergoing subtle but considerable change in the final years of German rule. Exile and old age had removed the stronger elements of traditional leadership by 1912, which partly explains the people's acquiescence in the abolition of the *Ali'i Sili* title. A new, more literate and Westernised generation of Samoans was coming of age and causing distortion to the indigenous authority structure; chiefs were complaining that they were finding it increasingly difficult to assert their authority over young Samoans. For his part, Schultz was worried that 'advancing democratisation' would undermine the social structure and increase the rate of social change, thereby loosening Germany's hold over the Islanders.[45]

The changes to the Samoan community were matched by a deterioration of racial attitudes among German administrative staff. In one of his last private letters to Solf before the outbreak of war,[46] Schultz remarked that his higher officials were now mostly old Africa men, distinguished by their 'mental laziness, complacency and a defective capacity for comprehension and adjustment'. He complained of getting bare support for his accommodative native policy because of the 'master race' attitude which these men adopted towards the Samoans. Such an attitude was particularly dangerous. The Samoans laid great stress on outer forms, honour and mutual respect in inter-communal relationships. Without them, Schultz argued, an isolated disturbance might easily become a mass riot; Schultz's period of office had already been marred by several ugly racial incidents. It was a sour note on which to end fourteen years of German rule, and it foreshadowed the communal collisions that would occur in the 1920s during New Zealand's administration.

Epilogue

Lauaki and his fellow exiles in Saipan were provided with land, seed, livestock, fishing gear and household utensils, and expected to procure their own living, as well as to participate in the labour corvée organised by the local German administration. They were given no idea of the length of their exile, though there seems to have been some expectation that it would last no longer than two years. Solf remained firmly opposed to the return of the chiefs until Lauaki's death, but in the end he left the decision to Schultz. Namulau'ulu Pulali died within the first year of banishment. The others were finally picked up on the orders of the New Zealand administration in Samoa in late 1915 and arrived back in Apia on 18 December. Lauaki was not among them: he had caught dysentery while on the voyage home and was landed at Tarawa, in the Gilbert Islands, where he died four days later. His body was later

71

removed to Samoa and buried at Fogapoa, Savai'i. By 1919 none of the originally-exiled chiefs was alive. Some died shortly after their return, others in the influenza epidemic of 1918. Lauaki's grave still exists, and occasionally washing is spread out to dry upon the basalt and coral mound. This is not an irreverent habit: the memory of Savai'i's most eminent orator chief lives on; his skills find constant emulation.

3

Ponape:
The Pattern of Spanish and German Rule

European knowledge of Ponape dates back to the sixteenth century. It has been suggested that the first contact was as early as 1526, when Loaisa y de Saavedra voyaged through the area, but no report of this exists.[1] The earliest documented sighting was by Ferdinand de Quiros in 1595. Irregular contacts were made by Spanish galleons and American whalers during the next three hundred years. By the year 1850, contacts had multiplied so quickly that an average of twenty-nine ships were putting in at Ponape annually, most of them whalers from the northern Pacific, seeking fresh provisions and recreation.

When the American Board of Commissioners for Foreign Missions (or Boston Missionary Society) founded its first station on the island, in the district of Kiti, in 1852, the Ponapeans were already well accustomed to Europeans and the trappings of their civilisation. Luxury goods had replaced iron as the most sought-after item of trade, and a fair-sized community of beach residents existed, consisting of ships' deserters, mutineers and escaped convicts. Andrew Cheyne mentions a white population of sixty in this 'rogues' paradise' when he arrived as a trader in 1842, and they combined to frustrate his attempts to found a trading empire on Ponape based on tortoise-shell, *bêche de mer* and various tropical plants.[2] While the beachcombing community formed a considerable acculturative influence on the Islanders, it never possessed the productivity or the power to challenge successfully the domination by the district chiefs. Commerce on the island generally remained in chiefly hands, and Europeans were required to function as trading agents or resident artisans and perhaps buy protection with a proportion of their earnings. It was probably from this situation that the Ponapeans acquired an early reputation for stubborn independence mixed with ferocity and duplicity. Ponape was never the home of the legendary happy savage who peoples the tales of early European travellers in the Pacific.

Initially, the Islanders were cordial to the Boston Mission, and the mission settlement was welcomed, despite the protests of the beach community, because the chiefs saw in it prospects of more frequent trade with European ships. But relations deteriorated quickly when the missionaries began evangelising. The Boston Mission had behind it thirty years of evangelical experience in Polynesia, and, with their strict Puritan traditions, its members viewed the indigenous cosmology and cults as diametrically opposed to Christianity, a system of evil which had to be met head on and eliminated. *Sakau* drinking, polygyny, and the absolute nature of chiefly authority were subjected to virulent attack, with the result that the mission encountered stubborn resistance in Kiti and in Sokehs.

The mission persisted, however, despite blockades and the burning of the Kiti station in 1865. During a smallpox epidemic in 1854, which carried off three-fifths of the population, the mission's inoculations and nursing work won it many apparent supporters, and its unrelenting campaign against the High Chiefs' powers gradually persuaded several powerful district chiefs to throw in their lot. By the 1880s, the Boston Mission was well entrenched in Madolenihmw and Kiti, ruling its adherents as a theocracy, controlling its own law enforcement agency, operating a kind of legislature and promoting private ownership of homesteads.[3]

By the 1880s also there was already a considerable German presence in the Carolines. In 1866 Alfred Tetens established an agency for Godeffroys in Yap, in the western Carolines, and this was followed by stations on Kusaie and on Ponape. By 1885 eighty per cent of the Carolines' trade, and indeed most of the commerce of the entire island sphere north of New Guinea, was in German hands.

It was natural, then, that this area should be a target for annexation when Bismarck's new pro-colonial policy began to operate after 1884. The flag was indeed raised throughout Micronesia, but Spain suddenly mounted vigorous protests, claiming that the Caroline and Mariana groups, though no official regime was installed there, had been part of the Spanish Pacific empire for centuries. Bismarck was at the time wrestling with the problem of his *Kulturkampf* against Catholicism and how to resolve it. The Micronesian issue offered him the perfect means by which he might make his peace with the Vatican. The dispute was therefore referred to Pope Leo XIII for his arbitration. In October 1885 the Pope decided in favour of Spain. It was not until eighteen months later, in March 1887, that a Governor of the eastern Carolines, Captain Posadillo, arrived in Ponape with fifty soldiers, twenty-five convicts and five Capuchin monks, to actualise the imperial presence.[4]

The Spanish were blissfully ignorant of their Pacific 'empire', and of the nature of the people with whom they were dealing. They came into immediate conflict with the Boston Mission over the site of their colony (Mesenieng), which the missionary Edward T. Doane claimed by right of prior sale. But the chiefs involved, Lepen Net and Souwenim Metipw, denied the sale, and Doane was sent to Manila under arrest for allegedly inciting the Islanders against Spanish rule.[5] The truth is difficult to isolate in this incident, but Doane's personal animosity to the Spaniards is well authenticated. To a missionary fired with ideals of the American Republic, Spain's Catholic State apparatus seemed the epitome of feudal decadence. Under such a regime the mission had a great deal to lose.

Meanwhile the Spanish were enjoying a short honeymoon with the Ponapeans, whom they called upon to provide working parties to assist in the construction of the colony. At first the Islanders complied willingly, but as time went on and they were repeatedly embezzled out of their wages by three unscrupulous European interpreters, resentment against the regime grew. Then, in July 1887, the Wasai Sokehs (High Chief of Sokehs) refused point blank to send any more working parties to the colony. The incident that occurred next is surrounded by conflicting evidence, but when the Governor sent a military detachment to the island it appears that the Wasai and his deputies refused to leave their assembly house. The Spaniards then fired into the air in an effort to persuade them otherwise. This was the signal for general consternation. Sokehs warriors grabbed the Spaniards' firearms and shot them down. Excited to fever pitch, the warriors followed up with a concerted attack on the new colony in which Governor Posadillo and a further eighty soldiers were killed.[6]

A new Governor, Don Luis Cardaso, arrived at the end of October with three cruisers and 700 soldiers, but the only action he took was to dispatch three of the suspected killers to Manila for trial. To the rest of the Sokehs people the Governor offered an amnesty, and by the beginning of 1888 relations were on an even keel once more, at least on the surface.

Comparative peace reigned until 1890. The Nahnmwarki of Kiti had already shown himself willing to accept a Catholic missionary in the district, probably to offset the growing influence of one of his chiefs, Henry Nanpei, who was the district's leading businessman and had become principal benefactor of the Protestant Mission. The first Catholic station was founded at Aleniang in June 1889. There was, however, a great deal of general coolness when Don Luis announced a plan to lay roads to the Catholic mission centres and establish military outposts in close proximity to them, so as to extend gradually an integrated network of Spanish control over the districts. The Capuchin Fathers were understandably alarmed at the likelihood of their work being identified with military rule and, when a road was cut from Aleniang into the stronghold of Protestantism at Oa in Madolenihmw in May 1890, they warned the Governor that the people would not stand for this two-fold infringement of their independence and their religious affiliation.[7] On 25 June, as a party of forty soldiers arrived to occupy the site for the garrison, they were attacked by the Madole-nihmw people and cut down to a man. A further forty sent the same day met the same fate. In the following months the rebellion grew, and the Spanish mounted a series of punitive expeditions involving several gunboats and hundreds of soldiers imported from the Philippines. These, however, only led to more serious reverses and heavy loss of Spanish life before Oa was taken and the rebellion broken.

The people of the northern districts of Net and Sokehs had had much more contact with the Spanish regime than the people of the south, to whom they were traditionally hostile. Since 1887 the Catholic Mission had been able to make several converts in Net and Sokehs. The revolt in Madolenihmw, and the barely-disguised distaste of Kiti and the other southern districts for the Spanish, caused anxiety among the northern people and forced them to consider an alliance of convenience with the administration and the mission. In consequence, indigenous feuds more and more took on the outward appearance of a confessional war between the Catholic north and the Protestant south. This occurred despite the deterioration of the Boston Mission's position after the 1887 trouble and its final expulsion by Cardaso in 1890.

Throughout the next decade the Islanders continued to defy the Spanish, especially in the south. Intermittent skirmishes and assassinations took place as successive Spanish governors tried in vain to reassert the imperial presence by road-building projects or schemes to disarm the population. On occasions the regime did gain the upper hand in military engagements, only to lose it immediately by a policy of appeasement, which was invariably interpreted as weakness. Reports from German naval vessels visiting the island in these years indicate that the colony lived in a state of constant siege. A buttressed wall with artillery emplacements encircled the entire European settlement at Mesenieng, while the land beyond was cleared to a depth of 500 metres so as to provide a clear line of fire. None of the 300-strong garrison dared to venture outside this fortress for fear of being shot down, and the soldiers spent most of their time drinking in the taverns. The administration also paid a salary or 'tribute' of about 100 marks a month to the various High Chiefs, to keep the peace; the leader of the Protestant faction in the south, Henry Nanpei, reportedly received 3000 marks a year.[8]

None of these measures altered things in favour of the Spanish. The Ponapeans maintained their military weight and effectiveness by means of the arms continually smuggled into the island by American whalers. Indeed, so low had the Spanish authorities sunk in the Islanders' estimation that this trade was carried on under the very nose of Spanish gunboats, which were under strict instructions to avoid provoking Americans because of the international differences between the two countries.

The Spanish-American war of 1898-99 in fact proved to be the nadir of Spain's abortive regime in the Carolines. A dispute between the Catholic sub-district of Awak in the north and the Protestant districts exploded into a general Protestant uprising in 1898, after the Spanish courts acquitted an Awak chief charged with murdering a Protestant. Politics and religion were inextricably linked in the affair. The Protestants in the south were determined to vanquish the northern districts and thrust the Spaniards from the island as a prelude to American occupation; the northern chiefs bore a particular antipathy towards the leader of the Protestants, Henry Nanpei, whom they suspected of ambitions to make himself the first 'King of Ponape'.

Nanpei was the most exceptional Ponapean of his generation. He had acquired the largest landed fortune on the island through an inheritance which was contrary to the Ponapean tradition of matrilineal succession. The inheritance was from his father, Nahnku, the former Nahnken of Kiti district. Nahnku had established a reputation for hospitality and assistance to visiting Europeans, and, in return, the father of Nahnku's wife, an Englishman by the name of James Headley, in 1863 left a testament ceding the full rights over a large area of land in Kiti, including several offshore atolls, to the Nahnken and his direct heirs. This document to private landed title, unconventional though it was, had been honoured by the Spanish regime, and was to be again by the Germans. Henry Nanpei continued his father's tradition of generous disbursement, and developed his estates considerably through trading and planting. He founded the first Ponapean-owned store, purchased more land, and planted it with coconuts and ivory nuts. In the late

1890s an Englishman visiting Kiti remarked with surprise on the substantial wharf, boathouse and storing facilities which Nanpei had built at the mouth of the Ronkiti River, and he described 'countless' planted coconuts flourishing in the river valley.[9] By the turn of the century Nanpei laid claim to 300 hectares in Kiti and to the Ant Islands offshore.

Nanpei had received an education from the Boston missionaries. Under their auspices, he had travelled to Hawaii and California, returning to Ponape with a rough collection of Republican ideas and quite Westernised personal habits. Nanpei was nothing if not adaptable. When the Spanish arrived he was not unfriendly at first, helping to mediate peace between the parties in the early conflicts, and even rescuing the Capuchin monks from attack during the 1890 war. For his services he was twice decorated with imperial insignia and he received a substantial stipend from the regime, reputedly the largest stipend paid to any of the island chiefs.

But Henry Nanpei was not prepared to commit himself unconditionally to the demands of his new masters. Always he was looking to the maximum political advantage, mindful of the uncertain basis of his estates in Kiti. He had made enemies among the Ponapeans because of his unconventional initiatives and his non-conformity to the rules of inheritance, and the struggle which absorbed him most was political, not religious. Nanpei recognised that the Spanish government was a poor guarantee of his position in Kiti, and of his growing power. In the end his sympathy with the United States made him an enemy of Spain. Exploiting his position as protector of the Protestant faction after the mission left in 1890, Nanpei used the mission schools to preach the virtues of American rule. He imported arms and ammunition into Kiti from Japanese trading schooners and allegedly used them as payment for the labourers on his land.[10] In 1898 Nanpei was the inspiration of the Protestant revolt, though typically he remained carefully in the background, in case the Spanish proved victorious.

In fact the Spanish forces, with the aid of Sokehs and Net, did manage to beat back the first attack on Awak by southern warriors in March 1898, but fighting broke out again a month later. Nanpei was arrested as the instigator of the disturbances, but the process against him faltered in the confusion surrounding the progress of the war between Spain and America. It was a time of uncertainty for the administration, which was besieged on all sides and expecting every day the arrival of an American naval force. The conflict with the Islanders dragged on into 1899, while

Spanish rule became ever more discredited. At last, in September 1899, a warship arrived with the news that Ponape (in fact the entire Caroline and Mariana groups) were to be sold to Germany.

Germany had never relinquished her interest in the Carolines. Bismarck's unsuccessful annexation bid had not impeded the activities of German traders in Micronesia during the Spanish period. Indeed, the agreement signed with the Spanish government in 1885 had specifically guaranteed freedom of trade and equality for German merchants in the area. Since German companies, the most prominent among them being the Jaluit Gesellschaft, had already built up extensive trading links by this date, it meant in effect that the *status quo* was shifted in their favour. The single Spanish firm, Factoria Española, did not develop to any extent during Spanish rule, and though there were other small traders on Ponape, and larger American and Japanese concerns in the western Carolines, they had not undermined German dominance of the markets. In 1899 the Jaluit Gesellschaft was exporting three-quarters of the 1500 tonnes of copra produced in the Carolines and it was urging the Foreign Office to acquire the group as a going concern before the Americans could do so.[11] In a fit of exhaustion, with the Pacific empire breaking down around it, the Spanish home government was yet determined to deny its island chains to the triumphant Americans. The equivalent of five million marks had been spent trying to subdue the Carolinians. To recoup that, the Carolines and Marianas were sold to Germany in June 1899 for a grand total of 17 250 000 marks. On 2 October a German expedition from New Guinea took formal possession of the Caroline Islands and brought the period of Spanish rule to an end.

The new German administration was forced to take up where its predecessors left off. The Spanish retreat left the Germans facing a thousand practised warriors in the five districts, and the problem of coping with large caches of modern arms and ammunition. It was a crude frontier predicament, which had prevailed without interruption for nearly two decades.

Official policy towards Ponape in the next seven years was influenced decisively by Berlin's consciousness of the island's past. With the Spaniards' experience in mind, officials of the Colonial Department were concerned lest any false moves or indiscreet demands by the local regime should lead to a general rebellion which only a full-scale land and sea operation could hope to suppress.

Of equal import were the economic considerations. Ponape was just not worth many risks. It was an insignificant, undeveloped corner of the colonial empire, with very modest potential as an economic or strategic asset. Though by far the largest island of the Carolines, it contained only eight per cent of the total population of the group (40 000), while the European population never rose above fifty during the German period. Ponape's high volcanic nature diminished its plantation potential, for there was only a narrow belt of level land between the mangrove-fringed reefs and the mountains, with a thin layer of topsoil lacking a coral base. This retarded the rapid growth of coconuts in particular. The constant, heavy rainfall hampered copra production, and the mountainous terrain of the interior made clearing and planting arduous and expensive. In addition, markets were a long way off and freights costly, and there was the ubiquitous problem of labour: because of the demands of yam cultivation associated with the competition for prestige in Ponapean society, the Islanders had little inclination to work for Europeans as wage labourers.

There were no large plantations on Ponape when the Germans arrived. Henry Nanpei, and a Portugese settler by the name of Dominic Etscheit, owned patches of irregularly-planted coconuts, but they were not geared to intensive production for export.[12] A few new plantations were established by Europeans in subsequent years, but their rate of development was slow; by 1904, six European plantations in the eastern Carolines employed only seventy-eight labourers.[13] The entire Carolines group in fact exported much less copra than did the neighbouring group of atolls in the east, the Marshalls. The Jaluit Gesellschaft had begun its trading in the Marshalls and had built up quite a sophisticated industry there. With German rule established in the west of Micronesia, the Jaluit Gesellschaft was given a concession in 1901 to develop the coral atolls of the eastern Carolines and the high islands of Truk. But Ponape was excluded from the agreement in recognition of its limited prospects and its fragile security.

With such a questionable asset, and for the sake of inter-communal peace, Berlin was at pains to avoid any policy which might cause unrest or provoke a hostile response from the Ponapeans, even to the point of sacrificing close administrative control and the economic mobilisation of the Islanders. The man whom they chose to lead the administration in the Carolines did not stray from this conception. He was Albert Hahl, Imperial Judge in the protectorate of New Guinea since 1896, and appointed Deputy Governor of the island sphere in July

Plate VI *Above right:* The Mountain of Sokehs. The murder of Boeder took place to the left of the mission buildings (from Spiegel von Peckelsheim, *Kriegsbilder aus Ponape*)

Plate VII *Below left:* Henry Nanpei in 1910 (from P. Hambruch, *Ponape*, Friedrichsen De Gruyter, Hamburg, 1932)

Plate VIII *Below right:* Melanesian police and German marines marching to war, Ponape, 1910 (from Spiegel von Peckelsheim, *Kriegsbilder aus Ponape*)

Plate IX *Left:* The ringleaders of the Sokehs revolt: Lepen Ririn and Soumadau (from Spiegel von Peckelsheim, *Kriegsbilder aus Ponape*)

Plate X *Below left:* Albert Hahl (by permission of the Hahl family)

Plate XI *Below right:* A Tolai of the early days, wearing shell-money necklace (from A. B. Meyer and R. Parkinson, *Album von Papua-Typen*, Stengel and Markert, Dresden, 1894)

1899. Hahl was well aware of the difficulties facing him on arrival in Ponape: 'We arrive in the protectorate with naked cheeks' he wrote to a colleague in 1899,

> and are supposed immediately to build houses [and] drill people whom we don't understand and who don't understand us . . . From the Spanish we'll learn nothing and will have nothing to take over; the ground is indeed chosen, but not sowed; at best with blood.[14]

In the light of Berlin's apprehensions, Hahl's strategy was to let the ground lie fallow awhile. From the start, his administration adopted a relaxed posture. Hahl arrived in Ponape with what the departing Spaniards considered a skeleton staff—a doctor, a harbour master, a police official and a mixed force of forty-six Melanesians and Malays—which prompted the Spanish Governor to urge Hahl to leave with him immediately, lest his puny group be massacred within a week.[15] Though the Ponapeans treated his small band of 'niggers' with open derision, Hahl was unconcerned, for he reasoned that any larger military display would only be cause for provocation. The Deputy Governor also took walking tours around the districts, deliberately without any military escort, in order to convey his peaceful intentions; and he announced that there would be no prosecution of any offences committed during the Spanish period, backing up his promise by negotiating a fragile peace between Awak and the warring Protestant faction.

Hahl's low-key approach succeeded in gaining a respite from conflicts for the first five years of German rule. It would be unfair to suggest that no substantial administrative priorities existed during this time. Hahl had drawn up a list of objectives, centring on the curtailment of the powers of the High Chiefs, on balancing the interests of clans and on completely restructuring indigenous land rights. According to Hahl's interpretation, the root of most social conflict in Ponape was the land tenure system, with its emphasis on matrilineal succession and the theoretical right of the High Chief to dispose of all land in his district. Gradual changes to land tenure concepts were taking place on Ponape, hastened by contact with the outside world, and Hahl recognised this development. He envisaged that in four or five years, when rumours of war had subsided and the Islanders were disarmed, Germany might lend her weight to the process and break the bonds of the feudal system. But the Deputy Governor was not sanguine about early changes. The Ponapeans he regarded in 1900 as 'distrustful, treacherous and apathetic', and the political situation as too delicate for ideas of economic and social reform.[16]

Where he was able to, without stirring passions, Hahl did sow seeds for the future. In continual discussions with the High Chiefs, which initially took place under armed guard because of their mutual suspicions, Hahl elicited a tenuous acceptance of a few vague principles of administration, like freedom of religious practice, preservation of the Ponapean 'constitution', and protection of individuals' property.[17] Significantly, the first signature sought by the Germans for the accompanying protocol was that of Henry Nanpei, not that of the High Chiefs. The High Chiefs were delegated local judicial powers in minor civil and criminal matters, while important cases affecting the districts were left to the Deputy Governor in concert with the chiefs. From the outside the 'package' seems a crude form of indirect German rule; in reality it had more to do with the policy of treading softly in uncertain places, and it left many disputes which otherwise would have reached German courts to be dealt with according to traditional sanctions and patterns of authority. Policing such an agreement was obviously out of the question.

Albert Hahl left Ponape at the end of 1901 to resume duty in New Guinea, this time as Governor—a post he retained until 1914. Although this gave him a continuing relationship with the island sphere (as its chief executive), his energies were concentrated almost entirely, and naturally, on New Guinea itself. His two-year acquaintance with Ponape must be seen therefore as a mere interlude in a long New Guinea administration. That does not diminish the value of his observations on Ponape, nor his conception of its problems, for Hahl was a man of astute perception and practical vision. But it did mean that Hahl was later to make decisions about Ponape based on a rather short, and difficult, tour of duty. His opinion of the people was no more flattering to them at the end of his stay than at the beginning. He left Ponape a disappointed man, after doing all in his power to win their trust and make them loyal subjects, without apparent success.[18]

His successor was Victor Berg, a forty-year-old colonial civil servant with some experience of German East Africa. Initially he shared Hahl's distaste for the Ponapeans, characterising them on one occasion as 'incorrigible layabouts and ill-civilised Yankee apes'.[19] Berg arrived with definite preconceptions about the job, and he earned a severe censure from the Colonial Department within his first two months, after a rashly-worded dispatch announcing his determination to assert imperial authority 'forcefully' and to meet local resistance with 'relentless' reprisals. He learned his lesson very quickly, however, after his superiors warned that any unrest during his appointment would lead to an immediate recall.[20] His administration thereafter was marked by a singular restraint and sobriety, and in both report and action he remained faithful to the official conception of his duties—to follow the lines of policy laid down by Hahl.

Only three events stand out in Berg's five-year tenure of office: a partially successful disarmament of the Carolinians, the beginnings of a long and wearisome dispute with the Catholic mission, and the manner of his death.

Despite Hahl's surveillance of whaling ships in 1900-01, an illegal whaler trade in consumer goods and arms did continue in Ponapean harbours into 1902 and 1903. After the farcical attempts by the Spanish to stop the arms trade, American whalers had acquired a nimbus of superiority over warships. Not even Hahl's threats of prison for those found trafficking with the whalers were sufficient to deter the Islanders. Lacking manpower and restricted by poor communications (it took six to eight hours for a report to reach the colony by boat from the southern harbours), the administration could rely only on occasional patrols by visiting naval vessels.

Therefore, the long-projected operation to remove as many of the Carolinians' firearms as possible was begun, not in Ponape, but in Truk, where the density of population was much higher (12 000 inhabitants occupied an area one-third the size of Ponape). Using the Samoan precedent of financial compensation, in late 1904 Berg, supported by the presence of SMS *Condor*, collected over 400 guns and a large amount of ammunition in less than three months.

Berg's idea was to use the Truk disarmament in turn as a precedent for a similar campaign in Ponape, not immediately, but in a few years when the Ponapeans were ready to trust the Germans. But Berg was presented with his opportunity after a very few months. On Maundy Thursday, April 1905, a typhoon broke over Ponape and left a trail of destruction in its wake: forty-six Islanders were killed in the eastern Carolines, over 300 were injured, and damage amounting to four million marks was inflicted on property and crops. On Ponape itself, all the breadfruit and bananas, and three-quarters of all coconut palms were destroyed; the administration's two-day-old motor schooner was thrown onto the reef and buildings suffered damage worth 150 000 marks; while the mission societies fared even worse.[21] At one stroke the economic potential of the area was set back years, and, although the ensuing threat of famine was averted, there was for a time an alarming scarcity of all but basic foodstuffs.

Berg decided to combine the task of reconstruction with a calculated offensive against the armament problem. His most powerful potential opponent, Henry Nanpei, was conveniently out of the way on a trip to Germany, and this increased Berg's leverage over the community. This time Berg offered thirty-five marks per weapon, ten marks more than in Truk, or rice and tinned meat at even higher values. Hand-in-hand with the arms purchase went the distribution of free coconut seeds and a campaign of planting and house reconstruction.

The results genuinely surprised the Germans. From May 1905 to May 1906, some 545 guns and thousands of rounds of ammunition were handed in, most for cash rather than goods. Ponape was revealed to be quite an armed camp, for the proportion of one gun to fewer than six Ponapeans was by far the highest in the Carolines and exceeded even that in Samoa.[22] Only one incident soured the operation, and that was the unscheduled arrival of a German warship, which led to rumours in the more suspicious areas, Sokehs in particular, that the Germans were planning to fall upon the now-defenceless districts. The surrender of arms dropped dramatically from that time, leaving a substantial number in the hands of Sokehs warriors, though several years were to elapse before the Germans discovered the fact.

Berg, however, considered the disarmament a success, and he was never to know otherwise, for on 30 April 1907, still in office, he died. Officially he died of sunstroke while out surveying—an unusual death for a man who had spent some nine years in the tropics. The Ponapeans themselves believe differently. Their oral traditions tell of Berg's digging in the ruins of Nan Madol and disturbing the tombs of the ancestral kings. He died a few days later, without any prior signs of illness, pursued to the end by the sound of ghostly shell trumpets echoing through the mountains.[23] It is a tale of retribution entirely in keeping with the brooding atmosphere of Ponape and its people.

The final years of Berg's administration had not been free of all recrimination. For the first time since the Boston Mission had left the island in 1890, the government in 1905 encountered a challenge from missionary zeal. A measure of confessional balance had been regained in 1899 when the Boston Mission returned to Ponape, but the centres of its operations now remained in Kusaie and Truk and only one or two missionaries were stationed in Ponape. In 1907 its work in the Carolines was taken over by the Liebenzeller Mission, an arm of the German evangelical *Jugendbund für entscheidendes Christentum*. In like manner, the mandate of the Spanish Capuchins was transferred to the Rhein-Westfalen Province of the Capuchin Order, and after 1903 German monks gradually replaced the Spanish.

Relations between the Catholic Mission and the administration were at their most cordial while the Spanish Capuchins were still on the island. Both Hahl and Berg were on very friendly terms with the Fathers, and their friendship was reciprocated; Hahl in particular was regarded by the Spanish Fathers as 'a sensitive and noble man'.[24] Ironically, with the arrival of the German Capuchins a less fraternal atmosphere prevailed, over an issue which had been evaded hitherto: the question of competitive proselytism.

The first collision occurred early in 1905, when the Capuchins sought approval to expand into Takaiu, an island section in the lagoon of Uh, where the mostly pagan and Protestant inhabitants had declared themselves ready to accept a Catholic station. Predictably, the evangelical missionary, Mr Gray, protested that Takaiu had always been a traditional Protestant preserve.

The dispute which Berg was now forced to adjudicate had ramifications beyond mere sectarian jealousy. Though it claimed over 1000 adherents, evangelical Protestantism in Ponape in the early 1900s was a hollow institution; even the Boston Mission on its return in 1899 acknowledged that the spiritual life of the people was 'all but zero'.[25] But religion had become over the years a powerful reinforcement of the political divisions of the districts. The complexion of one's faith was now a badge of political allegiance: the Catholic north against the Protestant south. To disturb that by insisting on the principle of religious freedom would create dangerous tensions in Ponape. It was a problem that Hahl never had to face even though he had succeeded in gaining the High Chiefs' assent to the principle in 1900. It was left to Berg, and he was only too aware of the Colonial Department's anxiety to maintain the *status quo*. He also recognised in Henry Nanpei a man who was *the* Church in Kiti, to whom the power was more important than the calling. Nanpei's support was vital to the administration. Under the circumstances, Berg would not sanction the Catholic Mission's plan without Protestant approval.

A confrontation with the mission was inevitable, especially after the Deputy Superior retorted that war was immaterial to the mission where converts were to be made. When Berg went on in 1906 to accept the action of the High Chiefs of Kiti and Madolenihmw, who stripped two of their chiefs of land and titles for favouring the Catholic Mission, the Capuchins were thoroughly outraged. Relations thereafter were steadily more strained.

The missionaries' stand is an important part of the Ponape story, for they were the real representatives of European rule at district and section level until 1907. The administration gained some knowledge of district relations through its consultations with important chiefs, but by and large until 1907 Hahl and Berg had been confined to rather negative policies: trying to reduce sources of inter-communal conflict, curbing gun-running operations and partially disarming the Islanders. Berg's death marked the end of this phase, for it coincided with the creation of the Colonial Office as a separate ministry, and with the new priorities of Secretary Dernburg: colonial self-sufficiency and co-ordinated economic and social development. After 1907 these pressures made themselves felt on Albert Hahl as chief executive of the island sphere, with portentous results for Ponape.

4

Reform, Rebellion and the Sunset of German Rule

The arbitrary nature of 'feudal' rule in Ponape, with its expulsion of tenants, banishment of dissidents and disputes over tenure, tribute and advancement, was an inexhaustible source of conflict which the Germans found difficult to control before 1907 because of the widely scattered nature of Ponapean settlement, the lack of roads and the dependence on slow boats for transport. The new Colonial Office initiatives gave Hahl in New Guinea the inducement to consider implementing the changes he had projected in 1900. Not just security, but also the need to stimulate indigenous production and raise Ponape's economic output—indeed the output of the whole island sphere—dictated positive action. In 1907 Hahl was sure he could introduce a new system of land tenure into Kiti district at least, because population pressure there was straining the available land, and because in Kiti lived Henry Nanpei, whom Hahl saw as a certain supporter of the German moves.[1]

The Governor undertook a tour to Ponape in September 1907 while the island was still without a new district officer. On 23 September, he announced to an assembly of chiefs the Reich's intention of converting the present land system into freehold ownership by farmstead tenants, and he managed to extract from the High Chiefs a written agreement that they would refrain meanwhile from dispossessing their present tenants of cultivated land.[2] Without offering any further information Hahl then departed, leaving behind him general confusion. Some sections of the population saw the agreement as a total abolition of chiefly powers; the High Chiefs feared that the agreement meant their position and prerogatives had been swept away by mere fiat.

When the new district administrator, Georg Fritz, arrived many months later, in April 1908, he found a highly unstable situation. In the absence of a strong hand, the leading chiefs had been spreading rumours that the Germans were planning to introduce new taxes and customs duties, and even forced labour camps.[3]

Fritz was a young, ambitious man, sensitive about professional status and esteem, who had just completed a successful tour of duty as administrator of the Mariana Islands. There, among the peaceful, passive race of Chamorros and Micronesians, he had with little difficulty set up a poll tax system, regulated the planting activities of the inhabitants, and introduced compulsory labour for the administration. Fritz was an official in the true colonial mould. He was eager to bring the 'realities of civilisation' to the *Naturvölker*, namely, the will to work for its own sake, joy in private property, and love of family, preferably the nuclear family. A patronising man, filled with the need to uphold the honour and prestige of the Reich among 'native races', Fritz was yet anxious to be, and to appear to be, fair, impartial and understanding.

Because the Marianas had been such a congenial area for his talents, Fritz came to Ponape unwillingly at first. His instructions from Hahl were to address himself to the land issue. Hahl wanted a survey of every farmstead and common on the island so that the needs of the people and of the administration could be gauged before effecting any changes. Fritz was in agreement with the Governor that things could be allowed to drift no longer, and that the seat of administration might just as well be shifted to another, more prosperous centre in the Carolines unless economic development were accomplished in Ponape along the lines desired by the Colonial Office.

Fritz himself foresaw the extension of his Marianas work to Ponape, including the levying of personal taxes and the imposition of corvée labour, but felt that it should be discreetly organised so as to overcome the resistance of the Islanders. He did not take kindly to Hahl's method of procedure, regarding the Governor's reform project of September as 'immature and unjust' and its disclosure in Ponape premature.[4] In February 1908 he had already informed Hahl of a scheme of his own which would transform the social system, and involve the Islanders throughout the Carolines in the tasks of development.[5] In areas where the chief and his tenants agreed, the absolute right of the chief over the commoner's land was to be abolished, as well as the constant obligations of tribute in produce and labour. In return, the main chiefs were to be compensated financially through a system of compulsory work which the government would organise for the emancipated tenants. The tenants would gain the freehold possession of their land, to be handed down in perpetuity to their heirs, but would be obligated to work on government projects for fifteen days each year at a wage rate of one mark per day. Half this wage would then be distributed to the chiefs as recompense for their lost income and privileges; the rest would fall to the government treasury. Fritz anticipated that, as the traditional leaders were incorporated into the administrative apparatus as officials and overseers of the public works, their 'pension' would be phased out and the tax of fifteen work-days on each Islander would accrue to the administration. It was a subtly-disguised system of mass taxation and corvée labour, designed, at one stroke, to reduce the independence of the chiefs and involve them more closely in administrative control, to accustom the people to ordered work, and to open up the island at minimal cost. Fritz later estimated that, with the extension of the scheme to the rest of the Carolines group, and with the added innovation of a direct cash or copra tax on the low copra-yielding atolls, the island sphere might generate 100 000 marks in cash annually.[6]

Hahl and Fritz had just managed to convince the Colonial Office in June 1908 that the reforms were essential to productivity, and to law and order, when suddenly the entire scheme was thrown into doubt by growing unrest over the reforms themselves. Not only had the latent dissatisfaction touched off by Hahl's visit spread throughout the native community, but Fritz was also becoming unavoidably embroiled in a major dispute between two Kiti chiefs, Henry Nanpei and Sou Kiti.[7]

Nanpei's legacy of land, his acquisition of the Protestant leadership, and his business ability had earned him a power base in his section, Ronkiti, which rivalled that even of the Nahnmwarki. In so doing he created enemies in the 'royal' line of chiefs. Among them was the section chief of Enipein in Kiti, Sou Kiti, descendant of a famous Enipein warrior of the same clan, who had conquered the Ant Islands off Kiti in a major district war of the eighteenth century. This connection, along with the titular headship of the goddess Naluk cult gave Sou Kiti significant historical rights to the Ant Islands, which Nanpei also claimed through his father's testament of 1863. Over the years, Nanpei had developed the islands, which were rich in coconuts and marine products, as the major base of his business operations, and he regarded Sou Kiti's claim with hostility.

The issue was revived in 1907-08 with Hahl's announcement of the proposed land changes. Though the Spanish regime in 1896 and Hahl in 1899 had recognised Nanpei's inheritance, his claims, particularly to Ant, strictly contradicted the traditional system of inheritance, and there were those from within Kiti itself who would gladly seek any charge to circumscribe Nanpei's power and wealth. Nanpei was particularly apprehensive of Sou Kiti as a political rival, for Sou Kiti was equally a man of reputation in Kiti. He was resolute, brave, loyal and clever; a warrior who had taken the Sou Kiti title after aiding Sokehs and Net in the Spanish wars and a leader who could mobilise many people in Kiti in his support. Because of this Henry Nanpei had a vested interest in seeing the German land reforms introduced. His chances of confirming his claims to the Ant Islands and their wealth were far greater if he supported the German plans than if he took recourse to traditional custom in Kiti.

At the same time, a new element complicated the dispute and aggravated Nanpei's dilemma. Sou Kiti was not a Catholic but he possessed clan relatives in the Catholic districts and was sympathetic to the Capuchin missionaries. They appear to have courted Sou Kiti to provide land in his section for a school and church.[8]

To Henry Nanpei this represented a serious threat: not only could Sou Kiti count on the Capuchins for active support in any campaign against Nanpei's estates, but a Catholic intrusion into Kiti would undermine Nanpei's position and considerable influence as Protestant head. It would also imply a certain triumph for the northern districts who identified themselves with the Catholic cause and treated Sou Kiti as an ally.

The district chiefs of Sokehs and Net were particularly wary of Nanpei. They continually suspected him of deliberately augmenting his landed estates and his prestige so that he would be in a position to demand recognition as the most powerful man in Ponape, strengthening the southern districts against the northern in the process. The German administration repeatedly seemed to these chiefs to be favouring Nanpei by seeking his company and advice and taking him as interpreter or mediator on tours around the Carolines.

Their suspicions hardened when, after Hahl's visit in September 1907, Nanpei reconstructed a group of his supporters which had grown up in the Spanish period as a direct result of the Boston Mission's attempts to introduce American ideas of party government and private property. This body of Protestant-trained chiefs in Madolenihmw, Kiti and Uh had acted, not always consciously nor without violence and coercion, as a vanguard of American ideas. On Georg Fritz's arrival, the group paraded itself as a new democratic movement which had formed ostensibly in response to social reforms. Its plan was to elect three chiefly representatives from each of the five districts, with Nanpei as 'chairman', to act as an 'advisory council' (*puin en lolokon*) to the administration in 'native affairs'.[9]

On one level the plan might be seen as a progressive initiative to have power shared in a colonial situation: but it is also necessary to recognise in it the operation of plain political self-interest: Henry Nanpei's primary aim was to capture a position and influence commensurate with his standing as Ponape's foremost land baron and entrepreneur.

Nanpei's uneasiness with traditional custom did not stem simply from the Ant Islands affair; he laid claim to parcels of land all over Kiti and in other districts as well. In fact Nanpei's status in Ponape was exceptional in every way. He was the son of a celebrated Nahnken, and enjoyed the title *Ipwin pohn warawar* (Born Upon the Ditch), which gave him considerable prestige;[10] he held the Nanpei title in three districts, Kiti, Madolenihmw and Uh; he was head of the Protestant faction in those three districts; and he possessed eminent kin connections in both Madolenihmw and Uh, who enjoyed the ear of their Nahnmwarkis.

For all his high birth, innate ability and the power and influence of his own making, Henry Nanpei remained a prisoner of custom. He had nowhere to go in the title system. Not being of the appropriate clan, he would never progress either to Nahnmwarki or Nahnken. As owner of a great deal of unconventionally-inherited land, he was always, in theory at least, vulnerable to sequestration by the Nahnmwarki of Kiti. It was logical, therefore, that Nanpei should initiate moves to counter and neutralise, if not abolish, the power of the High Chiefs, and secure for himself the maximum freedom of action. His proposed advisory council would achieve just those ends. With his followers from the three southern districts and their influence on the Nahnmwarkis, Nanpei would be in a position to manipulate both the traditional system and the German regime. The northern districts at least were in no doubt that Nanpei was out to destroy the Nahnmwarkis and entrench himself as an ally and protector of the foreign regime. From their vantage point in the north, the Capuchin Fathers agreed; indeed their Superior believed that Nanpei was out to create a new ruling line through which he and his descendants would become in effect hereditary Deputy Governors of Ponape.[11]

By July 1908 there was once more open animosity between the southern and northern districts, with the inexperienced Fritz totally confused by the complexities of the dispute. The isolation of Mesenieng, or Kolonia as it was now called, on the northern shores of Ponape added to Fritz's difficulties, for it effectively prevented him from discovering what exactly was going on in the south.

To counter this, Fritz began in May to construct a road from the colony to Kiti with paid out-islander labour. It had not gone more than 1000 metres, when, on 17 July, the road workers were thrown into consternation by a warning to stop work on the project or risk being attacked by Ponapean warriors. Five days earlier, people from Pweipwei and Paliapailong in Kiti had raided Sou Kiti's land in Tomworoahlong, destroying coconut and breadfruit plants and damaging some canoes and a house. Fritz was in Kiti investigating this incident when he heard of the furore at the roadworks. On top of this report came one from Nanpei: that the Catholic areas of Sokehs, Net and Awak were furious at the rumours of enforced land changes and new taxes, and were planning an assault not only on the European colony but on friends of the regime like Nanpei as well.

By now totally flustered and believing Ponape on the brink of rebellion, Fritz retreated to Nanpei's base in Ronkiti. At the same time he dispatched a message to the colony to prepare its defences and one to the Capuchin Fathers asking them to use their good offices to pacify the northerners.

The northerners, for their part, were genuinely nonplussed at the whole affair and then highly indignant at what they saw as a plot by Nanpei to discredit them. Two days after the unrest on the road project, the chiefs of Sokehs and Net gathered before Fritz in a demonstration of loyalty and obedience organised by the Catholic mission and Fritz promised that no changes to land tenure would be made until the chiefs approved.

None of these measures really solved the crisis or reduced the tension. When letters continued to arrive in Kolonia warning against a northern attack, Fritz contemplated calling in military support, but decided instead to tackle the island chiefs in a general assembly.

The assembly, on 4 August 1908, revealed how close to the edge of war Ponape had slid since the issue of land reform was raised twelve months before. The delegates from Madolenihmw came bearing rifles, the Uh people arrived in forty-two strongly-manned canoes, and rumour was rife that Nanpei and the Kiti district were waiting to fall on Sokehs. And Fritz did not help his cause by determinedly ignoring the recent incidents on which the northern chiefs in particular expected judgment. Instead, he simply welcomed the chiefs' queries about government policies and accepted the principle of Nanpei's advisory council, to comprise the five High Chiefs, section heads and one or two other representatives from the districts, who would all assist in the tasks of native administration.[12]

This proposal was greeted with stony silence, for the northern chiefs saw in it the triumph of a campaign carefully orchestrated by Nanpei. Both mission societies and Fritz, indeed most of Ponape, agreed that Nanpei was behind the series of false alarms in the previous few days. Nanpei appears to have paid the Pweipwei people, a group who could be bought at any price, to damage Sou Kiti's land in a traditional gesture of displeasure, with the hope that Sou Kiti would retaliate. Nanpei could then denounce his rival as a troublemaker and so destroy his claim to the Ant Islands.

Likewise, the incident at the roadworks in mid-July was Nanpei's work. His purposes in this case were labyrinthine. First, Nanpei did not want a road into Kiti, for that would compromise his freedom of action and enterprise; the warning of attack on the road workers was meant to be a deterrent. Second, Nanpei implicated the northern districts in the unrest hoping that Fritz would take action against them and the Catholic Mission. In drawing the disconcerted administrator to him in Kiti, it is possible Nanpei hoped to provoke a dispute between the Capuchin Mission and Fritz by convincing the former that Fritz was favouring Nanpei and his Protestant supporters. But, third, Nanpei had a genuine reason for seeking Fritz's protection, for Nanpei had enemies within Kiti itself who were accusing him of plotting with the administration to introduce taxes and change the land system in his own favour.

Nanpei was under siege from all sides, and through his manoeuvres he was attempting to manipulate circumstances to his advantage: the threat from Sou Kiti would be removed; Catholic pretensions in Kiti would be thwarted; and German support would be won for Nanpei's claims and his position in Kiti. Fritz's August assembly seemed to his opponents to confirm his success.

A few days later a new occurrence dashed all Fritz's hopes of regaining peace and stability by negotiation. It was imperative that Sou Kiti receive compensation for the destruction on his land if he were not to lose face to Nanpei. Traditionally the victim extracted justice by reciprocal force or intimidation. Fearing a major district collision, perhaps civil war, if Sou Kiti took matters into his own hands, the Capuchin Mission pressed the administrator to come to Sou Kiti's aid. In a secret meeting Fritz promised Sou Kiti that the government would compensate him financially and Sou Kiti expressed himself satisfied.

At this point, when the situation seemed most under control and the ways of the Ponapeans no longer a mystery, the frailty of German understanding was revealed. The mission's sources suddenly reported that Sou Kiti was disappointed with Fritz's offer and wanted a written assurance of support from the Government. Fritz baulked at the new demand. From his experience in the Marianas, Fritz had acquired a deep suspicion of Catholic priests, after observing the destruction of the Chamorro civilisation which the militantly-Catholic Spanish regime had wrought over the centuries. Fritz's reading of Ponape's past convinced him that the rivalry between the two Christian confessions lay at the heart of the district disputes, and he was almost frantic that the German regime should not take sides as had the Spanish. Any written agreement given to a Catholic sympathiser would, he was afraid, be used by the Catholic districts to incite the Protestants, and he minced no words in telling the Capuchins so.

There followed an acrimonious correspondence, the mission disclaiming all responsibility for the future behaviour of its adherents and Fritz accusing the Fathers of trying to enlist the administration in a religious war against Protestantism.[13] The estrangement became more complete when two letters, inspired by Nanpei, arrived from the Protestant High Chiefs in the south, begging Fritz to curb the activities of the Catholics and restrict them to the northern districts. By mid-August relations between the Government and the mission were virtually broken off and passions were so inflamed that Fritz felt it necessary to send for a warship and extra police to forestall the outbreak of fighting.

The cruiser SMS *Condor* sailed in, cleared for action, on 2 September, and 100 Melanesian police-soldiers from New Guinea landed. Fritz had already warned the Ponapeans of their impending visit, and had played up their reputation as 'black cannibals' to salutary effect. When Governor Hahl arrived in mid-September to assess the situation, a sullen peace prevailed, and he grasped immediately that the passive population he had known was now uneasy about German rule. In early October he telegraphed for a second cruiser and requested a further 100 soldiers, with the object of maintaining a garrison on the island until the tension had eased.[14] Some weeks later the gunboat SMS *Jaguar* arrived from Kiautschou.

Partly with Melanesian labour, partly with local volunteers, Fritz was able to resume work on the road to the south, an urgent project now in view of the unrest, and in six months a twenty-four kilometre road was cut through the island over the mountains into Kiti. A road ten kilometres long now also linked the colony with Sokehs. At the beginning of March 1909, the landing corps of the *Condor* and a detachment of the Melanesians marched ceremoniously from the colony to Kiti district to demonstrate the administration's new-found capacity for mobility; the journey took six hours! The Germans followed up with displays of firepower and close-quarter fighting by the warships. Arrangements were made to remove to the Marianas over 600 out-islanders stranded on Ponape since a typhoon in 1907 had destroyed their atolls, and who were in danger of being used as mercenaries in the district conflicts.

These measures restored at least some external respect for the power of the German regime, but they also heralded a new phase in its relations with the Islanders. The era of temporisation was over. The administration was now committed to a policy of economic and social development and to a more rigorous control over the political activities of the Ponapean districts. It was clear that for seven years Ponapeans had merely tolerated the Germans. Hundreds of firearms were still being hoarded in various parts of Ponape and there was a general feeling that serious disorder could occur at any time. Fritz felt obliged to institute armed patrols for men working on government projects, and the defence forces of the European colony were kept constantly mobilised in case of trouble. The Germans were approaching the state of siege which had prevailed under the Spanish two decades before.

Fritz and Hahl were of one mind that there was no going back from this position. The honour and reputation of Germany, not to mention that of her local officials, depended on the successful completion of the new social and economic tasks. Both men therefore pressed the Colonial Office for funds to establish a proper peace-keeping force in the Carolines which would ensure that all the reforms were carried through. A naval vessel stationed in Ponape waters, 200 soldiers, and a network of roads were the prerequisites they envisaged. Fritz also asked for an extra fiscal grant of 40 000 marks over two years to offset the cost of constructing the roads with voluntary labour, since the planned public corvée was momentarily out of the question.[15]

However, the recent disturbances had begun to raise doubts in Berlin about the wisdom of an aggressive forward policy on an island which possessed so little value for the Reich. In the circumstances, the State Secretary for Colonies, Bernhard Dernburg, considered cutting Germany's losses and withdrawing the government apparatus from Ponape altogether. The real 'epicentre' of the Caroline Islands, the focal point for traffic from the smaller islands, was Truk, the archipelago of high islands 616 kilometres to the west of Ponape, with a population of

20 000. Truk was, as Victor Berg had once described it, the 'Paris' of the island sphere, or what Zanzibar was to the negroes of the East African coast.[16] Its islands held half the population of the whole area; it had far better harbours and far richer economic prospects than Ponape, producing five times as much copra; and it was much closer to the more populous western half of Germany's island sphere. It is not clear why the Spaniards chose Ponape as a base in 1887, though its individual size, the difficulty of consistent water supplies in Truk and the fearsome reputation of Truk's inhabitants all played some part in their decision. The question of transferring the seat of German administration there had already been raised as early as 1902, but the same difficulties applied. By 1908, Hahl was using the insecurity of Ponape as the strongest argument against withdrawal. Hahl believed that unless Ponape was pacified there was a real likelihood of disturbances spreading to other islands in the group, like Truk. Germany had no choice: she was trapped on Ponape.

Dernburg accepted Hahl's argument and compromised. Germany would stay. But he refused Fritz's request for special finance, ordered the withdrawal of the extra troops, and in September 1908 instructed Fritz to follow Hahl's original policy and 'hold the ring', leaving development to the Ponapeans themselves. The naval authorities had already advised that a second cruiser was due to be appointed to the Pacific in 1909-10, which should ease the patrolling strain on SMS *Condor*.[17]

During the next nine months, the island colony stagnated as Germany resumed her defensive posture. In February and March 1909, Fritz was able to obtain the grudging consent of Kiti, Madolenihmw and then Uh to his reform scheme. The money argument was definitely influential in winning over the leading chiefs. In Kiti, for example, with over 200 men of working age, the Nahnmwarki would receive 1000 marks from the tax labour, with a further 700 marks divided among the Nahnken and his prominent colleagues. Since many chiefs were in debt, a guaranteed income from the Germans was an attractive proposition. Nanpei certainly used his influence to campaign for acceptance, an important factor since several chiefs were in debt to him. And the temporary presence of SMS *Jaguar*, as well as the belief that the districts could withdraw from the agreement if dissatisfied, seemed to have assisted Fritz in gaining the chiefs' assent.

Fritz got as far as beginning the registration of land holdings and organising the first work periods. But though the three southern districts completed their obligation for 1909, along with Net, which accepted the reforms hesitantly later in the year, the results were not encouraging. Anxious not to provoke the people, or the wrath of the Colonial Office, Fritz let the work proceed in haphazard fashion, with no European supervision and workers coming and going as they liked. As a result the project lacked any serious co-ordination or direction, and after the 1909 series was finished Fritz made hardly any headway.

Most people of the northern district Sokehs were not unsympathetic to the German innovations, but a small body of chiefs put up a stolid resistance and refused to accept them, at least for 1909. The dissidents were led by the leading trader and warrior of the district, Soumadau en Sokehs, section chief of Mwalok where the Sokehs ceremonial house was located.

Soumadau was not of the ruling clan, Soun Kawad, but his father had been a high ranking member of it, which gave Soumadau substantial prestige. Indeed, his prestige, energy and influence so eclipsed that of the weak and vacillating High Chief (Wasai Sokehs), that Soumadau was, in effect, the chief executive of the district. Soumadau was the embodiment of Sokehs' fiercely independent reputation. He had fought on the side of Awak in the war with the Protestants in 1898, and had led famous charges against the Spanish fortress. Sokehs district had long considered itself foremost among the five of the island. It had been the scene of the first uprising against the Spanish in 1887, and, though later forced onto Spain's side in distrust of the south, Sokehs continued to retain a sense of superiority over Europeans, jealously guarding its isolation on the small island which lay to the west of Kolonia. It was Sokehs which resisted Berg's disarmament in 1905; and Soumadau en Sokehs was even supposed to have been behind a plot to kill an acting administrator, Stückhardt, in early 1908.[18]

Soumadau was intent on safeguarding the integrity of the district against the southerners, and on this account he opposed the German reforms. There is also evidence to suggest that Soumadau was a committed traditionalist, and that in particular he was against the loss of traditional chiefly privileges and the possible destruction of clan control of land. This was despite the fact that he owned a western-style store in Mwalok and wore only European clothes.[19]

Many of the northern chiefs were suspicious of the German changes because they imagined them to be the inspiration of Henry Nanpei, whom they saw as benefiting from the new land distribution. With these misgivings in Sokehs, Fritz was unable to move them to accept the

German plans for 1909. And he was in no position to force them since not only had he promised that the reforms would be subject to district approval, but also he was now without military support again. However, after the mediation of the Catholic Mission, which assured the Sokehs chiefs that the reforms were 'a government affair' and nothing to do with Nanpei, they were finally persuaded to consider a work period for 1910 and let the survey of their land holdings go ahead.[20]

All in all, the Ponapeans still retained the initiative in 1909. Fritz's incipient system of close imperial control seemed to have been dealt a damaging blow, and the success of his innovations was very doubtful. Moreover, he was still tied by his agreement to the principle of a *Puin en lolokon*, Nanpei's advisory council.

Suddenly, in October 1909, Georg Fritz was transferred to Yap, to take over the government of the western Carolines. The reasons for the move are not known, though the Capuchin Order in Germany had considerable influence with the Centre Party and it is more than likely that the Order had been putting pressure on Berlin for his removal. There is little doubt that Fritz had come to Ponape predisposed against the Catholic Mission, and had allowed himself to be distracted from the real causes of conflict in Ponape by his involvement in religious sectarianism. Because of this his reputation suffered, and his later polemics against the priests did not help to redeem him.

But Fritz was nonetheless a competent and careful administrator, one who worked to gain a consensus of agreement about his reforms. Without that consensus he would not proceed, partly because he considered the Ponapeans a mercurial and unpacified people, torn by class conflict, inter-district envy and religious strife over which one could not ride roughshod. But Fritz's instincts were also fundamentally non-aggressive and conciliatory, and he disliked having to resort to military solutions: hence his agreement to implement his ideas not at his own, but at the Ponapeans' pace. If he did call for armed forces in the end, it was as a moral support rather than as a punitive instrument. Ponapean tradition is relatively tolerant of Georg Fritz. He grew with his job, though not to the extent that he was a match for Henry Nanpei, the island's *eminence grise*.

Ponape now received its fifth administrator in ten years. The new man was Carl Boeder, and he came directly from Dar-es-Salam in East Africa, where he had been involved in Germany's struggle against the Maji Maji uprising of 1905-06.

When he arrived in Ponape on 14 December 1909 a cloud of lethargy hung over the island. The absence of real rapport between Islanders and government, a chronic lack of finance, and continual changes in official personnel had brought most administrative activity to a virtual halt.

Boeder was in a difficult position, inhibited by the negative attitude of the Colonial Office, yet saddled with the reform initiative taken by Hahl and Fritz. His personality was ill-suited to the monotonous life of a small, close-knit island community isolated from the rest of the world; his experience in Africa was certainly no guarantee of success in dealing with Pacific Islanders. A correct and rather distant man, Boeder tended to assume that his personality and authority would ensure peaceful solutions to any problems which might arise between the two cultural communities. To the job of dealing with other races he brought goodwill, but he was authoritarian and demanding, and he carried with him from Africa the conviction that the rod was a legitimate and effective method of instilling 'colonial discipline' into fundamentally primitive peoples; in fact, rumours later circulated in Ponape that he had been in trouble in Africa because of his severity. With these attitudes, and despite the warnings of his predecessor, Boeder set out to re-invigorate the German presence on Ponape.

The new administrator was rather contemptuous of what he conceived as Fritz's weakness in dealing with Sokehs and the other districts over the compulsory labour question, and his first objective was to renegotiate the issue of Sokehs' approval of the reforms. Throughout February 1910 Boeder put pressure on the chiefs of Sokehs, mainly through the irresolute Wasai, to begin their work period at once, arguing that the Ponapeans could only enjoy increasing prosperity if they all worked hard and obeyed the government's orders. At an assembly on 16 March 1910 the reforms were publicly accepted, albeit under duress.[21]

The compulsory labour periods for all the districts got under way in April with remaking the old roads to Kiti and Sokehs. Of Fritz's road through the island to the south coast barely one and one-half kilometres was still passable, the rest was overgrown and fallen into disrepair. Boeder at least recognised that the road was economically and militarily of little use to the regime since the south could be reached almost as quickly by boat. But he planned to recut it nevertheless, since in his eyes inconsistency was the gravest sin which a regime could commit against its subjects. What Boeder really wanted was a new road around the coast, touching most of the sections, and then one along the foreshores of Sokehs Island, to give easier access to its interior.

The Ponapeans suddenly found themselves subjected to a new and distasteful regimen. For a start, their work was closely supervised by a European, Otto Hollborn, a former employee of the Jaluit Gesellschaft who had recently joined the administration. Sokehs in particular resented this: perhaps it awakened memories of the Spanish period. To quieten them, Boeder appointed Soumadau en Sokehs as a second overseer, to work in conjunction with Hollborn, at the rate of two marks a day. The results were only temporary. At the end of April 1910 the German administration demanded that Sokehs work a second period of fifteen days in 1910 to make up for the one that they had refused to perform under Fritz the year before. Despite the bitter protests of Soumadau, Wasai Sokehs and the Nahnken, Boeder and Hollborn insisted that the double obligation was all part of the package to which the Sokehs chiefs had agreed in February.[22]

The whole of Ponape was now greatly apprehensive about Boeder and the methods he used. Chiefs everywhere began to resent the fact, made clear to them for the first time, that the implementation of the new order meant that they must forfeit tribute from the people permanently. Tributary labour and the first fruits from tenants' harvests were the only sources of income for some chiefs, and consequently the money to be divided among the leading few chiefs after the work periods were over was small compensation for the majority. Boeder began to encounter resistance to the scheme, not only from the chiefs but from the common people also, who supported the chiefs' appeal to halve the amount of compensation and allow tribute to go on being paid. Boeder refused, and in addition he made it clear that voluntary acceptance of the reforms did not mean that the Islanders could withdraw at will.[23] Boeder's vision of a quickly-constructed network of roads for Ponape began to fade as people refused to work outside their districts and the organisation of work faltered in consequence.

The most persistent resistance came from Sokehs, which took great offence at the exaction of a second labour period. Boeder had ignored the fact that his predecessor, Fritz, had waived the fulfilment of the 1909 obligation for Sokehs, and he seemed deliberately to be provoking the district by ordering that this work period be used to build the projected road around the island, thereby compelling the people to destroy their coveted isolation and expose Sokehs to unwanted influences from the mainland. Throughout May protests and complaints about the administration's injustice continued to be made by Soumadau and Wasai Sokehs, and the smouldering unrest was manifest on the roadworks, where Sokehs labourers carried long knives and Hollborn had difficulty in extracting obedience. The Sokehs people, led by Soumadau, completed their first fifteen days ill-humouredly and demanded a month's interval to attend to their crops before beginning the second period. The administration could only get voluntary day-labourers to maintain the works when Soumadau's wage was raised to four marks a day. By the end of May there was a definite groundswell of opinion against Boeder and his subordinates.

Boeder was aware that something was afoot in Sokehs but discounted its importance, feeling secure enough to embark on an official tour of the Carolines at the end of May with half of the fifty Melanesian soldiers attached to the colony. No sooner had he left than the Superior of the Capuchin Mission hastened to Boeder's young deputy, the Secretary Brauckmann, with news that the Net people had warned of a plot by Soumadau to attack the colony on 31 May; simultaneously the people of Awak arrived to defend the colony. In the days that followed, Ponapeans began lurking around the perimeter of Kolonia or appearing in the settlement with their long knives, while Uh people, fearful of a revolt, came to remove their relatives from the government hospital.

Brauckmann initially gave little credence to the priests' report: relations between administration and mission had never fully recovered since the collision over the Sou Kiti affair. However Brauckmann was also inexperienced at deputising as chief official and seems to have willed any plots to be figments of the imagination. When he visited Sokehs and found nothing, he reported to the priests with some relief that he felt the matter was all 'idle talk'.[24] Those found in the colony with knives he arrested and then released immediately, though evidence he had received since his visit to Sokehs confirmed the likelihood of a conspiracy. There had, indeed, been a conspiracy, and it had failed only because Wasai Sokehs and the Nahnken were hesitant, and the Net people, traditional allies, refused to help.

Boeder's return on 24 June changed nothing. He, too, refused to take the matter seriously, declaring complacently that the unrest was simply 'the empty talk and bragging of some hotspurs' who were discontented with roadwork.[25] Rather than act against the 'hotspurs' in Sokehs, Boeder thought it 'politically more astute' to threaten them with naval intervention, knowing that a visit by the East Asian Cruiser Squadron was already scheduled for early July. The squadron arrived promptly on 2 July, but, contrary to the expectations of Boeder's staff and the rest of the European community, the administrator made no effort to punish those responsible for the growing agitation. Instead Boeder invoked the 'moral impression' which the collection of vessels was supposed to have, encouraging the Ponapeans to visit the ships and arranging for parades by the 400 members of the squadron's landing corps. That the mere external display of size and power was already an outdated sanction in the conditions of Ponape, Boeder does not seem to have considered, nor that his self-conceived tolerance might be taken as proof of weakness. Soumadau, for one, compared the Germans unfavourably with the Spanish who, though fearful, proved their bravery by fighting, while the Germans always talked about their soldiers, their ships, their glorious Kaiser, but did nothing.[26] Nevertheless, at the end of the banquets, the manoeuvres and the parades, Boeder once more felt master of the situation. He believed there was nothing to fear from the 'natives' in the foreseeable future, and to prove his point he decided not to go ahead with reinforcing the island's police troop as he had been planning.

Unfortunately for Boeder's optimism, the difficulties with Sokehs began all over again when the district was told it must now complete its second work period. Soumadau and the leading chiefs kept up their complaints and queries, while the road labourers continued to disobey Hollborn. In August, at a time when there was not a ship of any kind in Ponape and the island was effectively cut off from the outside world, the Wasai Sokehs demanded from Boeder an increase in the day wage of the road labourers. Boeder refused, threatened the High Chief with deportation and threw him bodily out of his office,[27] an action which was provocative in the extreme.

Worse was to come. After July 1910 Boeder introduced corporal punishment as a punitive sanction against anyone found guilty of lying, insubordination or 'shameless behaviour' towards whites. Despite the fact that, from this point on, clear warnings abounded that beatings would cause the Islanders to rise up against the Germans, Boeder made no concessions to indigenous sensibilities. He began to acquire a reputation for cruelty and contempt. A special convict uniform was introduced, and prisoners now had their heads shaved, a gross and calculating insult to the Ponapeans. A tradition exists that Boeder would use a drawn revolver to interrogate Islanders during a trial, occasionally shooting it off in their faces to frighten them; and that if he stumbled on a stone or a coconut while on an expedition he would fly into a rage and threaten to beat his guides and bearers.[28]

Then, in September, Boeder had the first thrashing administered, to Eliu Santos of Kiti, who lied to the authorities about a theft of money from Henry Nanpei. The ethnologist, Paul Hambruch, at that time travelling round Ponape, reported to Boeder that a secret society was now mobilising in all districts, with Soumadau as its leader, to plan the overthrow of white rule.[29] Boeder seemed oblivious of any danger, and disregarded persistent warnings by the Catholic Mission that Souma-dau was the main troublemaker and should be deported. The cruiser SMS *Cormoran* came and went in September without any action being taken.

Ponapeans say that Boeder counted Soumadau as a friend, and, if so, it is more than likely that Boeder felt he could control the Sokehs chief; after all, he had given him a well-paid job on the roadworks. But Boeder betrayed no understanding of the difficult position in which Soumadau now found himself. Soumadau en Sokehs was losing face. As overseer and virtual Chief of the district, he was supposed to protect Sokehs. But as Boeder's abuses mounted and he paid no heed to protests, Souma-dau's collaboration began to look shabby. This was not improved by the fact that he was getting paid handsomely for his supervision. To allow the fiction of his co-operation with the Germans to continue would only destroy Soumadau's credibility with Sokehs: he would lose his prestige, his influence, his ability to move Sokehs at all. Pressure was mounting for Soumadau to demonstrate his leadership more forcefully.

The pressure finally became intolerable on 17 October 1910. On that day, one of the Sokehs labourers, Lahdeleng, was sent by Hollborn to the administrator with a piece of paper alleging insubordination; Boeder had no hesitation in ordering ten strokes with a wire-lined rubber hose. The beating was administered by a Melanesian, and Lahdeleng was helped back to Sokehs, barely able to walk. On the island that night an emotional meeting took place, at which the marks of the beating were exhibited to all. Soumadau now had no choice but to prove he was a warrior chief, that he would not recoil in the face of so serious a challenge. He called for war to make away with the Germans as Sokehs had done with the Spaniards. There was some resistance from a party led by the Nahnken, who advocated compro-mise and co-operation with the regime. But the party of Soumadau and his brother, Lepen Ririn, had great influence over Wasai Sokehs, and it proved the stronger.[30] Lahdeleng, after all, was a member of the Soun

Kawad clan, the Wasai's own, and the imperative of retaliation was too strong to deny. Boeder had treated Lahdeleng like an animal in a culture where dignity and strength, courage and patience were the touchstones of manhood.

The entire district was caught up by the desire for vengeance, not simply in the passion of the moment, but because of regional loyalties and a peculiarly Ponapean feeling that fate dictated the destruction of Sokehs. There were no illusions about who would win in a head-on confrontation with the Germans. About a month before Lahdeleng's beating, a corner of Pan Kadara, the most sacred location in the stone city of Nan Madol, had crumbled. The corners of Pan Kadara were revered on Ponape as symbols of the various districts, and if any were to crumble it signified the impending destruction of that area. In this case it had been the Sokehs corner. Thus the Sokehs people knew and accepted that Sokehs must die, but, if so, they desired to die fighting, as men.[31] Their decision was probably strengthened by the belief that they could expect assistance from other districts because of cross-district clan relationships; Soumadau's own clan, Dipwenpahnmei, was the ruling clan of Madolenihmw and Net was ruled by Soun Kawad.

Early the next morning when Hollborn and the recently-arrived road engineer, Häfner, came to Denpei on Sokehs to begin work, they found Soumadau and his followers in war garb, their bodies oiled, wearing new grass skirts and carrying knives and rifles. The warriors began to converge on the two men, who immediately took refuge in the nearby Catholic Mission. While the angry Sokehs people surrounded the building shouting for Hollborn's blood, messengers were dispatched to the colony to raise the alarm. The first party was turned back and it was not until three o'clock in the afternoon that three mission helpers were able to get through. Boeder immediately rowed over to Sokehs with Brauckmann and five Mortlock Islanders. Thinking perhaps that a military display would only further provoke the Sokehs, or that they would immediately recognise his authority and submit to talking, Boeder brusquely refused his police master's plea that a troop of Melanesian police be allowed to accompany him.[32]

Boeder arrived at Denpei about four o'clock, where he was met by Hollborn, Häfner and the mission Fathers who had managed to slip out of the house. They were amazed that he was without military escort and tried to persuade him of the danger. Waving them away, Boeder went south towards Mwalok to confront Wasai Sokehs. He had gone only seventy yards when Lepen Ririn, Soumadau's brother, fell in beside him. Suddenly Lepen Ririn drew a gun and shot the administrator in the stomach. Mortally wounded, Boeder is reported to have appealed to Soumadau, who stood now above him: 'Ponape is good, Soumadau. Ponape is good', he said. Soumadau then replied, 'Ponape is good', and is alleged to have shot Boeder in the head.[33]

A frenzied crowd now rushed on the other whites. Brauckmann, Hollborn and Häfner were hacked down with knives or shot as they attempted to escape in Boeder's boat, and four of the five Mortlock Islanders were also killed. Only the two priests, Fathers Gebhardt and Venantius, managed to escape when they took refuge in the church and a group of loyal Sokehs women shielded them from attack with their bodies. After the killings, Boeder's body was mutilated by the people in a Ponapean gesture of contempt for a hated enemy. His hand was cut off and the body was thrown into the sea along with those of the others.

The Sokehs insurrection should have been the least likely such occurrence in any of Germany's Pacific territories. From the beginning, the Berlin authorities had insisted on a policy which would not provoke the Islanders, and their feelings on the subject were clearly expressed in the censure of Berg in 1902. The great reform scheme itself had not precipitated violence even though it represented a radical structural change in Ponapean society, by removing land possession from direct dependence on the hierarchy of power, and by implicitly subverting traditional authority. The changes initially were unpopular in all districts, though they were accepted in the end by the southerners. Even the resistance of the Sokehs leaders had been blunted by the time of Fritz's departure, and they had conceded that the changes might be instituted by negotiation at a later date. But then came Boeder and his methods. Initially Sokehs made the best of it, but Boeder's brutality and his injustice in foisting upon them a second work period in the same year aroused resentment beyond toleration. Not the reforms themselves, but the timing and manner of their enforcement brought about ultimate violence.

In the end, the uprising shows that, despite the dictates of official policy, the initiative for handling the colonised Ponapeans lay squarely with the individual officer in Ponape, in the same way that it did in Samoa and New Guinea. In Ponape, Boeder incorporated all the functions of colonial rule: legislative, executive and judicial. Measures like disarmament and the reforms of 1907-08 originated in the colony, not in Berlin. Most importantly, Boeder had been able to act for nine months virtually in contravention of guidelines laid down by Berlin, Hahl and Fritz.

There is no doubt he brought Sokehs' revenge upon himself. Boeder was an aggressive and ambitious administrator, yet he lacked the creative touch of a Hahl, or a Solf in Samoa; he had quickened the tempo of change without appreciating the consequences of the resulting unrest; he had been highly inconsistent in his behaviour towards the Ponapeans. In refusing to make concessions to a colonised people, in denigrating their sense of self-respect, and in dishonouring his predecessor's agreement, Boeder overstepped the bounds of moderation. That he could do so without censure from Berlin demonstrates that, in the final analysis, Ponape was too far from New Guinea, let alone Europe, for the actions of its executives to be supervised in detail.

For all the provocation, the insurrection had been almost spontaneous in execution, and the main objects of their hatred removed, the passions of the Sokehs people quickly subsided. This spontaneity, along with the feeling that the crimes against the district had been expiated, probably saved the colony. Max Girschner, the local doctor, was the most senior German official remaining, and he set out by boat for Sokehs as soon as the first confused reports reached him. Halfway there, he encountered the two priests who had been allowed finally to depart in a canoe. They advised him that the people were in 'a raging fury' and that there was nothing he could do, so Girschner returned to the colony to organise its defences.[34] No attempt was made by the rebels to shoot the doctor in his boat, though it would have been an easy matter, and would have left the colony at their mercy.

The Europeans were in a critical plight. There were less than fifty of them protected by another fifty police-soldiers, in a settlement with a two-kilometre perimeter and no walls. The rebels numbered at least 250 and it was soon evident that they were well armed. Some ninety rifles and new ammunition appeared from nowhere, as well as an old cannon and a case of dynamite stolen from the roadworks. Furthermore, the other districts on the island were as yet an unknown quantity, and no ship was scheduled to arrive in Ponape for at least six weeks.

The future of the little colony was firmly in the hands of Max Girschner, a man, ironically, whom Hahl had once judged as too 'soft, irresolute and vague' to handle the business of administration.[35] But Girschner had lived on Ponape for ten years and in that time he had earned the respect and affection of the inhabitants by his sympathetic attitude and his attention to their medical care. In the circumstances,

Girschner chose the only course he saw open to him: he gambled that the remaining districts were not party to the revolt and would respond to his call for assistance. Within twenty-four hours, some hundreds of warriors from Madolenihmw and Uh, as well as Net and Awak, allies of Sokehs, were encamped in and around Kolonia. Stone walls were built, barbed wire erected, the ground cleared, and sentries posted; Girschner even distributed 100 rifles to sentry parties. His measures did not meet with the unanimous approval of the remaining Europeans, some of whom warned that the 'loyalists' would take the earliest possible opportunity to make common cause against the whites.

It is difficult to penetrate to the truth of where most Ponapeans stood. There was no general support for the Sokehs in the aftermath of their act, not even from Soun Kawad members; only a few clan members from Kiti and one from Madolenihmw joined the rebels.[36] That traditional friends like Net and Awak hastened to the side of the Europeans was the result of fear: they understood, as indeed did the Sokehs themselves, the consequences of a collision with the Germans; and the influence of the Catholic Mission was also important in keeping the northern districts loyal to the Germans. As for the south, Girschner's call capitalised on the enmity which was now fixed between Sokehs and the southern districts, and, by offering an opportunity to take up arms against Sokehs, Girschner probably localised the revolt to the one district, at least for the time being.

But there were other, less visible signs that the other districts respected Sokehs for the action it had taken in defence of Ponapean virtues. Kiti, for instance, waited three days before sending any warriors to guard the colony, and it is the inscrutable Henry Nanpei who was credited with holding them back.[37] Nanpei is also widely regarded as having clandestinely supported the rebels with food and equipment from his stores throughout the ensuing campaign. Those guarding the colony made no attempt to counter-attack or even challenge the Sokehs. Indeed, the European camp was full of rumours that the 'loyalists' were actually succouring the rebels with food and weapons.

In the days and weeks that followed the uprising, the rebels themselves made no concerted assault on Kolonia, but confined themselves to nocturnal sniping and foraging raids. They even allowed a party of out-islander labourers and their Spanish overseer who were based on the Sokehs roadworks to return to the colony unscathed, and Soumadau made only a half-hearted demand for the surrender of the colony's weapons. These were all indications that the heat of the insurrection had been fanned and maintained by a relative few in Sokehs, and that it was more an explosion of frustration than a wholehearted rejection of foreign hegemony.

But the conviction of their inexorable destiny was too strong to permit the Sokehs to capitulate there and then. In the only attempt made by any of the Germans to talk with the rebels, Girschner on his own initiative sent a letter enjoining them to disarm, and pleading with those who had not participated in the murder to surrender. The reply was gracious but resigned: 'Thank you for your goodness, but we cannot come. We fear that we have committed too great a sin'.[38] Wasai Sokehs wrote explaining why they had been forced to act. Prison or exile they may have tolerated, but they would rather die than let themselves be treated 'like pigs'.[39] The Sokehs proceeded to dig themselves in on the inaccessible twin peaks of the island. They cleared a line of fire, erected fortifications, and waited for the invasion they knew must come.

They had to wait a long time. Not until the end of November, six weeks after Boeder's murder, did the post vessel, *Germania*, touch at Ponape and carry the news to New Guinea. It was a further month before Berlin heard. Meanwhile, Deputy Governor Oswald, who was administering New Guinea in Hahl's absence, sent 172 Melanesian police to relieve the beleagured colony. He also requested of Berlin a fleet of cruisers from the East Asian Squadron, and a new district administrator to take Boeder's place and to direct operations.

Berlin granted these requests immediately. Following the experience of the Spanish, the German authorities had assumed from the beginning that only a large-scale military operation would have any hope of restoring European authority if the Ponapeans were to rise again. They not only expected the most bitter resistance from the Sokehs people, but also concluded that any attempt to appease or accommodate them would simply add fuel to the fire. This campaign was to be more than a punitive expedition: it was an opportunity to pacify Ponape completely, and to establish once and for all Germany's hold over all of Micronesia. It was therefore agreed that the leaders of the Sokehs would be executed when caught, and the entire district banished from the Carolines.[40]

By 10 January 1911 the cruisers *Emden, Nürnberg, Leipzig* and *Cormoran*, together with SMS *Planet* from New Guinea and the armed schooner *Orion*, were all anchored in Ponape's north-western harbour of Langar, with over 300 inexperienced but enthusiastic German marines on board. In the following days no attempt was made to negotiate with the rebels. Instead, the ships proceeded to shell the heights of Sokehs, while Captain Vollerthun of SMS *Emden* worked out the plan of operations with the newly-arrived administrator, Dr Heinrich Kersting.

On 13 January, the marines made a completely unopposed landing on the northern foreshores of Sokehs Island, and prepared themselves for a struggle of several days to drive the Sokehs from the fortified heights. Then, on the same afternoon, Kersting arrived in the front lines and prevailed upon the senior officer to make an immediate attack on the enemy's main position, the Apalberg, arguing that surprise was the best way to overcome the stolid resistance of the Islanders. Before the main contingent of troops had been landed, and with the help of the Melanesian police who had to be prodded upwards step by step, the Apalberg was stormed and taken under heavy fire. The other peak of the island was captured soon after.[41]

The speed with which this initial victory was achieved surprised the Germans, but they were no less convinced about the difficulty of their task. Only two of the Sokehs defenders had been killed in the encounter and none were captured. More urgently, if the rebels managed to reach the mainland, they would be in a position to wage an almost endless jungle war with the German troops.

To forestall this possibility, a land and sea blockade of the little island had been set up at the beginning, consisting of the police troops, half the marines and the ships *Nürnberg* and *Planet*. This was all to no avail, for in the week following the conquest of the peaks, Soumadau and most of his band slipped through the cordon at night. Search parties combed the island for a week, seeking out probable hiding places. They caught thirty men and eighty-four women and children, but none had played a significant role in the revolt.[42]

Meanwhile the administration, under Kersting, proceeded to organise logistical support for the operations. Kersting's first task was to ensure that the unrebellious districts remained firmly in his control and were given no opportunity to consider throwing in their lot with Sokehs. If the stories of their collusion with the rebels while guarding the colony are true, then this was at least a possibility. The conduct of the 'loyalists' during that time had certainly not been without blemish. Several Islanders were guilty of robberies and pillage, and quarrels had broken out between the districts. When the first Melanesian reinforcements arrived and the Ponapeans were sent back to their farmsteads, the European community had heaved a collective sigh of relief.

By mid-January, the remaining districts were properly impressed by the size and earnestness of the German response. Kersting was anxious to drive home the impression that Germany would no longer be trifled with. He therefore warned the district chiefs that their only hope of preventing the war from ravaging their farms and possessions lay in co-operating with the government. They were to supply food for the troops, and guides and interpreters for the operations; they were to report rebel movements and to deliver any rebels they caught to the government.[43] In this way Kersting managed to set up, if by fear, a workable intelligence service on which the manoeuvres of the German troops were based. Near the colony, he also constructed camps where captured Sokehs could be detained, and arranged medical and general welfare services for them through the missions. For the later stages of the campaign, Kersting, largely on his own initiative, formulated a strategy whereby small detachments of troops would be stationed in various parts of Ponape and billeted on the 'loyalists', to search for and constantly harass the enemy. Kersting's experience in African bush wars in Togo had taught him that the only way to success in such wars was to take guerrilla tactics to his opponents.

In the last two weeks of January, the sorties on Sokehs Island were extended to the mainland, and the Germans occupied the sub-district Palikir, which had pledged its support to Sokehs. By 25 January there were 250 Sokehs men, women and children in German hands, among them five men directly involved in Boeder's murder. On 26 January this group of prisoners was transported to Yap. Palikir and its neighbour Tomara were then shelled by the waiting cruisers and the farms razed so as to deny the enemy any secure base for its activities.

Suddenly, on 25 January, the Superior of the Capuchin Mission received information that Soumadau and his remaining followers had entrenched themselves in the interior at Nankiop, where an old Spanish fortress was built on the side of a cliff. Nankiop was the symbolic centre of the Soun Kawad clan: its legendary place of origin. It was also an exceptionally difficult position to attack, with a tower and stone walls from which to fire, a high cliff at its back, and protected by almost sheer drops on three sides. It seemed that the Sokehs were making ready for a final, organised stand.

Next day, two companies of marines and Melanesians were sent to make a frontal assault on the fortress, while the landing corps of SMS *Emden* worked its way round by a secret path to attack the rebels on their most unexpected flank. 'Loyalists' sympathetic to Sokehs were able here to lend their assistance by leading the *Emden* corps along the most difficult and circuitous routes, so that it was three hours late when it arrived at Nankiop. By that time, the main force had suffered heavily from accurate Ponapean fire. At 5 p.m., as darkness was falling, the fortress was finally stormed, but, at the decisive moment, Soumadau and his men retreated up the cliff behind them, leaving three of the German forces dead and eight wounded, and without a single casualty themselves.[44] It was a pyrrhic victory, which worried Kersting and Vollerthun: if Soumadau were to repeat these tactics at every encounter, he could take a heavy toll of German life and remain virtually untouched. They did not yet know that the Nankiop encounter had virtually demoralised the Sokehs, and that their cohesiveness as a fighting force had been destroyed. From now on, the Sokehs were split into small groups which wandered aimlessly about seeking food and shelter, and trying desperately to avoid the German troops.

Kersting's harassment strategy had been put into operation by this time, and detachments of sixty men each were placed in Kiti, Tomara, Palikir and Nankiop. In addition, Kersting had the Ponapeans harvest all crops in the areas of fighting so as to starve the rebels gradually into submission. These procedures hastened the dissolution of the smaller and smaller bands of Sokehs, and, as hunger, sickness and the denial of solace from the other districts took their effect, surrenders became more frequent. By 8 February, another 137 persons, including Wasai Sokehs, had been delivered to the administration, leaving a core of about thirty or forty young and committed supporters of Soumadau.[45]

The group was reduced more and more to a nomadic existence as the German detachments carried out regular patrols. The ease with which the rebels had eluded the combined forces of Germany since the storming of Sokehs was proof that Soumadau possessed the potential to fight a long and effective guerrilla war, but it soon became evident that most of his followers lacked the tenacity and endurance, let alone the commitment, to suffer the constant hardships such a life involved. Some threw themselves upon the mercy of the Germans, which Kersting felt was due to the debilitating effects on 'Ponapean character' of prolonged contact with Western civilisation.[46] But he completely missed the point, for the hearts of the Sokehs were just not in the struggle. From the start they had accepted their lot: to be dispersed and destroyed by the sheer weight of Germany's might. It only remained to hasten the result.

The Germans never expected Soumadau and his close accomplices to surrender, since the rebels knew they could expect no mercy. Consequently, the administration was genuinely surprised when Soumadau and five of the ringleaders succumbed to their fate on 13 February 1911, and gave themselves up to the chief Nos en Net; the rest followed suit within a few days. By 22 February the last of the Sokehs warriors was in German hands.

The denouement was swift. A court-martial was convened on 23 February, the day after military operations were declared at an end. Representatives from the two missions and the trading community joined with Kersting, Girschner and a naval officer to try summarily those accused of the murder of Boeder and his companions. Though each of the leading Sokehs figures was given a full opportunity to defend himself, the tribunal was interested less in the justice of the result, which was already a foregone conclusion as far as the judges were concerned, than in the necessity to make an example which would deter malcontents in the future. The bulk of the evidence revealed that resentment of Boeder's actions had run deep and wide, and there were no regrets that he was dead. It also became clear that there had been a lingering, almost desperate belief that the Germans might be driven out as had been the Spaniards. After all, until Boeder's arrival, none of the districts had really experienced the strong hand of Germany. Deputy Governor Oswald had concluded when he first heard of the uprising:

> In the final analysis they didn't fear us and didn't believe we were earnest in our threats ... We suffered from the mistakes of the Spanish. Perhaps if we had begun energetically this would have been avoided.[47]

But the court-martial tribunal was not interested in why the revolt occurred, only that it had and must therefore be punished. The trial lasted only a day and the court agreed that seventeen Sokehs should be executed, several others sent to prison with hard labour at the Angaur phosphate works, and the remainder of the district banished *en masse* to the Palau group. Ironically, the only call for clemency towards those to be executed came from the navy's representative. Though Kersting himself acknowledged that Sokehs had suffered under Boeder, his concern for 'consistency' of punishment, together with the 'deterrence' arguments of the missionaries and traders easily won the day.[48]

The very next day, 24 February, fifteen of the condemned prisoners, handcuffed together and escorted by Melanesian police, were marched down to Kumunlai, an old cemetery and cult place outside the colony.

Plate XII *Right:* To Bobo (on left) (from the Fellmann Collection, Mitchell Library)

Plate XIII *Below:* A New Ireland war party (from A. B. Meyer and R. Parkinson, *Album von Papua-Typen*, Stengel and Markert, Dresden, 1894)

Plate XIV *Above:* A leader of the Baining massacre, 1904, possibly the adoptive fa[ther] of To Marias (from the United Church Archives, UPNG)

Plate XV *Below:* The execution of one of the leaders of the Baining massacre, 190[ ] (from the United Church Archives, UPNG)

There they were lined up against a makeshift fence strung between coconut trees and tied with their arms outstretched, 'as Christ crucified'.[49] The Melanesian soldiers (for the tribunal had decided that German soldiers should not be subjected to this undignified ritual) ranged themselves in two lines, one standing, one kneeling. Soumadau was refused permission to speak to the expectant crowd, but in a quiet voice he greeted the people and urged them not to follow the Sokehs example. Before he could finish, the first volley of shots rang out; the soldiers kept firing until all were dead. Then the bodies were thrown into a common grave and the crowd, now hushed, was told to return to their districts.

With the ending of the Sokehs uprising, Germany's occupation of Ponape had a little over three years to run. It was a period of remarkable tranquillity on the part of the Ponapeans, considering all that had gone before. The key to their docility lay in the retribution suffered by Sokehs; in that sense German policy had succeeded. Not just the execution (which shocked many Ponapeans), but the size and capacity of Germany's response was a revelation to most people, accustomed to the odd biennial visit of a light German cruiser.

But it was the quantity, rather than the quality, of the amphibious operation that had cowed the Ponapeans. The navy does not deserve the credit claimed by its Public Relations Bureau for the rapid completion of the campaign. Sokehs Island had been stormed by a few officers and the Melanesian police before the main body of German troops had even landed, and the rebels had little difficulty in slipping through the navy's cordon and escaping to the mainland. For over a month, the rebels successfully eluded the troops, who seemed to have a singular capacity for getting lost in the jungle. Such was their awkwardness, and their profligate use of ammunition, that the German navy was the butt of many jokes among 'loyal' Ponapeans during the operations. Kersting was more justified in claiming that the work of the administration, in organising support facilities and mobilising the districts, had put the greatest pressure on Sokehs.[50]

Kersting was in a position to capitalise on the Ponapeans' subdued temper. Heinrich Kersting took his job as administrator of the eastern Carolines very seriously. Indeed he had, perhaps, an exaggerated view of his role in the government of empire, for he foresaw himself as 'Chief of the Island Sphere', commanding a sea-borne administration which would trip from island to island dispensing edicts and advice. Nevertheless, Kersting showed every sign of respecting the sensibilities of the island people, and he combined an authoritative presence with sympathy for the plight of Pacific Islanders under German rule.

He wasted no time in reasserting the priorities set in 1907, in a way which would excite least distrust and resistance. Time was important to Kersting: if the implementation of his predecessors' reforms were allowed to drag on, there was the danger of their objectives being diverted. He therefore discarded the plan to survey all land holdings on Ponape prior to issuing certificates of freehold tenure. Instead 'commissions' of Ponapeans themselves were charged with the task of setting off the limits of each farmstead, erecting boundary markers and making maps of each district. The commissions of seven, several to a district, consisted of section chiefs, title holders and the more important district representatives. Most of their work had been completed by September 1911. It was an original method of evading the conflict which would have inevitably accompanied a European survey of Ponape, a survey which it was estimated could have taken twenty years.[51]

Hand in hand with the reform of land tenure went the regulation of inheritance rights. The Germans did not like the traditional system of matrilineal inheritance, whereby land fairly automatically went to the descendants of the mother's brother after the death of a tenant, or was divided up among several matrilineal descendants. The new land deeds provided that land should go to the oldest male heir of the tenant, and all landless male, as well as female, relatives were expected to farm it for the profit of the entire family. In this way the government hoped to eliminate the multiplication of small, uneconomic, scattered pieces of land. Each family was also required to plant 100 coconuts on its farmstead before the new land deed was issued.[52]

All these measures were intended to give individual Ponapeans a greater stake in their own productivity and the incentive to improve it. To guarantee that, Kersting now turned his attention to the demands which High Chiefs could traditionally make on the time and resources of their commoner tenants. Instead of the customary twenty-two feasts, and the offerings of first fruits and special canoes, which a section was expected to provide each year to the Nahnmwarki and Nahnken, the land deeds stipulated that only one feast, a Feast of Honour, need be given by a section to its Nahnmwarki; all further feasts were nonobligatory. Moreover, a High Chief could call on a commoner to provide only one day's work twice a year. The High Chief was required now to work his own farm, though he was still paid a 'salary' from the proceeds of the annual work periods, which never faltered under

Kersting. Kersting refused to abolish this annuity, arguing that it was an absolute precondition for continuing good relations between government and people.[53]

It was not Kersting's intention to emasculate the High Chieftainship or eradicate its authority completely. On the contrary, he was anxious to preserve the bases of social control and intra-district stability. Kersting emphasised the importance of the Nahnmwarkis by promulgating regulations in 1911 which gave the chiefs power to try and to sentence districts people guilty of a range of offences, from disrespect to the High Ones to stealing and bodily harm.[54] Thus he was implementing the scheme Fritz had projected in 1908: to draw the Nahnmwarkis out of their isolation into the administrative system and delineate their duties exactly. The Nahnmwarki was transformed into a *Kaiserliche Richter* (Imperial Judge), but a petty *Richter*, along the lines of the *pulenu'u* in Samoa.

In emphasising the importance of the Nahnmwarkis, Kersting protected the Ponapean social system to some extent. Islanders were made aware that their new autonomy and economic freedom did not eliminate the duty of submission to customary social sanctions, or to lawful demands from their High Chief. And, indeed, patterns of social behaviour continued much as they had in the past, despite German attempts to alleviate the more demanding aspects. People kept offering first fruits and special gifts to the Nahnmwarkis, while feasting on a grand scale remained an integral part of district relationships and the chiefly prestige competition.

It would be erroneous to regard this division of roles between the Germans and the High Chiefs as a new balance of power in Ponape. The island, its people, their authority structures remained very firmly in German hands after 1910. There was no talk now of an advisory council. Henry Nanpei's designs had been suspect from the beginning. The mass of the Ponapeans was not behind such an innovation and Nanpei probably recognised, as did Hahl and Fritz, that in an open break with the Nahnmwarkis the people would follow them, not Nanpei. Any chance of the council's gaining German approval was in any case lost in the confusion of the revolt and its aftermath.

However, Nanpei did not suffer from the abandonment of his creation, nor from the revolt, though his attitude to that event was ambivalent, to say the least. With the German triumph and Kersting's program, Nanpei finally gained indisputable title to the Ant Islands and his various estates in Kiti. Ponapeans claim that he did even better from the new system, for he persuaded several tenants on his lands to claim only modest portions as their freehold, arguing that the Germans were going to tax people according to the area of their land. Nanpei is then alleged to have claimed for his own whatever private land was left.

The future now lay with Henry Nanpei, whether Germany ruled or not. In the final years before war broke out, he increased his standing with the Germans, sending his sons to be educated in Germany, and visiting the headquarters of the Liebenzeller Mission himself, where he was fêted as 'Defender of the Faith' against the Ultramontanism of the Capuchin Mission. Since the removal of Sokehs, the old power struggle between north and south more and more took the form of a personal confrontation between the Catholic Mission and Henry Nanpei. Nanpei regarded the priests as the one remaining danger to his position. With his advisory council lost and Germany well in control of district relations, Nanpei's access to power as leader of the Protestant faction was considerably more exposed to any renewed campaign to extend Catholic influence. Catholicism he regarded as a particularly subversive political force because of the hold which traditionally it asserted over adherents, especially through the chiefs.

After the exile of the Sokehs district, the Capuchin Fathers did cast about for areas in which they might carry on their mission to spread the Gospel. The rebellion they regarded as the perfect argument against continued confessional demarcation of the island. To them it was obvious proof of their oft-repeated arguments that religion was not the cause of Ponape's major disturbances and therefore they could envisage no objections to peaceful and indiscriminate proselytism after 1910.[55]

Nanpei saw things in a different light, and he opposed vigorously their intensified expansion campaign. His attacks on the mission were carried into the Protestant press during his second visit to Germany in 1912, and in late 1913 he even brought a libel action against the priests. In all this, Nanpei managed to enlist the sympathy of Heinrich Kersting, who regarded the chief as a Ponapean of unusual enterprise and sophistication, and whose own relations with the Catholic mission were growing less and less cordial.

Kersting would not argue the moral rights and wrongs of divided spheres of influence when, from his secular point of view, the stability of the island depended upon maintaining them. Kersting knew that the Protestant chiefs in the south were worried for their continuing influence, especially in the wake of the traumatic social changes now taking place, and he would not risk their fear sparking off a new explosion against the Catholic Mission. As well, Kersting was increasingly impatient with the mission's approach to education, which he saw as narrow and partisan. A grand scheme for the island sphere possessed Kersting, in which he, as Ruler, would give the education of the Islanders into the hands of the Reich and build a new generation of colonial subjects dedicated to material improvement.[56]

The administration's relations with the Capuchins worsened to the point of estrangement as the mission resorted to a series of petulant actions after 1912 in defence of its prestige. The priests became convinced that the government was collaborating in a conspiracy to degrade the mission in the eyes of the Ponapeans, and they ostentatiously disdained to cultivate relations with the rest of the European community. When the new Bishop of the island sphere came to Ponape for the first time in 1913, the mission deliberately refused to issue invitations to Kersting and the other Europeans; even the officers and crew of SMS *Cormoran* were ignored.[57] The reputation of the Fathers had not been enhanced when, in 1912, the Superior of the mission was convicted of a libel action which Georg Fritz had brought against him in 1908, and fined 900 marks. On top of this, Kersting had been forced to investigate charges that one of the priests had committed adultery with a Kiti woman. In Awak there were mounting complaints that the resident priest, Father Fidelis, was encouraging the people to lie to their chiefs. How much these incidents were inspired by the hostility of Protestant chiefs is difficult to assess, but the result was that the moral authority of the mission was considerably weakened in the eyes of Protestants, Catholics and the administrator alike.

Ponape was outwardly 'pacified' in 1914, but was a long way from being a prosperous and loyal corner of the empire. Germany had obeyed the Ponapean dictum *inta puain inta* ('blood buys blood') and had won the right to impose law and order throughout the island. But law and order and communal peace were not one and the same. The Pacific Islanders of Micronesia, and Ponapeans in particular, remained as distant from their rulers in 1914 as they had been in 1900. True, changes had been made and accepted: some 1100 individual land deeds had been registered, confirming tenants in the possession of their farmsteads;[58] roads encircling Sokehs, and around the mainland to Madolenihmw—projects considered not feasible only a few years before—had been constructed; the annual work periods after 1911 had been performed without demur, and the chiefs had agreed that from 1914 on the work periods should be replaced by a cash tax; the

Nahnmwarkis had retained their authority, and were vested with new powers. Indeed Ponapeans of later generations looked on the German period as being the most innovative of their history. But in terms of enduring social harmony and economic development, Ponape was not much further advanced than it had been when Fritz arrived in 1908. No-one was sanguine about the island's future. The only certainty was that Germany was committed, by fear of withdrawal, to staying.

Even that certainty was destroyed by the outbreak of World War I. In May 1914 Kersting left Ponape on leave. On 14 July the East Asian Squadron, under Graf Spee, sailed in without warning and stayed for several weeks, 'reprovisioning'. It was to be Ponape's only contribution to the German war effort. On 6 August, with war declared, the squadron cleared for action and sailed away. Exactly eight weeks later, Ponape, with the rest of the Carolines and Mariana islands, was occupied by the Japanese.

Epilogue

Over 400 men, women and children of Sokehs were sent into exile in 1910, at first to Yap in the western Carolines. There the men were forced to work very hard and bear the harshness of the police whom the German administrator put in charge. Food was insufficient and of poor quality, and conditions only improved after Hahl visited Yap and angrily ordered better treatment. The exiles were later removed to Palau where former warriors had to work in the Angaur phosphate mines while the women and children lived at Aimeliik, on Babelthuap.

When Japan occupied Micronesia, the Sokehs were free to make their way back to Ponape. Now their cup of bitterness was filled to overflowing for they found that the Germans had settled 1200 out-islanders from the Mortlocks, Pingelap and Mokil on their land. These brought specialist skills in fishing, canoe-building and navigation, but they have been regarded ever since as interlopers, especially by those Sokehs now confined to the mainland.[59]

5

The New Guinea Islands
War and Commerce Under Company Rule

It was not until the 1870s that European traders began to exploit on a large scale the rich coconut groves and the concentrated coastal populations of the Bismarck Archipelago for the copra trade, or the abundant marine products such as *bêche de mer* and pearl-shell. German traders were among the first. When Eduard Hernsheim, a Hamburger attempting to set up his own trading empire in the south-west Pacific, anchored in Port Hunter, Duke of York group, in October 1875 to establish an agency, he found that the native inhabitants were well accustomed to the visits of white traders and could understand pidgin English. He also found that Port Hunter had been chosen already as the logical site for a first settlement by the Reverend George Brown, who had arrived in August to begin work for the Australasian Wesleyan Methodist Missionary Society.

European penetration of the islands of New Guinea developed from these foundations. The coasts of the Gazelle Peninsula and New Ireland were the earliest choice of whites seeking profits. New Ireland is a long, and, at points, extremely narrow island to the north-east of New Britain, overlapping the eastern extremes of the Gazelle Peninsula and stretching away to the north-west. The south, with its straight coasts, reefs and poor anchorages did not attract much interest, except for the labour trade, but in the north there were areas of flat or gently undulating land and dense populations where a resident trader could make a living.

The Gazelle Peninsula is a distinct structural land unit at the northern end of New Britain, separated from the rest of the island by a major fault line. There, in an area of 777 square kilometres live the Tolai people, estimated in German times to number some 40 000, effectively isolated from other New Britain groups except for the Baining and Taulil people in the mountains to the west. On the east coast of the Gazelle Peninsula lies Blanche Bay, formed from a giant exploded crater. Around the shoreline of the old crater, hills rise steeply, some as high as 610 metres, except in the north of the innermost bay, Simpson Harbour, where the coastal flat is wider. Here, later, arose the town of Rabaul. Three dormant volcanic cones lie on the outer fringe of Blanche Bay, to the north and east. On the inner rim are three active volcanoes, Rabalan-kaia north of Simpson Harbour, Matupit on the south-eastern arm of Blanche Bay and Vulcan across the bay in the west, this last emerging from the waters in the 1870s and erupting again with devastating effect in 1937. The setting and atmosphere of Blanche Bay is one of tropical grandeur, a composition of towering heights and vivid colouring, from the deep blue of the fine harbours, through the varied greens of the forests to the sandy browns of the mountainsides.

On the steep coasts of this great volcanic lake Europeans tried to gain an early foothold. Barely two years after his arrival, George Brown had established seven mission stations on the Duke of Yorks, eleven on New Britain and five in New Ireland, though most were precarious holds and none was situated away from the coast.[1] In this earliest phase of permanent settlement, the New Guineans dictated the pattern of the relations and the rate of development. Local groups on the coast were particularly jealous of their traditional economic ties with inland tribes. Some coastal 'big men' were able to reinforce their own power within their residential groups and subject inland neighbours through their monopoly over European goods and the introduction of firearms which, as in Samoa, became an integral feature of the early copra trade. European traders were restricted to the lowest type of barter commerce in order to acquire copra. Large quantities were impossible to buy in any one place since the New Guineans generally refused to prepare it themselves, and it was left to the individual agent not only to collect the coconuts but to cut and dry them as well.

In the event of a collision with villagers, there was little redress for the isolated trader. Each came as an individual, with his own economic status and goals, and each was forced to live on local terms, making adjustments for the specific area and circumstances in order to ensure his safety and a livelihood. To live on tribal territory and succeed in collecting plenty of coconuts, these men were dependent on local goodwill and co-operation. Most took New Guinean wives, perhaps several wives, who then worked at drying copra. Traders' resources were few, and the majority were agents for larger firms which provided house, boat, implements and the necessary provisions on credit. In return, the agent collected his coconuts or pearl-shell quota to pay off his usually high debts, hoping to make enough profit to sustain a tolerable existence a little longer.

Such men often were outcasts from their own society, men of

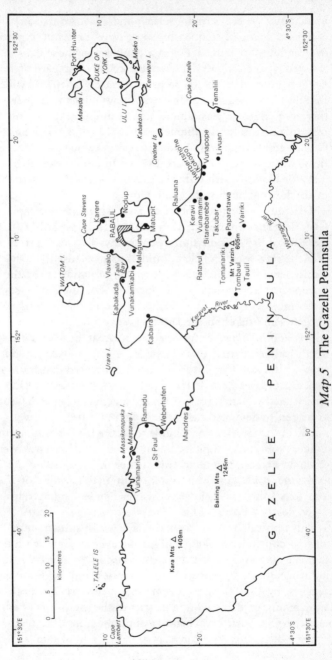

Map 5   The Gazelle Peninsula

uncommon energy and indiscipline. Confrontations with New Guineans occurred frequently. Some were the result of mutual misunderstanding, for language was a problem in those early days. Many resulted from a trader's drunkenness and his disregard of local custom. Traders invariably carried firearms themselves, and they made it clear that they expected trouble from the New Guineans. In a tense situation, therefore, violence was almost a self-fulfilling expectation, both sides resorting to arms at the slightest notice. Ten of the twelve agents in New Guinea employed by the Godeffroys firm came to a violent end during those earliest years of the late 1870s.[2] In terms of security it was every man for himself, with only the dictates of his own conscience and the instructions of his firm to guide him.

The most violent clashes occurred when the newcomers, be they traders or missionaries, tried to move inland. In April 1878, four Fijian teachers of Brown's mission, recently installed inland from Ratavul in Blanche Bay, were murdered and eaten, because the local 'big man', Talili, feared that he would lose his monopoly over the supply of European trade goods to the interior. For the six to seven whites, including George Brown, scattered along the eastern coast of the Gazelle Peninsula and the Duke of York Islands, the event had much wider implications. Talili wielded a great deal of influence in the north-western corner of Blanche Bay, and enjoyed a reputation as a ruthless despot. The Europeans were convinced that his move against the missionaries heralded a general assault against all Europeans. In fear at their isolation they organised an expedition with George Brown as leader, to demonstrate to the Tolai that Europeans were strong and intended to stay. Brown was able to secure the support of those coastal Tolai at Nodup, Matupit, Malagunan and Kabakada who were already, to some extent, bound to the European presence by the ties of the exchange trade, or who were traditional enemies of Talili. They attacked Talili's area, burnt down his hamlets, pillaged his stores and killed nearly a dozen of his followers.[3]

This reprisal, and the formal peace which subsequently Brown was able to conclude, broke Talili's hold over the interior north-west of Blanche Bay and heralded a new phase of expansion and European influence, both by Brown's missionaries and by European entrepreneurs. By 1880 the first two mainland converts had been baptised at Vunamami, or Kinigunan, a district to the south-east of Blanche Bay, and the first Tolai preacher was appointed. In 1881 there were forty praying sites, fifty-five converts and 514 school pupils. By 1886 the number of converts to Methodism in the Gazelle Peninsula and the south of New Ireland had risen to 4000. The local mission was by then divided into three circuits, each supervised by a white missionary and operating a school for prospective New Guinean teachers.[4]

Brown, who had borne the burden of expansion, left in 1881. He had done little himself to set up schools for New Guineans, preferring to plant Methodism widely by travelling and stationing preachers, but he had helped to overcome the particularism of Tolai village centres nonetheless. By the time he departed, the traditional hostilities of many contiguous coastal districts around Blanche Bay were broken and people were mixing freely, at least while under the shadow of the mission's presence.

By 1880 commercial competition had accelerated to the extent that there were now five firms active in the area. The two main trading companies, Hernsheim and the DHPG, successor to Godeffroys, set up a network of agencies along the coast of the Gazelle, from Vlavolo on the north coast, to Vunamami in the south-east. Hernsheim alone set up thirteen between the years 1877 and 1883, as well as nine on New Ireland and several on smaller island groups to the north and east. By 1884 these two firms were reportedly exporting between 1350 and 2000 tonnes of copra from the Archipelago.[5]

They did not have business with the New Guineans all their own way. The rates of exchange for tropical produce rose sharply in these years: where, in 1875, a length of tobacco would secure twenty-five to forty coconuts, by 1880 it was only fifteen, and knives, axes and firearms had replaced red cloth, glasspearls and empty bottles as the most sought after items of trade. Firearms particularly were coveted by ambitious 'big men'; there were said to be 700 in Tolai hands by 1887.[6] New Guineans also demanded amounts of native money (*tambu*) in exchange for their produce, and Europeans were forced more frequently to finance trips to Nakanai on the north coast of New Britain to buy the raw material from which it was made.[7]

The most important economic and social development of this stage of relations between Europeans and New Guineans was the opening up of the Kokopo coast from Cape Raluana to Cape Gazelle, south of Blanche Bay, and the establishment of the first plantation at Ralum by Emma Forsayth and her business partner, Thomas Farrell.[8] The alienation of large amounts of land became a new and ever more crucial point of contention in the eastern Gazelle Peninsula. Land within the boundaries of the local residential group (a series of hamlets called a *gunan* or *pakanagunan*) was controlled by the Senior (*alualua*) of the matrilineage (*vunatarai*) on which residence was based, and any individual member of the descent group had a claim to land not in use. The *alualua* was not only genealogically senior within the group, but was also a man of enterprise and leadership who combined in himself authority over all aspects of indigenous life, with the exception of the principal cults. He could, for instance, delegate the use of uncultivated land belonging to the *vunatarai*. During the 1870s and 1880s, particularly strong *alualua*, who were also 'big men' through their entrepreneurship and warrior skills, 'sold' land in this way to Europeans, in order to acquire firearms for campaigns against other hamlets, or goods to be distributed for the purpose of building up support for their position of influence. The prevailing uncertainty about a 'big man's' power increased the opportunities which a shrewd New Guinean possessed of carrying off such a transaction over the heads of his fellows. It only became clear later that group rights might have been infringed on a large scale.

It is important to distinguish between purchasing the right to use *vunatarai* land and actually owning it. The conception of possession extended only to land that was utilised immediately, and the rights reverted to the descent group once the land went fallow. Nor did the transfer of land to an outsider necessarily remove the original owners' rights to use fruits and trees planted there, or include sections with particular cultic importance to the group. The Tolai were reasonably aware of what they were doing in selling small blocks of land for the immediate use of a mission or trading station, though they may not have understood what a 'sale of land' meant in terms of European law. Their understanding definitely stopped short in the case of enormous areas which were not taken into use for several years. And when European purchasers deliberately obscured the meaning of such contracts, as was the tendency in the early 1880s, then they could expect only great bitterness and determined resistance after the land was finally cleared for plantations and the villagers expected to move.

There is an interesting description of the typical land purchase procedure in Eduard Hernsheim's *Memoirs*. He claims that it was simply a matter of signifying to the nearest native group the land desired and walking around it to gain a rough measure. Then after 'the natives' had marked a European contract paper, suitable trade goods were distributed. Hernsheim concludes with the pointed observation:

That the natives signing the paper were the actual owners of the
land or understood the contents of the contract was naturally
impossible to prove, and only actual occupation could guarantee
possession.[9]

Such a process obviously begged numerous questions about the true
ownership of the land and the right of the vendors to sell, but most of
the early land acquisitions in the Gazelle seem to have been made in this
way. Thomas Farrell claimed to have 'bought' 2050 hectares of land
extending along the coast and inland from Cape Gazelle to Ralum Point
for £50 in trade goods, as well as other areas on the north coast and
inland from Port Weber; Richard Parkinson, the German-English
planter and ethnographer who moved to the Archipelago from Samoa
in the early 1880s after marrying Emma's sister, is supposed to have
purchased the entire districts of Kalili and Vairiki for just £10 in trade.[10]
Farrell and Emma were careful to draw up written agreements and have
them endorsed by the New Guineans; some of their purchases at least
were concluded on board British warships with the captain as witness.

Ralum's trading competitors were not outdone in the rush for land
which occurred between 1882 and 1885. Eduard Hernsheim purchased
1640 hectares in New Britain and the Duke of York Islands, plus a
further 3280 hectares in the north of New Ireland and 780 hectares in
the Hermit group. The DHPG laid claim to nearly 820 hectares in the
Duke of Yorks. One of Farrell's own traders, Octave Mouton, a
survivor of the Marquis de Reys expedition, had purchased 2050
hectares of his own around Vunamami by 1888.[11]

But it was Ralum which led the way in developing commercial
plantations on a large scale. By 1886 Ralum already had 180 hectares
under cotton, coconuts and various experimental plants, with a work
force of hundreds. In the next few years the plantation was to expand
dramatically, gradually taking over land on which no occupational
claim had been made at the time of purchase. That it could do so
without resistance, at least until 1890, was largely the influence of
Emma. As the owner of Ralum, she acted out the local expectations of
a 'big man', giving occasional feasts and dances and providing trade
goods for coconuts, so that a mutually profitable market system
developed.

In November 1884, a German warship, SMS *Elizabeth*, sailed into
Blanche Bay to hoist the imperial flag over New Britain. The process
was repeated on New Ireland, in the Admiralty, Hermit and Anchorite
groups, and at three places on the north-eastern coast of mainland New

Guinea. The area was now under the formal protection of the Reich. The administration and development of the new protectorate was left to the New Guinea Company, a chartered firm under the hand of the powerful Berlin financier Adolf von Hansemann, whose immediate interest lay only in the mainland, or Kaiser Wilhelmsland as it now became. Hansemann and his Board had plotted a golden and profitable future for their tropical foster-child, in which the Company was to act as land broker and adviser to thousands of imaginary German settlers who were expected to flock to New Guinea from the homeland and the Australian colonies.

The Archipelago was expected to play second fiddle while this dream was materialising and for the first few years the only signs of Company activity in the islands were a magistrate who resided first on Matupit, then in Kerawara, then at Kokopo, and a bewildering array of laws to govern every facet of 'civilised' life in the tropics. No attempt was made to impose effective control through an administrative staff, a police force or a communications network; and to all intents and purposes the administration of the Bismarck Archipelago existed in name only well into the 1890s.

There had been a certain measure of informal and arbitrary control at the centre of permanent white settlement around Blanche Bay, where European settlers had been able to take matters into their own hands, at least prior to 1884. Richard Parkinson had mediated in disputes between groups of coastal Tolai and, in some cases, had dictated peace with the aid of his own police force—150 Buka men drawn from Ralum plantation. When New Guineans had attacked a European in the area, punitive expeditions had been mounted swiftly and carried out with severity.

This changed with annexation, as relations between the coastal Tolai and the European planting community entered a phase of mutual accommodation and economic advantage. The Tolai were quick to recognise the need of the plantations for large quantities of native foodstuffs to feed their labour lines. As a result, they began to expand their gardens and produce a surplus to sell to the plantations. There are several striking descriptions of the markets which were held every third day at Ralum, with perhaps 200 women gathering from as far away as twenty kilometres to sell yams, taro and bananas under the watchful eye of their armed menfolk.[12] In 1886 Ralum was supplied in this way with 159 tonnes of taro and yams, and local gardens were being extended regularly as the labour force increased. Even this was insufficient to meet the needs of the plantation, and Emma was forced to send boats along the coast to buy more and more produce. The copra trade was also proving a source of ample profit to the New Guineans, and native copra production rose from zero in 1870 to 1371 tonnes in 1884.[13] By and large this 'production' meant simply collecting the available surplus of coconuts to sell, for since market gardening and coconut collection already provided them with a new and constantly rising standard of living, the Tolai were not interested in increasing the planting of coconuts. They were also unwilling to offer themselves for wage labour on the plantations. In 1890, when 1044 recruits were obtained from New Ireland, only 130 could be enticed from the whole of New Britain.[14]

The same year saw the first major encounter between the coastal Tolai and the plantation owners over land on the Kokopo coast. Ralum now was occupying systematically its land holdings to the west and east, and linking them by roads. But in doing so, it began to encroach seriously on the goodwill Emma had built up among the Tolai. One of the roads from an outstation to Kokopo, the site of the New Guinea Company's holdings, was being built along the foreshore, cutting through local fishing grounds and a men's *tubuan* cult place. The Tolai had given clear warning that they resented this two-fold infringement: trade goods distributed for the purchase of some houses lying on the route had been returned, and the number of women visiting Ralum market from the affected districts had dwindled considerably over a period of weeks.[15]

But the road building went on, under the supervision of John Moses, a Filipino overseer who was arrogant and unpopular with the local people. In March 1890, when the road reached the houses to be demolished, a group of Tolai attacked Moses and clubbed him to death. It was only the beginning. Four major districts along the coast and in the hinterland—Vunamami, Keravi, Bitarebarebe and Tingenav-udu—formed a coalition in late March and attacked Ralum. They were only narrowly beaten off. The Europeans, under Richard Parkinson, replied with two large reprisals, in which five whites and over eighty foreign labourers took part, and they succeeded in driving the Tolai forces into the interior, destroying some sixty hamlets and killing eight warriors.[16] Peace was finally negotiated in April with the exchange of pigs and shell money, but the ringleader, the 'big man', To Ruruk, was not captured and executed until a year later.

Although district fishing rights were safeguarded and various local complaints were corrected in the negotiated agreement of April, 1890 marked the beginning rather than the end of confrontations between the Tolai and the Gazelle Europeans over land. The Tolai were prepared to make peace in 1890 after compensation had been offered, and because they recognised the growth of the New Guinea Company plantation at Kokopo, now called Herbertshöhe, as a new opportunity for marketing produce and copra. However, as a result of the 1890 clash, the Tolai were forced to vacate immediately, in favour of Ralum plantation, all the coastal land between Malapau (a western outstation) and Ralum that already had been set aside in pre-annexation contracts of sale but not yet occupied. By the middle of 1893 Emma had increased her cultivated area to 240 hectares of cotton and 350 hectares of coconuts. The New Guinea Company possessed about 165 hectares of cotton and coconuts east of Ralum and was now occupying land in the districts of Malagunan and Tingenavudu.[17] Octave Mouton had also begun planting on his estate in Vunamami district.

The Tolai were further alienated by the behaviour of imported labourers who harassed local women and stole market produce, and there was general resentment of the German station manager at Herbertshöhe after he closed down for a time the native market at Kokopo plantation, depriving neighbouring Tolai of their regular trading incomes.

In early July 1893 tension reached a new peak, and the first reports of clashes between villages and Company police began to come in. It was at this moment that an enterprising young sorcerer further inland, Tavalai of Ulagunan, claimed to have discovered an ointment which could repel bullets and actually turn them against the person shooting.[18] 'Big men' from the affected areas hastened to Ulagunan to pay the 1000 fathoms of shell money which Tavalai demanded for his ointment, and by mid-July a conspiracy to attack Herbertshöhe and subjugate the whites had been fashioned. There were several reasons why inter-district co-operation should succeed at this point. Firstly, Tolai settlements were already susceptible to occasional alliances through inter-marriage, trading arrangements, and ritual links in the *tubuan* and *ingiet* cults. Secondly, in 1893 there were also widespread feelings of uncertainty as European plantations took over land which they claimed to have purchased years before. Finally, the attack on Ralum in 1890 had shown the Tolai that resistance was feasible only when they possessed something to fuse the different groups together: in this case the ointment proved to be a perfect integrating mechanism.

Plate XVI *Right:* Pominis of Papitalai
(from *Hiltruper Monatshefte*, 1933)

Plate XVII *Below:* Men from Pak
Island, Admiralties Group (from
H. Nevermann, *Admiralitäts Inseln*,
1934)

Plate XVIII *Left:* A Wampar man during German times (from R. Neuhass, *Deutsch Neu Guinea*, 1911)

Plate XIX *Below:* Men from Siar, near Madang, in the 1890s (from A. B. Meyer and R. Parkinson, *Album von Papua-Typen*, Stengel and Markert, Dresden, 1894)

In September 1893 some 300 warriors from the districts of Mala-gunan, Tingenavudu, Ulagunan, Bitarebarebe, Biretava and Vairiki attacked Herbertshohe. The Germans barely managed to repel them. Punitive raids were repeatedly mounted on the districts, and inflicted heavy casualties (over forty Tolai were killed), but the warriors refused to be subdued. Smeared with the magic ointment and singing a ritual chant, they flung themselves at the plantation, rooting out cotton bushes as they went and offering fierce resistance to the troop columns of New Irelanders under European control.

In October the New Guinea Company's Governor, Georg Schmiele, arrived from Kaiser Wilhelmsland to try to negotiate a settlement with the Tolai, since the disruption of the native food markets was having serious consequences on the Company's labour force at Herbertshohe. Meetings were arranged with the 'big men' of the leading districts, and Schmiele demanded nominal amounts of *tambu* as a traditional surety, but at the last moment the Tolai feared betrayal and the negotiations broke down. Skirmishes continued on into November amid rumours that the entire coastal area south of Blanche Bay was awaiting the final defeat of the white men. The hitherto peaceful villagers between Herbertshohe and Ralum began to stir, and the Europeans' last line of defence, the imported labourers on the plantations, were more and more disconcerted at the fanaticism of the enemy.

On 29 November the small German cruiser, SMS *Sperber*, arrived off Herbertshohe, and Schmiele made a last attempt to bring about a negotiated settlement. It failed: only Bitarebarebe district, well inland from Herbertshohe and comparatively unaffected by European expansion in 1893, was willing to consider peace. The other districts kept up their resistance into mid-December, when a combined expedi-tion of German marines, European settlers and New Ireland labourers was launched on them. Only then, after the Europeans and their allies had penetrated beyond known settlements, shooting and burning as they went, did the Tolai cease hostilities and declare their submission.

Naturally enough, the New Guinea Company and most of the settlers attributed the ending of the war to the *Sperber* expedition and to the bombardment of coastal villages which the ship had carried out at the same time as the land attack. From the Tolai standpoint, European pressure was less decisive. Sources close to the Tolai suggest that they, and not the Europeans, decided that it was no longer practical to continue the uprising. In his memoirs Octave Mouton describes the final, combined expedition in some detail, and in quaint but telling prose recounts a decisive moment in the hunt for the massed Tolai forces.

> Later we arrived at a village on a hill there the natives came from all directions uphill to attack us with the exception of one side which showed level ground the rest could not be approached by climbing to reach us, the native police were uncontrolable and I and the officer and the other whites told them not to use our ammunition wastefully, the natives came from all directions, at last through the level side we saw a fellow painted red and white and carrying no arms all he had in each hand a bunch of croton like a bunch of flowers, he did not last long as soon seen he was shot, from that moment we could have heard a pin drop after a while, no sooner the wizard dropped all we could hear was the rush of natives through the bush, I cut off one of his ears to show the natives of Kinigunan, so that the fact that they really believed the wizard and evidently he believed it himself because he was unarmed and like a priest leading his followers . . .[19]

Tavalai had become a victim of his own delusions.

The Tolai themselves report an additional reason for their change of heart: an *alualua* called To Bobo, from Vunabalbal, managed to obtain some magic ointment and took it to the Germans who smeared their forces with it before going into battle. Not only did it strengthen the resolve of the Melanesian troops, but in the eyes of the enemy it also made them invulnerable; thus the Tolai sued for peace.[20]

Without doubt, Tavalai's death and the use of his ointment against them were greater shocks to the Tolai than the whistle of a few artillery shells. In the calmer light that prevailed after the war there were Germans who saw this. The *Sperber* expedition quickly became notorious as an example of how not to hunt New Guineans. From the beginning it was a fiasco: the New Guinea Company manager, Paul Kolbe, led a party which got lost in the bush on the way in, then proceeded to fire on a detachment from the *Sperber* on the way out; while the Tolai managed to evade a decisive battle altogether. In addition to all this, the captain of the *Sperber* was openly cynical about the success of his bombardment since all the target villages were behind a hill; the only casualty seems to have been a man who dislocated his neck in shock at the whistling shells![21] If Europeans had any dominating effect on the ending of the 1893 war it was because, as Schmiele recognised, the Tolai were becoming economically dependent on the whites and this was a powerful motive for them to accept peace rather than total victory.

The war of the bullet-proof ointment was an important departure in
the history of the Gazelle Peninsula. For the Germans it inaugurated
a new phase of expansion in the European economy. By 1897 European
plantations in the eastern Gazelle had grown to 1295 hectares of
planted land, and the Big Three companies were exporting 2325 tonnes
of copra. Ralum alone was said to 'own' almost the entire districts of
Kabaga, Ravalien, Ulagunan, Tingenavudu, Bitarebarebe, Malagunan
and parts of Kabakaul and Vunamami.[22]

As for the Tolai, they had shown themselves a force to be reckoned
with. They had not won the war, but neither had they been defeated
totally. With the bullet-proof ointment, a feature similar to the Maji
Maji of East Africa a decade later, the Tolai had for a time successfully
opposed European self-confidence and superior technology with an
unconquerable morale.

In addition, the co-operation which the districts had achieved in war
did not disintegrate entirely with peace. Because of the gradual economic and political consolidation imposed on the Gazelle through
missionary activity, and through the spread of trading and planting, the
confederation of districts behind Herbertshöhe tended to survive under
strong leadership. Some Tolai already had accepted that the whites
could not be driven out, and that they must find some compromise
solution to the problem of coexistence. One of these was To Bobo, the
alualua who had helped to bring the war to an end by procuring
ointment for the Germans. In 1894 he became head of the Vunabalbal
clan after the death of his elder brother, who had unified the area against
Herbertshöhe. As a Methodist preacher and 'big man' in his own right,
To Bobo came more and more into prominence as virtual leader of the
old confederacy based on his district Vunamami. He was a man who
recognised the need for peaceful adjustment to the expanding European
economy.[23]

Few Europeans showed much understanding of the problems which
faced leaders like To Bobo, or of the resentment which the Tolai
harboured against the growth of European settlement. In the aftermath
of the war, even the normally responsive Emma of Ralum declared that
the only way to guarantee peace in the Gazelle was to give the Tolai 'a
sound thrashing and drive them away from our lands'. Georg Schmiele,
the Company Governor, was one of the few who tried to understand.
A man who alienated almost every white settler in New Guinea by his
stiff and priggish manners, Schmiele nonetheless was peculiarly sensitive to the changes being forced upon the Tolai by the pressure of white

development. As early as 1891 he had recommended that several 'trusted agents' be appointed to act as intermediaries between the racial communities. No action was taken. Now he recommended them again, and foreshadowed the establishment of reserves to protect the Tolai from the complete loss of their land. This time the Company accepted his ideas, but too late to enable Schmiele to implement them himself: on his way back to Germany in 1895, Schmiele died of fever in the East Indies. His ideas remained shelved until the arrival in January 1896 of Imperial Judge, Albert Hahl.

Hahl was a man of mixed qualities. He possessed a humane spirit, with a genuine interest in the varied cultures of Germany's Pacific empire, and his open, at times egalitarian personality marked him off from his Prussian compatriots. But he combined these qualities with a detached, even a callous sense of the brutalities of colonisation, which allowed him to regard conquest as a legitimate instrument of civilisation.

When Hahl arrived in New Guinea, there existed to all intents and purposes no systematic administration, for the New Guinea Company was engaged in negotiations to transfer permanent political control of the colony to the Reich and considered itself obliged only to a holding operation in New Guinea. Hahl, in whose hands the 'administration' now lay, immediately began moving among the Tolai in an effort to understand their language and customs, and to win them for the ideal of German colonialism. He had already set about defining the goals of the regime. The protectorate's future lay in its contribution to the economy and prestige of the Reich. In Hahl's vision, economic development depended, first, on strengthening the purchasing power of New Guineans in an ordered administration, and, in the long term, on educating them in the service of European capital.[24] These were predictably eurocentric objectives, though they were balanced by a wish to protect New Guineans in the process, a wish which increasingly conflicted with the aims of trading and planting firms in New Guinea.

Albert Hahl early established a tradition of direct, personal and dynamic administration by constant travelling, by initiating contacts with outlying communities, by leading expeditions and police tours and by helping to resolve parochial disputes. Within three months of his arrival, Hahl could converse with the Tolai on the Gazelle Peninsula, and this stood him in good stead, for he was quickly besieged by Tolai leaders anxious to arrest the further encroachment of plantations on village land.

Hahl was aware that many indigenous groups had not grasped the implications of land purchase contracts and that certainly they had not anticipated European settlement and plantation agriculture on the scale it had reached. To Bobo, in particular, was able to persuade Hahl that Vunamami hamlets should be allowed to hold on to their extensive coconut stands as well as subsistence land. The Governor then agreed to negotiate with the owners of Ralum for the establishment of a reserve for Vunamami villagers who were currently occupying Ralum ground, despite the plantation's legal claim to the area. Hahl also set out to dissuade Emma from carrying out a plan to resettle the inhabitants of nine further hamlets on non-Ralum land in the interior in order to take up already-purchased land for new plantings. Such a move would disrupt the traditional basis of the local economy and remove a vital source of food supplies for the plantations. An even more immediate danger, which Hahl recognised, was the likelihood of a new wave of resistance in the area south of Blanche Bay as the populations of the interior came under unwarranted pressure from bitterly anti-white refugees migrating inland from the coast.[25]

This danger did not disappear until well into the 1900s but, as a result of Hahl's early efforts, which were successful though not without struggle, some reserves were excised from land already purchased by Europeans. Vunamami, for instance, was left with 147 hectares out of its original territory of 287 hectares, an area not inequitable in terms of 1896 land use.[26] The reserves were not gained without conditions: Hahl decreed that they should revert to their European 'owners' after fifty years if the New Guineans had not planted coconuts or populated the area more densely in that time. To Bobo's method of meeting these conditions was to lower bride prices by fiat in order to encourage marriage and increase the population, thus reinforcing Vunamami claims to the land; he also led the way in planting coconuts regularly and processing them into copra.

To Bobo prospered under the eye of his new patron, the Government. And among his own people he continued to grow in stature, for his innovations convinced his followers that he was acting for the common welfare, not just his own ambition. Through his leadership he helped the Vunamami confederacy come to terms with the growing colonial apparatus, and ensured that it could contribute to the shaping of its future.

But Vunamami was far from the only beneficiary. The Tolai of the eastern Gazelle prospered as a people for the rest of the German period.

Up to and beyond 1914 they enjoyed a steadily rising per capita income. They supplied eighty per cent of all native-produced copra in the Bismarck Archipelago, and about fifteen per cent of New Guinea's total copra exports.[27] At the same time they strove to remain as independent of the European wage economy as possible, refusing to enlist for wage labour on plantations where, in most cases, they were regarded merely as chattels and not as voluntary employees. A few did enter service for the government or the police force, for here, under Hahl at least, the relationship was more reciprocal and they could retain a sense of economic and social partnership.

Land problems around Blanche Bay and on the north coast of the Gazelle were only one facet of Hahl's concern to provide the security necessary for trade and plantation agriculture to flourish. A second requirement was control of existing native trade routes from the interior, and the construction of new roads at strategic points. The Tolai possessed a very extensive system of markets running inland from Blanche Bay, but the mutual suspicions and hostilities of local settlements made the system vulnerable to sudden disruption. Capitalising on the Tolai's attraction to better market access and economic gain, and with the aid of shell money, iron and Methodist Mission influence, Hahl induced local villagers in 1896 to build a road from Herbertshöhe to Raluana. This road enabled him to secure the trading links which ran from the hinterland to the Kokopo coast.[28] A network of roads was also the first stage in any future taxation project.

By the end of Company rule in 1899, additional roads or riding paths had been constructed around the rim of Blanche Bay to Simpsonhafen (the later site of Rabaul), from Simpsonhafen to Nodup on the north-east coast, and from Herbertshöhe south-west to Vunakokor, sixteen kilometres from the sea in the Varzin mountains. Hahl did not find the same ease in getting the Tolai to maintain the roads: that required constant supervision; and by 1898-99 he was using New Guinean prisoners to complete much of the work.

The final element in Hahl's security program was the appointment of Schmiele's 'trusted agents'. Control by reprisal had always been an inadequate policy, even if at times it was the only way for the meagre government apparatus to exercise its authority. In August 1896, in areas of the Gazelle Peninsula and the Duke of York Islands where the Methodist Mission in particular wielded a decisive influence for peace, Hahl nominated the first individual New Guineans to convey his wishes to groups of hamlets; among them was To Bobo. The new officials, whom the Germans called originally *lualuas* but later *luluais* after the Tolai name for a district war leader, were given limited administrative and police powers to supervise road construction in their localities and to adjudicate small, local disputes. Fines of up to twenty-five marks or ten fathoms of *tambu* could be imposed, but villagers had the right to appeal against decisions to the Imperial Judge at Herbertshöhe.

The system of *luluais* was designed basically to encourage the peaceful solution of difficulties, and to act as a lever through which the government could 'draw' New Guineans to work within the colonial economy as road builders, plantation labourers and, later, taxpayers. To delegate a more autonomous 'chiefly' power to these agents was impossible, for the social and political authority of the traditional *alualua*, on which the appointments were based, was generally well circumscribed, and the Germans soon found themselves dealing with numerous complaints against *luluais* for exceeding their authority. Moreover, as the system expanded and single villages were given government *luluais*, the new appointees were not always the natural clan elders or 'big men' of their districts, so that some experienced difficulty in exerting their newly-ascribed authority. By 1900 Hahl had appointed forty-four of the new officials in the Gazelle and twenty-three on the Duke of York Islands, the only areas which his administration could reach effectively.[29]

But if racial relations in the Gazelle Peninsula were improving in the years after 1893, it was not simply the work of the German government. Missionaries had been spreading the Good News during the 1880s and 1890s, and they share credit, at least indirectly, for an increase in stability.

When the war of the bullet-proof ointment began, the Methodists were permanently entrenched throughout the northern Gazelle, in the Duke of York Islands and on southern New Ireland. Three white missionaries and forty-odd Pacific Island assistants, including the first New Guineans, were ministering to over 5000 followers. By 1899 and the end of Company rule, the number of New Guineans regarded as being supporters of the Methodist Mission had risen to 10 419. The mission occupied ninety-five outstations (over fifty in the Gazelle Peninsula), run by twenty-nine Polynesian and sixty-six New Guinean assistants. In addition there existed a major seminary for the training of local teachers on Ulu Island in the Duke of York group, which was giving an elementary education and promoting economic and political co-operation among the Tolai village groups.[30] At the level of the hamlet, the Methodist Mission probably exercised greater influence in the 1880s than did the other mission society, the *Herz Jesu Mission* (Mission of the Sacred Heart or MSC).

The first Sacred Heart priests arrived in Matupit in September 1882 to re-establish the Vicariate of Melanesia, which had been virtually abandoned since 1855. Three priests and two brothers made up the original party, and they settled first in Nodup, on the north-east coast. Within a few years, the headquarters of the mission was transferred to an area of land east of Herbertshöhe on the Kokopo coast, to which the name Vunapope ('seat of the Popies') was given. By 1891 the Mission of the Sacred Heart had its own Bishop of New Britain, Ludwig Couppé, a Frenchman of indomitable spirit and tireless energy, plus a complement of five priests, six lay brothers and five nuns.[31]

The same year, the Colonial Department, under pressure from the Imperial Commissioner residing in Kaiser Wilhelmsland, Fritz Rose, officially separated the areas in which the two missions could evangelise: the Methodists were allocated the area to the north and west of Raluana point, the MSC the area to the east and south. Within a very few years both parties, as well as the Berlin authorities, acknowledged that the demarcation was an absurdity. In its sector, the Sacred Heart Mission found only a small and scattered population, so continued to operate in areas destined for the Wesleyans; by 1897 Couppé claimed 3700 baptised adherents in the Methodist districts of Malagunan and Vlavolo alone. At Vlavolo rival churches stood only 400 metres apart, and the Catholics freely admitted they had at least thirteen churches in Methodist areas.[32] The official division into spheres of influence was finally removed in April 1899.

The Catholic Mission was not free in the early days from clashes with the Tolai over land, especially on the north coast at Vunakamkabi near Vlavolo. Nevertheless, Catholic missionaries, like the Methodists before them, soon gained acceptance as men set apart from those seeking cash profits in New Guinea. Because of its efforts to mitigate the effects of the 1893 war on villagers behind Herbertshöhe, the Sacred Heart Mission was soon allowed by the Tolai to expand inland from Vunapope, and the first inland station was set up at Takabur in the district of Tingenavudu. Similar intervention on the north coast, where the mission obtained a pardon from death for the 'big man' organising resistance against them, paved the way for the conversion of the entire district; Couppé also was not far behind Schmiele in actively campaigning to reserve land for the Tolai in areas they had already sold.

In taking upon itself the functions of protector and advocate, the Catholic Mission won the trust of many Tolai. At the end of 1897 it could point to eight stations on the north and east coasts and hinterlands of the Gazelle Peninsula. With a staff now of forty Europeans, over 4000 baptised New Guineans, and two trained catechists, the Catholic Church in German New Guinea was becoming a formidable power.[33]

Because of its resources and strongly centralised character, the Catholic Mission was able to exert as much, if not more physical control in its areas of influence than the German administration during the 1890s. The first road on the Gazelle Peninsula was actually built by Couppé, from Vunapope to Takabur in 1896, while the following year the mission armed its own labourers with private firearms to defend the Vunakamkabi plantation. Couppé was also the spirit behind Hahl's raids in the late 1890s on the north coast settlements of Massawa, Massikonapuka and Ramandu. These raids were designed to break the indigenous slave trade which centred on the technologically backward and largely defenceless Baining people. Many of the freed victims were delivered to the Catholic Mission for rehabilitation, while land was confiscated from the slave traders and they were driven out of the region. Couppé's plan of conversion was to collect these former slaves, as well as orphans and the illegitimate offspring of white settlers, feed and clothe them, and then educate them in Catholic orphanages. Later they would be settled in self-supporting peasant communities in the interior, and through inter-marriage and instruction, provide the core of a new Christian people in New Guinea.

That the mission, rather than the administration, could take the initiative in developing relations with New Guineans was in large part due to the impotence of officials like Hahl. Throughout the 1890s, the New Guinea Company refused to accept full responsibility for the internal security of the New Guinea protectorate, arguing that it was the job of the Reich to protect settlers from New Guineans and the navy to carry out police actions and impose European control when and where the Company desired. In the Bismarck Archipelago the Company did provide a police force of thirty-six Solomon Islanders, but, equipped with antiquated Mauser rifles and forced to work most of their days in the Company plantation, the Company police force was no more than an empty gesture towards the problem of security. The gesture was even emptier when the Company refused to supply its own administrators, or those of the Reich, with a boat large and fast enough to transport the police quickly to areas of unrest.[34]

Europeans rash enough to live away from the centre of white settlement in the eastern Gazelle had to fend for themselves. At the fringes of contact beyond the Kokopo coast, the New Guineans remained totally in control until the end of the century. Despite his road into the Varzin Mountains, Hahl could not entrench German influence there because of the power and hostility of the 'big man', To Vagira, who was in the habit of spearing anyone found trying to acquire European goods. On the north coast, the Kabaira people resisted successfully all attempts to punish them for attacks on whites, even a major naval expedition as early as 1886. In fact this incident was a good example of the limitations of naval intervention in German New Guinea. Five hundred men were landed from three warships in June 1886 in order to capture hostages in retaliation for repeated acts against Europeans. Over several days they searched the district back and forth, only once contacting the inhabitants at close quarters and failing to capture anyone. In the following years fourteen Europeans were killed in Kabaira, and as late as 1899 the people were still resisting European encroachments on their land.[35] The slave traders of the north also continued their predatory raids on the Baining people despite Hahl's efforts, and unrest continued there into the early years of the new century.

Nowhere were the limitations of the government more clearly visible than in New Ireland before 1900. Hostility between coastal groups and Europeans had existed since the early 1880s over the labour trade. Besides forcible removals, occasional shootings and the indifference of some recruiters about returning ex-labourers to their proper destinations, trade was carried on in arms and ammunition. This only aggravated the conflicts.

The New Irelanders took their revenge by attacking resident traders. Three Europeans were killed in various parts of the island in the last three months of 1885, another two were driven from their trading posts, while all of Farrell's stations on the north coast were plundered and burned. In September 1886 Hernsheim's agent, Hermann, was murdered by the Kapsu people because his predecessor had burned their huts in a drunken rage; Hermann's successor, Hoppe, shared the same fate in December 1888. In the area around Tubtub, another three traders had been dispatched by March 1890.[36] Part of the trouble was the non-return of labour recruits, who had either died on the plantations of Samoa or extended their contracts; partly it was the desire of New Irelanders for firearms and ammunition with which to vanquish traditional tribal enemies; while several incidents can be traced directly to excesses and acts of violence by traders.

During the 1890s the deteriorating state of relations drove many traders out of New Ireland. By the end of 1891 only four were left on the north coast. With the New Guinea Company abdicating its responsibility for their security, these men were forced to rely on the infrequent visits of German warships or take the law into their own hands. When they did organise their own expeditions, the New Guinea Company promptly fined them for unauthorised use of force; if they waited on the navy, it invariably proved to be as inadequate a deterrent to New Irelanders as it had been to the Tolai. Before Hahl's arrival, only one naval reprisal was in any way effective. In other reprisals, either detachments became lost, or never managed to find the right village, or the villagers fled into mangrove swamps where the sailors could not follow them.

Despite the continual pressure of the New Ireland traders for a hardline attitude, and the arguments of imperial officers for a small police force to be stationed permanently in the north, nothing was done in these directions by the Company or the Reich. Hahl's arrival hardly helped either, in spite of his energy and good will. Without finance, sufficient personnel, or a proper police corps, Hahl could carry law and order only as far as his whale boat would take him. In 1899 the situation away from the east coast of the Gazelle Peninsula was the same as it had been two decades before: it fell to individuals to ensure their own safety, a task which many undertook with more belligerence than diplomacy.

6

The Reich and Race Relations in the New Guinea Islands

In 1899-1900, the Bismarck Archipelago sector of German New Guinea was still very much a trading colony, with more than half the export copra coming from trade with the New Guineans. Plantation agriculture was, however, expanding at a rate which would transform New Guinea into a genuine plantation colony by 1914. When the imperial government assumed full administrative responsibility for the protectorate in 1899, European plantations covered a planted area of 2582 hectares; Ralum alone had grown to 1010 hectares. The New Guinea Company had earned 80 000 marks from cotton in 1898, and in the same year exported its first ten tonnes of plantation-grown copra.[1] A population of 200 Europeans now lived in the Bismarck Archipelago, scattered from the Solomon Islands to the Admiralty group.

Albert Hahl was called back from Ponape in 1901 to take over as Governor of German New Guinea after the first Imperial Governor, Rudolf von Bennigsen, had resigned. Von Bennigsen was an old-style Prussian army officer, whose scarred face betrayed the number of duels fought in his youth. His formula for control of the protectorate was brutally direct and simple: expansion by pacification; and his short tenure of office is notable for several bloody campaigns against recalcitrant New Guineans. A man whose sense of honour was absolute and unyielding, von Bennigsen is said to have resigned in a fit of pique, after Bishop Couppé persuaded Berlin to reverse a decision by the Governor not to sell land to the Catholics in the Duke of Yorks group, a Methodist preserve.[2]

Hahl's approach to the job was more methodical and less openly violent. Though he too was convinced of the need to 'pacify' and 'control' the population in order to attract investment to the colony and encourage expansion, his program was not designed to cow the inhabitants, nor simply to keep the peace and let development take its own course. By opening up the land and incorporating the people into an ordered administration, Hahl hoped to mobilise them for the developing economy, either as labour for the plantations or copra processors for the traders.

His plan was not as well articulated as Solf's in Samoa, nor was it founded on a particular moral image of the New Guineans as a whole. Violence he regarded as an inevitable component of colonialism, a political problem not subject to clear-cut moral judgments or judicial decisions. Hahl considered that, in the long run, violence would only be eliminated by the growth of a sound administration, and by education. Thus Hahl preferred to treat individual acts of violence by New Guineans as acts of war, not as criminal offences, and his chief concern was to restore public peace and order in the quickest, most effective way.[3] If this sometimes involved punitive expeditions or police hunts, with the threat of reciprocal violence, then so be it.

In 1901, after the virtual bankruptcy of Company rule, Hahl had to start from scratch. His problems were compounded by the continuing shortage of finance and personnel, and by the conditions of the country itself: the multitude of cultural groups, of languages, and the physical obstacles—reefs, swamps, rain forests and mountain ranges. These forced Hahl to concentrate his scant resources in the most advanced area, the Bismarck Archipelago, leaving the large plantation concerns under the New Guinea Company to carry out the opening-up process on the mainland. Outside the areas of white settlement and established sources of labour, Hahl intervened only when unrest was of a widespread nature, and then only with a reprisal. Where direct rule was out of the question for some time, he accepted as unavoidable the death of individual white people if they fell foul of local tribes.

Such a policy meant that the Germans' administrative effort in the Archipelago for the first five years was centred on the Gazelle Peninsula, northern New Ireland, and regional stations in southern New Ireland and Bougainville, these latter acting largely as labour depots. Direct rule, based on Hahl's original appointment of *lualuas* or *luluais*, was extended to all these areas, with a district officer keeping the area under surveillance and mobilising the inhabitants for government tasks. To give weight to his authority, and to impose control by conquest where tribes were at war, the district officer was provided with a complement of about fifty New Guinean police, drawn predominantly from the Solomon Islands area.

Administrative innovations after 1900 included organised public works and a poll tax. The former was an integral element of the direct control idea: in particular, the construction of roads was intended to inprove access to villagers so that they could be taxed. In November 1903, a Government Instruction (*Anweisung*) authorised officials to co-opt all able-bodied men in the areas of control for up to four weeks a year to assist in the construction and maintenance of roads, or to work on government plantations.[4] By 1914, using this ordinance, the Germans had built a network of roads in the vicinity of all their main settlements, though outside the Gazelle Peninsula none of the roads stretched very far into the interior. In the Gazelle there were 209 kilometres of road between the Warangoi River and the Baining Mountains by 1911: a series running north and west of the Kokopo coast linked most of the inland districts and reached beyond the Varzin to Taulil, while a proper shoreline road was constructed between Herbertshöhe and Rabaul. There was also a road from Rabaul over the Ratavul pass to Talili Bay on the north coast, and from Weberhafen to Massawa on the north-west coast, and into the Bainings.

Not all these roads, whether in the Gazelle Peninsula or outside, were constructed with willing co-operation. More-or-less stern resistance occurred in areas where villagers saw no immediate advantage accruing (for example, in Bougainville), or where it was part of a wider and deeper protest against white presence flowing from the loss of land resources (as was to be the case at Madang, on the mainland). The coastal Tolai helped build the first roads willingly enough, because they were paid for it, and because roads gave them better access to markets. After 1900, however, their attitude changed, particularly under the corvée regulations, when it became clear that they were being used to extend the road network mainly for the regime's purposes. Their growing distaste for roadwork made the Tolai particularly amenable to Hahl's second new measure, the head tax levy.

When Hahl introduced the head tax to New Guinea in 1906, it was designed to act as an alternative to forced road maintenance and to push more villagers onto European plantations. For this reason Hahl delayed its introduction in the Gazelle Peninsula at least six months, so that he could exploit free Tolai labour in order to finish his road-building program. Such was the Tolai dislike for the roadworks that Hahl knew they would gladly grasp any opportunity that delivered them from it. With their comparatively large cash reserves from trading, the Tolai would have no trouble paying a tax the moment it was imposed, leaving Hahl with insufficient labour to carry out his projects.[5] His fears were well-founded. When the tax was finally introduced into the Gazelle in 1907, the Tolai offered no resistance; even when in 1910 it was doubled in many areas from five marks a year for every adult male to ten marks, people continued to pay it willingly in preference to working on the roads.

Between 1900 and 1914 Tolai demand for consumer goods rose swiftly, and their material prosperity continued to grow. A district like Vunamami saw its per capita income treble during the period, despite rapid population growth. European-style businesses began to proliferate as Tolai took up carpentry, or purchased European boats, carts and horses to use as commercial transportation. Copra production rose steadily all this time, especially after the plantings on reserves like Vunamami began to bear; by 1909 some 'big men' were receiving up to 300 marks a month from the sale of copra. Up to 1914, four-fifths of the native copra produced in the Archipelago continued to come from the Tolai people, and they were responsible for perhaps one-third of all consumer imports into that area. By 1913 the value of clothes and textiles purchased by them amounted to 240 000 marks, and they seemed to have little difficulty in paying for the European cigarettes, tinned goods, clothes, even houses, which had become status symbols; several influential men were reported to have saved up to 10 000 marks in silver, one-mark coins.[6]

Progress and prosperity were accompanied by a selective resistance to the European economy. The Tolai still refused to accept wage labour on a large scale unless it involved an elite position like domestic servant or policeman, where a sense of partnership existed. Only those on the inland fringe of Tolai settlement offered themselves as contract labourers, in order to share in the economic opportunities which were lacking on the frontier. By 1910 a mere ten per cent (or 1095) of the able-bodied Tolai population were indentured as labourers or soldiers, and the vast majority of these were employed close to home in the Gazelle itself.[7] The head tax failed to alter this pattern of economic behaviour, for up to 1914, at least, the coastal Tolai were prosperous enough to meet all the levies from their manifold enterprises.

Disputes over land continued to occur as European plantations expanded their plantings. At the end of 1902, Europeans claimed 53 480 hectares of land in the Gazelle, only 5330 of which were planted with coconuts, coffee, cotton and kapok.[8] Though a dozen land reserves for Tolai had been set up by 1902, eight of them around Blanche Bay, the basis of their existence was precarious. Hahl had to fight plantation owners for every metre and every tree in seeking native enclaves in areas where wholesale land alienation had occurred in Company days. Even when he was successful, the reserves possessed no legal basis, being subject to the continuing goodwill of the land's European owners. For instance, on the Vunamami reserve in Ralum, To Bobo faced constant pressure from Emma throughout the 1890s. Finally, in 1901, after appeals by To Bobo, Hahl had the area properly surveyed and concrete markers erected, by which time reserves in Ralum amounted to 1000 hectares for some 2000 Tolai.[9]

Then in 1902 and 1903, imperial ordinances were issued in Berlin, giving colonial governors the authority to attach special conditions to the European right of ownership of native land, and to expropriate legally-acquired land from private persons in order to ensure to local inhabitants the possibility of an economic existence. By a regulation of July 1904, Hahl put the first of these into effect, probably using as a basis the agreement he had reached with To Bobo concerning the Ralum reserve in 1896. The conditions elaborated at that time, by which the Tolai were allowed to keep their reserves, thus became official policy and enabled the administration between 1903 and 1914 to set aside over 5740 hectares of previously-alienated land for the residence and use of New Guinean groups. In 1914, seventy reserves totalling 13 115 hectares existed in German New Guinea.[10]

These measures did not altogether eliminate conflicts over land, for the rights of native users of enclosed land were not made hereditary or transferable, so that interests created by continued occupation failed to be preserved. Moreover, abuses continued to occur in the process of acquisition, especially in areas not under permanent government control. Officially, purchases of land for Europeans were made by the government after assessing a customer's claim in relation to local needs. In practice, a company or group with an interest in a particular area was allowed to make an arrangement with the often inarticulate and helpless local people, and the claim to a sale of land was then simply confirmed by the administration. Official investigation and government purchase were all too often an empty formality.

The last great war in the Gazelle Peninsula, in April and May 1902, can be traced directly to the omissions of German land policy. It occurred in the Varzin Ranges, an area which, under To Vagira's influence, had evaded German control and remained hostile to Europeans since the 1890s. Armed intervention was necessary in July 1898, and two more expeditions were carried out within twelve months of the imperial takeover, after To Vagira had raided a neighbouring district and captured fifteen prisoners for a cannibal feast. None of the administration's attempts to subdue him had been successful.

Because of the entrenchment of the large plantations on the Kokopo coast, those seeking to take up land in the eastern Gazelle had to move further inland beyond the borders of the New Guinea Company and Ralum. One such was a German planter, Rudolf Wolff, who in October 1900 settled on 500 hectares of land purchased from the local 'big man' To Kilang at the foot of the Varzin near Paparatawa, about three walking hours from Herbertshöhe. For a while relations with his neighbours were good, as Wolff inaugurated a prosperous exchange trade in copra with several inland districts, but in March 1902 To Kilang disputed the conditions of the original land sale. He claimed that Wolff was clearing an area not included in the agreement, an area which involved a *marawot*, land sacred to the *ingiet* society.[11]

This was not the first case of New Guineans in the area reclaiming land which they had sold in the recent past, so during the next few weeks Wolff joined with the Mission of the Sacred Heart, which was fearful of impending unrest, in trying to have the dispute adjudicated by the administration. Government officials, however, treated the matter in a dilatory fashion, seemingly unaware of any urgency. With an official survey of the disputed land being continually delayed, Wolff's Tolai neighbours were becoming more and more antagonised by his failure to control labourers who were pilfering local poultry. Finally, when Wolff took the imprudent action of firing his gun to frighten off a young warrior who was a relative of To Vagira, the latter persuaded To Kilang that it was time to take matters into their own hands.[12]

First an ambush was laid to catch and kill Wolff but this failed, so on 3 April some two to three hundred warriors from the districts of Paparatawa and Tomanariki surrounded his home while he was absent and fell upon his wife with their axes as she bargained with them over a pig. They then killed the planter's baby daughter and ransacked the house, taking with them thirteen rifles and 1000 rounds of ammunition. Wolff himself nearly shared his family's fate when he rode up to the house to investigate and found a solid wall of warriors brandishing their weapons. Only by charging his horse through their ranks did he manage to escape.

While all this was happening, the Governor lay stricken and delirious with an attack of black-water fever. The Herbertshöhe administration was in the hands of a young magistrate, also by the name of Wolff. Like most of the colonial Powers, Germany lacked experienced administrative personnel. Wolff was a good example of the authority bestowed on officers who showed initiative in the field; an example, too, of the effect which a single individual could have on the pattern of racial relations in his area of German New Guinea. Wolff interpreted the murders as proof of wide-ranging, acute resentment against white rule, and he suspected that some 1200 people in the districts of Paparatawa, Tomanariki and Viviren were involved, at least tacitly.[13] Instead of mounting a quick police raid to seek out the ringleaders, as was the normal practice, Wolff responded by arming and releasing onto the Varzin districts 2000 labourers offered by white planters.

It was a decision which the Colonial Department later described, with masterly understatement, as 'injudicious'.[14] In fact Wolff with this one decision turned what had been a local incident into a racial campaign, a total war in which leaders of the Tolai finally rejected any idea of coexistence. Old inter-group hostilities, dormant since pre-contact days, were rekindled as coastal people fought inland tribes and New Irelanders and Solomon Islanders invaded the territory of the Tolai. A war of indiscriminate slaughter followed, in which innocent men and women were shot and missionaries threatened, the hostilities pene-trating far inland to the newly-contacted Taulil people and reaching back to pacified districts where the lives of whites and New Guineans alike were in fresh danger; even pacified Tolai in reserves between Herbertshöhe and the Varzin showed solidarity with the offenders by signalling troop movements to them with drums.[15] For their part, Europeans aided and abetted the reprisals because, in their eyes, the slaughter of a white woman and her child represented the ultimate desecration of the white race. Even the Catholic Mission allowed itself to be drawn into the fighting when the war threatened to envelop its stations in the more settled districts.

The war lasted into May 1902, with no quarter given on either side. To Kilang and To Vagira resisted fiercely, despite the superiority in firearms of the European forces. To Kilang was driven inland to the Taulil people, traditional enemies, who ambushed his party, killed his son and promptly cooked him. To Kilang himself escaped, but fell eventually in a battle with police near Paparatawa mission station. To Vagira, enemy of the white people to the last, went on fighting even when his own people were ready to deliver him up. It was not until 18 May that he was killed in a gun battle with the police. With To Vagira's death and over eighty dead and wounded, the Varzin rebels were finally subdued. Peace was formally sealed with the administration on the Empress's birthday, October 1902.

There is no doubt the whole affair would have been handled differently had Hahl been at the helm. Total response was not his trademark, though once the campaign had become a general one Hahl showed no hesitation in using it to extend control over an area which had thwarted him for some years. As a result of the victory, the Germans placed a police post at Paparatawa, confiscated half the district land, and constructed a road from the Varzin to Weberhafen on the north coast, thus opening up the ranges and incorporating the Varzin into the regional organisation. By 1904 they could claim to have the entire one-language area of the northern Gazelle Peninsula in their control, with 107 districts organised under government *luluais*.[16]

Now only one area of European settlement in the northern Gazelle remained beyond the direct supervision of Herbertshöhe. This was the Baining Mountains in the north-west, and here, two years after the Varzin war, an incident occurred which showed up the fragility of German notions of control, even when an area was formally within the regional organisation. The Baining Mountains had been opened up only in the late 1890s by the New Guinea Company and the Catholic Mission, the Company with an experimental plantation at Massawa-hafen and the mission with 500 hectares at Weberhafen. The Catholics also had sponsored Hahl's anti-slavery raids in the 1890s, and were heavily involved in the 'pacification' of the area. By 1900 the coast, to all appearances, was peaceful, with four mission stations in the region. One of them was St Paul, an artificial village among the Baining people, some hours inland from Massawahafen and the furthest point of German contact from the north coast.

St Paul was founded as the Sacred Heart Mission's first 'industrial village', in which slaves and orphans adopted and educated at Vunapope were gathered together with land and tools, and expected to function as cells of Christian peasant-farmers and artisans amongst their heathen compatriots. One of their number in St Paul was a Baining man, To Marias, who, after fourteen years as a ward of the mission, found himself at variance with Church policy and alienated from the way of life now expected of him. To Marias wanted to divorce his wife, a mission convert, in order to marry his lover Sa Vanut, who was already wife to another man. When the Director of St Paul, Father Matthäus Rascher, refused to sanction the divorce, the two lovers fled to To Marias's adoptive father, 'big man' in a nearby village. At

Rascher's behest, both were brought back to St Paul on the end of a rope, where Rascher proceeded to beat To Marias for his sins while a nun dealt the same punishment to Sa Vanut.[17]

The incident only brought to the boil the mood of desperation among a small group of the Bainings. Not all the redeemed slaves welcomed the new order of things—the European dwellings, the precepts of Christian morality, the Western work ethic and the paternalism of a priestly regime. To To Marias in particular the 'industrial village' represented pain and humiliation. Whether he also saw it as an unwarranted deviation from the life the Baining people had always led; whether he regarded Rascher as a powerful rival who had to be eliminated if he himself were to stake a claim to authority over the area, is not clear. Certainly the mission stood in the way of To Marias's freedom and independence. But the discontent went beyond To Marias's particular grievances. Threats of violence had already been made by other Bainings against the mission in 1901, for, in setting up a large plantation at Weberhafen, it had tended to divert traditional market exchanges on the coast in its direction and away from the Baining people, who depended on coastal markets for their fish and trade goods.

Matthäus Rascher himself must bear some of the responsibility for worsening relations. An autocratic disciplinarian who tolerated no opposition, nor suffered fools gladly, Rascher was not popular even among his own mission *confrères*. Rascher clashed several times with Bishop Couppé, for instance, who was also a man who liked to get his own way. Numbers of Rascher's colleagues regarded him as obstinate, impatient and distant, though these may have been simply the outward shortcomings of a man whose superior attainments lifted him above his fellow workers. Albert Hahl admired Rascher's pioneering spirit, and respected greatly the work he had put into learning the language and customs of the Baining people. But Hahl, too, considered Rascher rather too complacent, particularly where his authority with the Bainings was concerned.[18]

The Bainings themselves had their own reasons for disliking Rascher. Not only was he given to administering beatings for all sorts of failures in his little flock, but he also organised the much-disliked public road works for the area. Thus he faced the added danger of being identified more with the secular government and its demands than with the disinterested aims of the Catholic Mission. Rascher did not believe that the Baining people could give any serious trouble. In his pioneer grammar of the Baining language, he wrote that the Bainings were 'more unwarlike, more irresolute, more untalented and undeveloped than the coastal inhabitants'.[19] Even after signs of sullen hostility had been evident for some time and the first rumours of a plot against his life became common knowledge, Rascher refused the Governor's offer of a police detachment for protection until things cooled down. All this suggests that the priest was naïve about the extent of his authority, and guilty, in Hahl's words, of a 'lapse in intellect rather than an infringement of morality or law'.[20]

The lapse was to cost him dear, for To Marias was fashioning a conspiracy against his life. Where Christianity hung lightly on New Guinean shoulders, more as a socio-economic alliance than as the product of inner conviction, Rascher's determination to preserve the Catholic ideal of marriage was hardly likely to be accepted with equanimity. Soon after his detention and punishment, To Marias had planned to attack the mission station on 7 August 1904, but the attack had to be put off at the last moment because of the arrival of the New Guinea Company plantation manager, who was well armed. The opportunity came again on 13 August. On that morning, after breakfast, as was his wont, To Marias asked for Rascher's rifle in order to shoot pigeons for the mission's kitchen. While Rascher, feeling unwell, lay on his bed, To Marias stole up to the priest's window and shot him in the stomach. It was the signal for the conspirators to fall upon the rest of the missionaries. Three brothers and five sisters were cut down with axes as they went about their daily tasks; at the same time on a lonely station at Nacharunep some kilometres west of St Paul, Baining people murdered a Trappist monk, Father Rutten, as he sat reading his breviary. Those Bainings who were regarded as particular supporters of the priests were also killed, though several managed to escape to the coast and raise the alarm.

The importance of this episode lies less in the fact that some New Guineans were unhappy with the trappings of European rule than in the way it exposes the tenuous control which the Germans exercised over New Guineans in the early 1900s, even in an area comparatively long settled and formally included in the regional organisation. When the report of the massacre reached Herbertshöhe on 14 August, Hahl and most of his executive officers were absent on patrolling duty in the far reaches of the protectorate; there were only twenty police at Herbertshöhe itself. The immediate dispatch of sixteen of these to the north left the centre of the colony without any administrative leadership or security forces. At the same time, labourers on a European plantation on the north-east coast made plain the uneasiness between whites and New Guineans at large when, on learning what had occurred, they wanted to cease work 'because all the whites were dead'.[21] When Hahl returned and could divert more police to the area, it still took a month of regular expeditions into the Kara range and the Krau valley, where the insurrection was centred, before the rebels were suppressed. Many of them came from the village of To Marias's adoptive father, and at least fifteen were killed in encounters with the administration's forces, among them To Marias himself whose head was taken triumphantly to the coast. Seven of the participants in the massacre were eventually hanged, while more than twenty were given long prison sentences. In death the rebels achieved a small, if bizarre, victory over Hahl, for he was indiscreet enough to pack off the heads of three of the executed Bainings to Freiburg University for 'scientific examinations', for which he was roundly condemned by almost the entire German press.

Recriminations followed the Baining massacre thick and fast. Newspapers in Australia and in Germany made it front page news for days, and friends and enemies of Catholicism speculated endlessly about the reasons for the slaughter. The Superiors of the Sacred Heart Order themselves were understandably anxious to play down the role of Rascher in the affair, and the Provincial of the New Guinea Mission, Father Linckens, argued defensively that the massacre was a case of racial hatred, an episode in the black-versus-white struggle in German New Guinea.[22]

Hahl would have none of it. He refused to consider the attack as more than an act of violence directed against the immediate cause of resentment; a limited affair carried through by a small unrepresentative group of the Bainings. The time he took to ferret out the murderers and bring them to justice makes this clear: Hahl wanted no repetition of the Varzin war in 1902.

This was not the last of the trouble in the 'industrial villages' of the Baining Mountains. There was a revival of hostility in 1905 when the priests took local children away to school without their parents' knowledge or consent. And in 1911 the mission once more received a threat from a local 'big man'. Government troops made several more forays into the area after 1904, but by and large the north-west Bainings were much more tightly organised by the time war broke out in 1914, and sufficiently 'pacified' for 200 local people to be working on government projects and private plantations.[23]

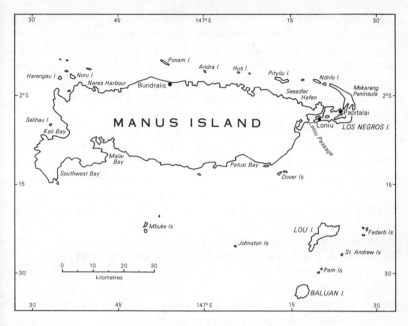

Map 6 Manus Island

The Baining massacre was the last major collision on the Gazelle Peninsula, and with its resolution the problem of physical security receded into the memory of a frontier past for most of the planters in the Gazelle. Questions of economic development, of finding more and more New Guinean labour for the plantations had been urgent before 1904, and now they became the major issue in the settled areas. Hahl had already moved to strengthen the planting economy by exerting control over proven recruiting grounds outside the Gazelle Peninsula. The first choice for a new government settlement from which to carry this through fell naturally on northern New Ireland, a prime source of recruitment for Gazelle plantations in the past, where by 1900 sixteen trading stations also flourished, plus two small plantation businesses producing 1000 tonnes of copra annually.

Early in 1900 the imperial administration established its first regional station there, at Kavieng on the north-east tip of the island. Under the iron hand of Franz Boluminski, a district officer whose fiery eye, awful presence and ruthless energy remained fixed in the memory of the population for more than a generation, it took only five years to transform northern New Ireland into a model province of empire, a

151

stable, organised and easily accessible area stretching from Kavieng to Pinubit, 155 kilometres to the south. It was in northern New Ireland that Hahl first levied his head tax; the area also provided a steady stream of villagers to European labour lines, so that by 1914 seventy per cent of the adult male population was estimated to have recruited for European service during German times.[24] Local European plantations prospered from the surge in recruiting: between 1902 and 1914 planted areas in northern New Ireland expanded some tenfold with the help of casual and contract labour from neighbouring villages.[25]

The success of the Kavieng station reinforced Hahl's conviction that permanent government presence was the key to development, and it encouraged, too, the Berlin authorities to provide greater funds for the establishment of regional stations in other areas. In 1904 and 1905 two more were founded on the frontiers of control in already proven recruiting districts: Namatanai in southern New Ireland and Kieta in Bougainville. The pacification process in both areas proved to be more arduous and bloody than at Kavieng, and in the end the Germans could claim tight control only over districts in the immediate vicinity of their stations, though roads were built along the coastlines and *luluais* installed over a wide area. Even under these uncertain conditions economic expansion went on. By 1911 there were seven plantations in southern New Ireland, and by 1914 two large concerns in Bougainville.[26] In both areas the native inhabitants were taking advantage of new opportunities by hiring themselves out as day labour, and by regularly planting coconuts to ensure an independent cash income for the future.

With these two areas under direct rule and at least formal control, Hahl's attention after 1906 swung to the western half of the protectorate. This left the Admiralty Islands as the only large group in the archipelago without a permanent regional organisation, a deliberate decision because of the untenable position which the imperial government inherited there in 1900.

The Admiralties lie off the northern coast of New Guinea. The main island is Manus, eighty kilometres long, with a maximum width of 27 kilometres. It is by far the largest island of the group, mountainous and well-forested, with alternating steep coastal slopes and swampy bays. The other islands lie to the south of Manus, grouped in a semi-circle beginning in the east; the largest of these is Rambutjo. European activity during the German period was concentrated in the east of

Manus and on the out-islands. The crescent-shaped Los Negros Island lies at the eastern end of Manus, separated by the very narrow Loniu Passage. Seeadlerhafen, where the Germans were to make their head-quarters, lies within this crescent; so too do Papitalai village and harbour, and Loniu village, one of the largest settlements in the group.

The Germans found three major social groups in the Admiralties. The Usiai were subsistence agriculturalists scattered in small groups in the interior and were considered by the others to be a dependent and inferior lot. On the coasts lived the Matankor, who combined agri-culture with fishing. The third group were the Manus, a truly maritime people who lived in lavishly-constructed pile settlements built over the waters of swamps and bays. The Manus were—and still are—great sailors, in the old days taking their giant outriggers into the west and as far south as the Gazelle Peninsula; only for sago, taro, beans and timber were they dependent on land dwellers. The three groups together were estimated by the Germans to number some 13 000.[27]

Contacts with the Admiralties had been many and frequent since the early seventeenth century, and by the 1880s the inhabitants had acquired the reputation of being particularly independent and wild. Cannibalism here was supposed to be the worst in the Pacific, and continual blood feuds between the Manus and the land dwellers endangered the security of most European passers-by. The Forsayth concern was the first to establish a trader in the group in 1881; Hernsheim and others followed in the 1890s. They survived only with difficulty, becoming the pawns in a series of payback murders carried out by different Manus groups. The Manus made a specialty of cutting off European schooners close inshore and then massacring the crew to get to the weapons store. These were then used to give one party an advantage in the on-going struggles between rival settlements, with the result that the victims in their turn took to plundering passing boats in order to retaliate with arms of their own. Six European traders were murdered one after another in the decade before 1900; in 1899 there were three punitive expeditions to punish raids on whites, all of them unsuccessful.

When the imperial government took over the protectorate only two German and three Scandinavian traders resided in the islands, and there was every chance that they would soon be murdered or driven out. In the circumstances, with little finance and no ready investment capital, with an intransigent population and a negligible number of labour recruits from the area, the Germans would not consider extending direct rule to the Admiralties in the early years. For most of the period the administration sought merely to contain unrest by occasional repression, a policy which proved more and more inadequate with the passage of time.

The first visit by the new Governor, Rudolf von Bennigsen, in July 1899, set the pattern. Although friendly contact was made with the people of Mouk Island, von Bennigsen used force against the inhabitants of St Patrick Island to punish them for repeated attacks on Europeans. Within three months of his departure, another three white traders and several New Guineans had been killed, and a schooner plundered. The reprisal for these murders was one of the most savage the Germans ever carried out in New Guinea. Von Bennigsen and his naval reinforcements from SMS *Seeadler* employed a minimum of restraint, raking settlements with machine gun fire, setting loose a party of Manus auxiliaries to plunder the villages, and then destroying the houses. Twenty-five people were killed in an initial assault on the inhabitants of St Patrick Island; several attacks on Pitilu Island off the north coast of Manus claimed another twenty lives.[28]

Von Bennigsen's brutal methods failed to stop the predatory raids by these groups. Until 1911 a major expedition to the Admiralties took place at least every eighteen months to punish the people for some misdemeanour. Another three Europeans were killed during that time, besides several Chinese and Malay traders, and their Melanesian assistants. Continued bombardments, police raids and the destruction of property had no lasting effect. When a warship appeared, a cunning system of signal fires from island to island warned of its approach, and guilty villagers had time to ferry themselves and their valuables to safer places.

In the early days, Hahl tried the expedient of stationing troops in the group temporarily, but without success. War-like villagers scattered by the police only became wandering raiders, and the Mouk-Mandrian, Rubal and Pak peoples in the east of the islands simply turned from marauding the centres of European trading to terrorising friendly islanders in the vicinity; a hundred people were reportedly killed in a single raid on Ponam Island, north of Manus.[29]

What the Germans faced in Manus was not just aimless savagery or conservative resistance to change. It was rather a contact situation common to many parts of New Guinea. Patterns of hostility and alliance which had prevailed in the past among the various groups of Admiralty Islanders were now being influenced by the intervention of importunate, white newcomers, who claimed the authority to order the lives of all villagers and possessed technological marvels capable of changing forever the old way of life. The long confrontation between one Manus Islander, Pominis, and the Germans is a striking illustration of the New Guinean ability to exploit the new sources of power while giving precedence to relations with neighbouring groups of islanders.

Pominis was from Papitalai, on Los Negros, a shore-dwelling group of Manus people who relied on canoes for fishing, transport and fighting; who obtained meat from the sea, from hunting, from breeding pigs and dogs, and from cannibalism; and who traded frequently with other Manus communities in coconut oil, dogs' teeth and clay pots. In the early days of German contact with Manus, Pominis seems either to have recruited for Herbertshöhe as a labourer or been taken there as hostage after a punitive expedition. Once in Herbertshöhe he became acquainted with the Catholic Mission, acquired an elementary education and offered himself as a convert, ultimately reaching the rank of catechist. Sometime before 1904 he was returned to Papitalai, where, from all accounts, he began evangelising, built two schools and set out to educate his village.[30]

As the only educated, bilingual member of Papitalai, Pominis took the lead in adjudicating disputes with neighbours; perhaps the possession of a rifle gave him added authority. When, soon after his return, Papitalai was attacked by its long-hostile neighbour, Loniu, it was Pominis who led a retaliatory expedition. Loyalty to freshly-acquired foreign ethics was of no practical use in dealing with such traditional hostilities, and Pominis was quite prepared to use customary methods. Unfortunately, from that point on Pominis found himself condemned by local Europeans as the worst kind of half-educated savage, branded as a cannibal and accused of organising raids on schooners.

In March 1904 the German cruiser SMS *Condor* arrived off Papitalai, and the captain ordered Pominis to go with him to Herbertshöhe 'to be questioned'. Pominis showed himself willing at first, but at the last moment he was overcome by apprehension and retired into the interior, emerging only briefly to offer half his land as compensation for any wrong he had committed.[31] His offer was refused, and a police party finally captured him with the help of people from Pitilu Island.

In considering what to do with Pominis, Governor Hahl, as was his custom, took a pragmatic, political view of the matter, rather than one based on a strictly legal interpretation of the charges. Hahl did not normally interfere in local disputes among New Guineans unless they occurred in areas under government control, or posed a serious threat to the reputation of the regime. In his eyes, Pominis, the catechist turned war leader, constituted just such a threat; he was seen as a political delinquent who must be removed. Hahl wasted no time. Without formal court proceedings, he convicted Pominis as a menace to public order and banished him to Kavieng for ten years.[32]

Hahl's 'political' approach to such disputes enabled him to find the quickest and tidiest solution to the problems of inter-communal peace, but it also laid him open to charges of expediency and miscarriage of justice if his solutions compromised the interests of European colonists with powerful friends at home. The reputation of the Sacred Heart Mission was directly affected by the banishment of Pominis, for it had succoured him and trained him, and now his activities were being blamed on its proselytising policies. The tenacious Bishop Couppé was a fair match for Hahl. He would never let the good name of the Order be so tarnished. Accordingly, Couppé used his considerable influence within the German *Zentrumspartei* to have Pominis's case reopened. It was not long before an investigation by the Colonial Department discovered that Pominis's conviction had been secured in irregular fashion: no defence counsel had been provided, nor had Pominis been informed of the verdict against him.[33] Hahl was rebuked for his haste. Pominis was released. Couppé could be well satisfied. Now Pominis returned to Papitalai, this time as the thin end of the missionary wedge to sound out the possibility of purchasing land for a station.

Pominis's case demonstrated, as Police Master Full concluded, that the administration could get its fingers burnt by taking sides in what were basically 'native feuds'.[34] But if the Sacred Heart Mission thought that, as a result of its intervention, Pominis was now *their* man, they too were mistaken. For in the years after 1905 Pominis became more and more a law unto himself. Visiting Europeans used his linguistic talents, and he became a valued guide and interpreter for government and private expeditions to Manus. New complaints against him, that he had abducted a woman from a nearby village and planted a skull on a stick next to the Christian crucifix in Papitalai, were an unintended testament to his growing individualism. Papitalai eventually became too small for Pominis, and, after quarrelling with the 'big man', Songan, he agreed to leave the village and set up a new one with his followers on Mokareng Peninsula. By 1912, when Couppé arrived to buy land, Pominis had achieved a leading position as spokesman and intermediary for his people.

The Catholic Mission was afterwards to claim that, under Pominis's authority and through his good offices, it had purchased some 500 hectares in the Papitalai area.[35] If this was so—and the Papitalai villagers were disputing it as late as the 1960s—then the Catholic Mission had been duped by its protégé. For later investigations into land dealings on Manus make it eminently clear that Pominis had no such authority to dispose of land, since genealogically he was from a junior branch of land controllers in Papitalai; at most he could dispose of ten or fifteen hectares.[36] If Pominis did transfer 500 hectares to the mission, then he did so without any reference whatever to the rights and interests of the real owners.

It is evident from these transactions that Pominis was by now independent of all his sponsors, traditional and European, without either his own people or the Catholic Mission being certain where he stood, or what he was up to. The first to find this out was the mission. In November 1913 two priests and a brother arrived at Papitalai to claim their estate and till what they thought was prepared ground. Instead they found a wilderness. Pominis, who was supposed to set up a house and plantation for the newcomers, was nowhere to be seen. For three years the priests laboured fruitlessly in Papitalai, the people indifferent to their presence and unaware that much of their community land was assumed by the priests to belong to them. Finally, in 1916 the mission abandoned Papitalai altogether and moved its station to Bundralis, sixty-four kilometres to the west, on Manus. Pominis remained a maverick to the last. While the priests struggled dispiritedly at Papitalai in the years after 1913, he lived at Mokareng as a 'Catholic pagan', the teachings of his youth all but abandoned. Only many years later, when his compatriots had all become Catholic, did Pominis return to the fold.

All this was in the future. The disorder and aggression which had been a marked feature of the early German period in the Admiralties gradually gave way to an acceptance of German hegemony. The turning point in the eastern out-islands seemed to come after 1905: at the end of that year, after three Buka labourers had murdered their German employer, the people of Pak Island surprised the Germans by taking the law into their own hands and killing the labourers themselves.

The next step was the extension of direct rule to the Admiralties. The first *luluais* were appointed in 1909, significantly enough on Pak. Two years later, a permanent government station was erected in Seeadlerhafen; the decision to establish the station probably was hastened by the need to compensate for the exhaustion of old recruiting grounds. German law and order spread so quickly from then on that by 1911 European businesses had begun to take a secure grip without the worry of warding off attacks. Hernsheim by then owned more than 980 hectares of land in the Admiralties, nearly half of it under cultivation; boat building and pearling were two of the industries already established; and the final sign of pacification was the jump in labour recruits, from a mere seventeen in 1905 to 823 in 1913.[37]

Manus was an outer point in the gradually-expanding economic frontier of German New Guinea. When war rudely shattered the colonial enterprise, that frontier, though yet slender and irregular, was outwardly impressive in extent. European businesses laid claim to more than 185 000 hectares of land, 34 190 hectares of which were plantations under cultivation; planted areas had increased by fifty per cent between 1908 and 1912 alone. From a little over 2950 tonnes at the beginning of imperial rule, copra exports had risen to 14 260 tonnes in 1914; total trade amounted to 16 000 000 marks.[38] Governor Hahl had mapped out a development program for the years 1914 to 1917 which, under the benefit of large but decreasing Reich subsidies, would round out the local administration with new stations in southern New Britain, Bougainville and on the main rivers of the mainland; build up the police force, especially the expeditionary corps used to open up and 'pacify' new areas; and increase government schools and health facilities for New Guineans. Within ten years Hahl hoped to have the colony independent of imperial subsidies.[39]

This neat, European model of progress was, however, under strain from the New Guinean end. Resistance to German control still hampered settlement in the Bismarck Archipelago and on the mainland, and New Guinean self-sufficiency was proving an obstacle to the conception of development which Hahl and the planters held. To begin with, the extension of regional stations throughout the protectorate and the appointment of native intermediaries were no guarantee of complete German control. Though it was basically a system of simple, direct rule and *luluais* were little more than levers through which to mount police action or levy taxation and forced labour, the regional organisation fell short even of these modest goals in many areas. Not all *luluais* were able to gain the respect of their groups; and astute 'big men' tended to avoid the office altogether because of the dangers associated with unpopular government demands. The Germans also had to deal with many cases of partiality, excessive zeal and ignorance on the part of their agents.[40]

The root of these problems lay in that these managerial positions were generally the first institutionalised, political offices in New Guinea societies, and cut across customary categories of leadership and power. Leaders of local groups were not the only instruments of social control, and what influence and policy-making roles they did possess were usually circumscribed. They could not and would not sacrifice the co-operation of individuals on whom they depended for daily support, by making demands in the name of a new abstract authority.

The other main instrument of mobilisation, the poll tax, also had a limited effect. Official figures indicate that the tax was paid fairly readily throughout New Guinea. Revenue rose steadily from 76 370 marks in 1908 to 301 550 marks in 1914, and reports mention only minor resistance to the tax, probably because it removed some of the forced labour obligations to which people like the Tolai took particular exception.[41] But the head tax was not generally achieving the ends for which Hahl had designed it, namely to force ever larger numbers of New Guineans onto the labour market and thus accustom them to the plantation economy. The coastal Tolai experienced little trouble meeting the tax from existing trade incomes, while, on New Ireland, villagers in both the north and the south were engaging in day-labour at local plantations to earn it, then returning to subsistence gardening and coconut cultivation in their home villages. Indeed, the head tax had started an upsurge in local coconut plantings so that New Guineans might enhance their own trading incomes.

The labour question posed the most serious of all the threats to the model of progress that Hahl and the planting community conceived for New Guinea. New Guineans, it is true, underwent much greater pressure to offer their labour to white planters than did Samoans or Ponapeans. In May 1913 Hahl estimated that ten per cent (or about 20 000) of contacted villagers were engaged in some capacity in the service of the non-New Guinean population,[42] a high percentage for a colony in New Guinea's stage of development, with a people fragmented by topographical, cultural and social factors; in the Kavieng area alone more than fifty per cent of the male population had already recruited for European work.

These figures, however, only give an indication of the size of the economically-active population, those who participated at different stages in the European economy. They do not prove that there was a vast army of New Guineans *assimilated* into the plantation economy by 1913. In fact no recognisable 'urban' work force existed in German New Guinea, no pool of permanent wage labour. Employment with Europeans was in general a temporary experience: the majority of New Guineans returned to their villages after completion of contracts or casual labour, and resumed subsistence gardening. Plantations in the Gazelle Peninsula were also suffering in 1913-14 from the preference of people in old recruiting areas to work locally. In 1913 three-quarters of all the recruits from northern New Ireland worked on local plantations, and this region, like southern New Ireland, Bougainville and New Britain, experienced a relative decrease over the years in the numbers of recruits it contributed to the total labour force.[43]

Whether this relative economic independence would have continued had the war not intervened is at least doubtful. For the fragmented societies of German New Guinea were confronted by a growing class of pan-German planters, which could, and did, place considerable pressure on the policies of the colonial government. Theirs was a crude philosophy of colonisation: they considered that colonies belonged to the immigrant settler, not to the native inhabitants, nor to the local administration. They saw the 'native' as a negligible quantity, a mere commodity to be exploited in the search for profit; and they viewed the government's first priority as protection of settlers, doing all in its power to help them achieve prosperity, in this case by securing more and better labour.

Inevitably these beliefs and their intolerance brought the pan-German settler clique into conflict with Hahl, who sought to develop New Guinea with an eye to the people of the land and their future. Hahl appreciated that village New Guineans had a claim to just and sympathetic treatment, and to some protection against the consequences of radical social change: hence his work to ensure that villagers in areas of wholesale land alienation should have reserves on which to fall back. He also fought to regulate the processes of labour recruitment, for, with a practical sense of the colony's future, he was concerned at the depopulation of some areas brought about by excessive recruiting. In 1909-10 he wanted to close the entire protectorate to the recruitment of women, and he periodically placed an embargo on 'worked out' areas so that population balance and local economic activity would not be damaged permanently by premature depletion of labour.[44]

But in the end it was the size of white settler communities, and their ability to mobilise support back in Germany for their sectional interests, which determined the degree of colonial exploitation. German New Guinea had a European population of more than 1000 by 1913. Of these, some 350 were traders and planters, and the vast majority of them were concentrated around the centres of government activity in the Gazelle Peninsula and northern New Ireland. Giant companies like the New Guinea Company, the DHPG of Samoa fame, and Rudolf Wahlen's Hamburg South Sea Company (HSAG), possessed equally giant stakes in the economy of the colony. A branch of the highly nationalist German Colonial Society had been functioning in New Guinea since December 1903, and a Planters' Society since mid-1904, while an additional pressure group was found in the Governor's Council, though until 1914 it was subject to Hahl's appointments and possessed no legislative powers.

Exploiting every avenue of access to the home authorities, the planting community managed often to impede Hahl in his efforts to protect New Guineans from the effects of European penetration. Because of their influence, Hahl was permitted to close only northern New Ireland and Nusa to the recruitment of women, instead of the whole protectorate. In 1913 the settlers' unceasing demands for labour and the chronic shortage of finance forced Hahl to renew the recruiting drive in already hard-pressed areas, with the result that there were major outbreaks of violence in southern New Ireland and at Aitape on the northern mainland. Hahl was caught also between the conflicting pressures of competing entrepreneurs. When, occasionally, the smaller settlers found themselves on the Governor's side against the interests of large-scale capital enterprises, it was usually the latter which triumphed, not Hahl. Thus he failed to get abolished the continued privileged access of the New Guinea Company to labour resources on the mainland, or to curtail the right of the DHPG to recruit labour for Samoa in the Archipelago.

Because of his attempts to procure equitable treatment for the inhabitants of New Guinea and to conserve them into the future, Governor Hahl attracted the contempt and genuine animosity of many of the planting community. When he left New Guinea in 1914 at the end of his term of office, prominent settlers bade him good riddance as 'one of the best hated men of the protectorate'.[45] And yet, in their basic ideals and ultimate objectives, German planters were much closer to Hahl than they realised or were willing to accept. At heart Hahl was in sympathy with the needs of settler-entrepreneurs. Though he claimed

161

in his farewell speech in April 1914 to have recognised the importance of the relationship between the two races for the future of the colony,[46] it was not a claim based on an ideal of equality for New Guineans in their own land. Rather it was an admission, and a warning, that the prosperity of New Guinea lay in the Germans' ability to tap the labour of the population by creating an ordered existence. Hahl was adamant that New Guinea life and thought must be assimilated to that of the German people if the Reich's national ends were not to be subverted. With this in mind, it is easier to understand Hahl's assumption that violence was a natural and inevitable part of the colonising process.

7

The Mainland
New Guineans under Company and Empire

The New Guinea mainland's north-eastern quarter was known to European explorers at least two centuries before German settlement. Tasman, in 1643, Dampier, in 1700, and D'Entrecasteaux, in 1792-93, all touched at various points on the coasts north of the Huon Gulf. In 1827, three years after the Dutch took possession of the western mainland, Dumont d'Urville entered Astrolabe Bay, which was named after his ship. Until 1871 nothing came of these early visits except for a temporary Catholic mission station on Umboi Island.

In 1871 a Russian naturalist, Nikolai Mikloucho-Maclay landed at Bongu on the south coast of the deep and open Astrolabe Bay. Here, on land which rises gently for nearly two kilometres from the coast, he set up camp and remained for three periods of time between 1871 and 1883. Maclay's initial reception was far from friendly, for the local inhabitants were fearful of his fair skin, his clothes, and of the obvious power of the Russian cruiser which had brought him to the area. However the Russian possessed a new material culture which drew people to him, and his serenity in the face of hostility, his readiness to accept death for the advantage of gaining knowledge, finally earned him the respect of the Bongu villagers and of settlements along the length of Astrolabe Bay.

Maclay enhanced his acceptability by being prepared to make suitable gifts to the people, and to engage in the local system of trade and exchange. Visitors from as far away as Karkar, the wooded, volcanic island north-east of Cape Croisilles, came to trade for Maclay's stock of steel axes and adzes, nails, mirrors, cloth, paint and the seeds of new plants. As a source of wealth and the master of new and apparently 'superhuman' knowledge, Maclay came to be revered as a *tibud* or demigod. The New Guineans of Astrolabe Bay and the Rai coast further south seem to have had some experience of white people before Maclay's arrival, for the people of Bongu and of Siar, a small island to the north, possessed an image of a land across the horizon called Anut, peopled by whites who lived in large houses, and owned iron axes and knives. Maclay was connected with Anut: New Guineans

163

therefore concluded that he was one of its deities, come to give them the new material culture. Even after his departure, Maclay continued to exercise the patriarchal role with which he had been invested, pleading with the British and Germans at the time of annexation that the Papuans of the Rai coast should be left independent. When he said his last farewell in 1883 he warned the Bongu villagers about Europeans who might follow him, hinting that only those who identified themselves as his brothers should be accepted as 'good'.[1]

The people of Astrolabe Bay were therefore ready for the visits of Otto Finsch in the early 1880s. He came as an exploring agent for the New Guinea Company, the newly-established German consortium run by Adolf Hansemann in Berlin. Shouting 'Oh Maclay' everywhere he landed along the coast, Finsch was able to make friendly contacts and buy land in the area, in particular, much of the landing area at Bongu and a 148-hectare forest section. In late November 1884 the German flag was raised in Friedrich Wilhelmshafen, a small but sheltered harbour some thirty-two kilometres north of Bongu, and a Company claim was made to the land surrounding it, which appeared 'uninhabited, uncultivated and apparently no one's property'.[2] By this time Finsch had already explored much of the mainland coast, discovering and naming the Sepik River (Kaiserin Augusta Fluss), Dallmannhafen, Berlinhafen, Hatzfeldthafen and Deutschlandhafen, and at all these points he had taken 'unowned' land into possession, mainly to establish Germany's claim to the area. As a result of Finsch's enthusiastic reports, the New Guinea Company chose as the site for its first settlement, Deutschlandhafen (now renamed Finschhafen), a densely-wooded harbour sheltered by a small peninsula near the south-eastern tip of the Huon Peninsula. Presumably because of its geographical prominence, Finschhafen was expected to be the node for traffic from the north and east, but especially from the south, for the mainland (Kaiser Wilhelmsland) was to be the scene of the New Guinea Company's great experiment in planned colonisation from Australia.

The first party of employees, consisting of five Europeans and thirty-seven Malays, arrived at Finschhafen on 5 November 1885. They received an enthusiastic welcome. One old man clasped the captain of the Company vessel to his breast and greeted him as a long-lost friend, obviously mistaking the newcomers for manifestations of local ancestor spirits.[3] On this understanding, the whites immediately purchased land in the vicinity of the neighbouring village and put up their houses. With gifts they bought the patronage of the 'big man', Makiri, though unbeknown to them his authority extended only a few kilometres inland and was limited even in his own tribe.

The New Guinea Company initially was irrepressible in its optimism. The Directors in Berlin issued instructions to their first Governor (*Landeshauptmann*), Admiral Freiherr Georg von Schleinitz, to set about opening up the land. Once coastal stations had been secured, expeditions were to penetrate into the interior of the island to determine its topography, note the amount of free, 'unowned' land, and learn the language and customs of the inhabitants. Existing trade was to be protected and encouraged, and a system of roads constructed to maintain communications for the planned network of inland stations. The Company anticipated no real difficulties from the New Guineans: they possessed 'neither the strength nor the will' to resist, and the Directors envisaged a wholly peaceful occupation of the country and the willing co-operation of its residents.[4]

The colony was soon overrun by an army of officials trying to administer numerous impracticable regulations derived from Prussian civil and criminal law. There were bureaucratic absurdities and disorganisation aplenty. The pioneers in Finschhafen found that they could not erect their tents because someone had left vital components at home; neither had they been supplied with any eating utensils. A huge machine to process china grass was sent out long before it was known whether china grass would prosper in New Guinea; it didn't. Company regulations as early as January 1886 fixed the price of copra, and tried to cover every possible contingency, even to the return of empty packing cases.[5] Land purchase regulations were particularly unrealistic since all acquisitions, at predetermined prices, had to be approved first by the Berlin Directors, a process which could take six months; moreover the Directors insisted on retaining all subsoil rights. Land, and many more amenities, could be purchased in the Australian colonies at lower prices and with easier credit.

No attempt was made to formulate a realistic policy towards the native inhabitants. From the beginning, the New Guineans were regarded as part of the natural resources of the land, to be exploited with a minimum of outlay. Ordinances were drawn up in 1887 and 1888 to regulate relations with coloured labourers, but these were designed less to protect the recruits than to make easier the work of organising them. The first draft of the disciplinary ordinance composed in New Guinea in 1887 was an unwieldy instrument of 185 provisions; von Schleinitz explained away its heavy emphasis on corporal punishment with the observation that, from childhood, Pacific Islanders, Malays and Chinese 'were accustomed to blows and other severe punishments'.[6] One of its compilers had suggested that up to 200 strokes a month be allowed for some infringements, and the mandatory death penalty for many others. When finally issued in October 1888, the ordinance was tempered somewhat by the Colonial Department's reservations, but it still sanctioned the reduction of food rations, confinement and floggings. The regulation was revised in 1900, but the attitudes which had informed it before then continued to find expression in the actions of white employers well into the period of Australian rule.

The Finschhafen people refused to accept lightly the one-sided relationship which these plans implied. At Finschhafen the local residents never provided more than occasional day labour, at first for the novelty of working with iron implements, and then to acquire iron themselves in order to trade with inland tribes for traditional valuables like dogs' teeth. But within a couple of years of the Europeans' arrival they became reluctant to work for them at all, out of fear, Makiri claimed, that they were contributing to the growth of the whites' power and restricting their own independence.[7] From October 1886 onwards the Company was forced to import labourers from the Bismarck Archipelago. Increasingly harsh treatment from Company officials alienated the Finschhafen people further. The foreign labourers from Asia and the Archipelago repeatedly abducted women and plundered plantations. But particular offence was given by the Austrian station manager, Julius Winter, who in 1890 organised a raid against a mountain village of the Kai people when they resisted his attempts to obtain a concubine for his black personal servant. The resulting destruction helped to poison relations among tribes in the entire Finschhafen area.

By 1890 local distaste for the New Guinea Company had intensified to such a degree that a black recruiter was murdered in nearby Busum village. On another occasion the Germans received quite a scare when all relations were suddenly broken off by villagers, and a fleet of strange war canoes appeared in the harbour. Gradually, the local residents pulled back away from the station, selling their land and houses to the Company. However, they continued to resist attempts by Europeans to penetrate the hinterland, for traditionally they had enjoyed a monopoly over trade with inland tribes and, since the arrival of the

Germans, had become prosperous entrepreneurs through the flow of trade goods into the interior.

The Finschhafen settlement never prospered. It was little more than a collecting point for an army of officials who had less and less to do when the expected land rush failed to materialise. Attempts had been made at systematic agriculture, but they foundered on the hard coral base of the soil. Then, in early 1891, a malaria epidemic struck, killing thirteen Company officials and more than thirty labourers in a few weeks. Plans had already been mooted to move the Company head-quarters elsewhere, so Finschhafen was abandoned for Stephansort, some 193 kilometres further up the coast, where the shores of Astrolabe Bay curve northwards.

The pressure on coastal inhabitants increased dramatically now, as the New Guinea Company moved into the area in a grand manner, taking up land which its agents claimed to have 'purchased' in earlier years. One agent in particular, Johann Kubary, manager at the Bongu station (now Constantinhafen), exploited the favourable impression which Finsch had created in 1884 to set the Company's land-buying program in motion.

Between 1887 and 1889 Johann Kubary sailed the coast from Constantinhafen to Friedrich Wilhelmshafen 'purchasing' most of the coastline of Astrolabe Bay, an area of 32 780 hectares. Most of these purchases were carried out in a cavalier manner, judged even by the standards which the New Guinea Company set itself. From the people of Bilibili Island, south of Friedrich Wilhelmshafen, Kubary presumed to buy all the mainland coast between the Gogol and Gum rivers. The transactions were concluded, not by careful surveying and the signing of contracts, but by Kubary's sailing along the coast in his pinnace noting the names of river mouths and prominent features, without at any time landing; Kubary then distributed a trivial collection of trade goods to the Bilibili Islanders. This process was repeated with the Islanders of Jabob, between Bilibili and Friedrich Wilhelmshafen. From them, Kubary purported to buy all land between the Gum River and Friedrich Wilhelmshafen, using his boat to note features, dispensing trade to the Jabob, and then posting up a sheet of paper on a coconut palm to conclude the 'sale'.[8]

In this way, for a mere 256 marks 90 pfennings in trade, Kubary claimed on behalf of the Company 5500 hectares of coastal land to a depth in places of 5000-6000 metres, land which neither the Bilibili nor the Jabob had any right to sell, nor any idea that in co-operating with

Kubary they were doing so. For his part, Kubary acknowledged that his exercise had given the Company only nominal rights over the soil, rights designed mainly 'to pave the way to a friendly understanding [with the people]'.[9]

Kubary's casual business deals did not end there, for the purchases were not registered until 1896, a procedure which contravened the Company's own instructions. Nevertheless the New Guinea Company moved in to take up the land of Friedrich Wilhelmshafen in 1891 and renamed the harbour area Madang. It encountered a small population of some few hundred people living in four major villages, Siar, Bilia, Graged and Panutibun, divided into patrilineal clans, and practising a simple root and fruit crop horticulture supplemented by fishing, hunting and trading. They were a people whose male cults, the *mulung* and *meziab*, played a vital role in social control, and who, through common initiation, feasting and dancing, achieved a limited consciousness of unity and mutual assistance across the four villages.[10]

The inhabitants at first accepted the German newcomers as *rentiers* of the small plot on which the first house was built, but when the whites began clearing vast tracts of land nearby, the 'big man' of Bilia protested to the recently-arrived Lutheran Mission. It was to no avail: the Company insisted on the authenticity of its claims, and the occupation of the harbour's entire foreshores was set in train. In 1893 occurred the first dangerous confrontation over land. Administrator Schmiele set out to erect a quarantine station on Oertzen Island at the edge of the harbour, where the Siar people had fruit trees planted and claimed fishing rights off the reefs. Despite the offer of compensation, the Siar refused to countenance any encroachment on this preserve, and armed themselves to take back the island by force if Schmiele persisted. In the end, with Schmiele, too, in no mood to withdraw, only the intervention of the Lutheran missionary Bergmann, and his threat to leave the Siar to their fate, stopped the Islanders from attacking. Bergmann was becoming an important intermediary in the mounting disputes between the villagers and the New Guinea Company; at least twice more he had to come between the Siar and the rifles of the Company police to prevent violence.[11]

To the villagers around Madang it was soon apparent that the German settlers could not be Maclay's brothers from Anut. Since the Germans obviously possessed a superior culture—and firearms—the people contrived to resist them in their own way, by remaining as independent of the European economy as possible. Marketing produce and artefacts brought them a satisfactory standard of living, and they refused to enlist as plantation labourers, preferring work done in their own gardens at their own pace. They were also able to prevent the Company from restricting the prices they demanded for food supplies and ethnologica by exploiting new arrivals and visitors to the area who were willing to pay higher prices. In a certain sense, the Europeans were the economically weaker people in the 1890s, for they needed increasing supplies of native produce to feed their workers, yet they did not find a permanent or increasing demand for trade goods from the local inhabitants. A limited amount of iron and trinkets satisfied the Madang villagers' needs, the surplus being used for personal-profit trading in traditional valuables with inland tribes. Moreover, since stands of coconut were very sparse on the central coasts of the mainland, there were few resources on which to base a trading exchange of mutual advantage. By 1893 the New Guinea Company was forced to look beyond Madang for its supply of contract labour. Between 1887 and 1894 only about 600 mainlanders recruited for work locally, compared with the 2836 brought from the islands.[12]

The Company's inability to mobilise a local labour force can be traced directly to its failure to extend political control and bring as many of the mainland populations as possible within the framework of an ordered administration by direct rule. Throughout the 1880s and 1890s, the Directors in Berlin kept on insisting that the obligation of defence against internal unrest, as well as external attack, lay with the Reich, not the Company, and they looked to the imperial navy to act as a kind of mobile police force at the beck and call of officials in the protectorate. Several collisions occurred in the early years over the role of the navy and the Company's right to requisition vessels for punitive expeditions. To solve the problem this was causing in all of Germany's colonies, not just New Guinea, the Foreign Office and the German Admiralty in April 1887 set firm limits to the navy's police role and issued specific procedural instructions. As a start, captains of warships had to give adequate notice of their arrival, while the Company Governor was required to make a formal, written requisition and to take all preliminary measures necessary for any military action. But the new regulations left to the navy, not the Company, the final decision whether or not military intervention was physically possible.[13]

Since the New Guinea Company in following years continued to neglect the question of an effective security force of its own, this last clause made further arguments inevitable, especially since in many cases the naval officer was forced to make a political judgment before acting. For instance, in December 1887 Admiral Heusner of the East Asian Cruiser Squadron refused a request to punish New Guinean villagers near Cape Lambert, since there was some doubt in his mind whether they had murdered a German trader. Heusner went on to reject a similar request against people at Hatzfeldthafen, arguing that it was probable that Europeans were to blame for recent unrest, and impossible anyway for German sailors to punish a mountain-dwelling people effectively.[14]

That sailors, even marines, were not equal to the task of hunting down New Guineans frequently made captains hesitate to expose their men and ships in punitive expeditions. Some of the earliest confrontations admittedly were bloody affairs, in one case so bloody that Bismarck suppressed its publication for fear of political repercussions.[15] But only rarely did marines operating on land inflict serious punishment on New Guineans. In most cases they had difficulty even making contact, as at Kabaira in 1886. One of the problems in bringing the power of the navy to bear was the relative immobility of European-trained soldiers in very rugged country and tropical jungle, where New Guineans avoided large concentrations and movement was along narrow paths where troops were susceptible to ambush. Jungle fighting was still a relatively undeveloped skill for European troops in the late nineteenth century, and German marines were continually hampered by their uniforms and cumbersome equipment, while military formations were adopted which were more suitable to large-scale movements in open spaces.

Formidable difficulties accompanied the organisation of naval expeditions: native bearers were impossible to hire for more than a few days at a time; whites with an adequate knowledge of an area to act as guides and interpreters were scarce; above all, it was impossible to keep secret the preparations for an extensive campaign, for the report of a warship's arrival spread like wildfire and the villagers who were the object of the exercise were immediately on the watch. Even if a naval raid were launched inconspicuously, the ship was usually so large and so slow that the victims had ample time to escape to the jungle with their valuables. New Guineans lost their initial awe of warships very quickly, so that before long even artillery bombardments did not overly concern them. Around Aitape on the north coast of the mainland, villagers were known to collect unexploded artillery shells after bombardments and rework them into sago pounders, and if villages were hit by shells they could easily be rebuilt. Perhaps the epitome of contempt for the punitive power of the German navy is best expressed in the words of a New Irelander in 1890:

> What name you speak belong man-war. Man-war he all same one bloody fool, he no save kill 'em kanaka. He make fire house, never mind. He no save go bush. Kanaka he no 'fraid belong man-war. Man-war he come, kanaka he go bush alright.[16]

One man who recognised the inadequacy of the navy as police force was Fritz Rose, the Imperial Commissioner who virtually ran the colony during the interlude of imperial administration from 1889 to 1891. After surveying the New Guinea Company's record, Rose felt acutely the need to start again from scratch, to establish shipping communications, to create harbours and landing places, to cut roads and to improve relations with the inhabitants. Above all, Rose could see that the protectorate was in for serious trouble between the New Guineans and the growing German interests, especially in Astrolabe Bay, where, as he put it, the people 'feel themselves cramped; and ignorant of the existence of a regime which also protects their interests, they will be moved easily to arbitrary acts of violence in their distress'.[17]

Rose wanted to make that regime more apparent by placing New Guinean intermediaries in each settlement along the coast and in the interior bordering the mountains. He was the first official to press the New Guinea Company for a sensibly-sized police force and a sea-going vessel able to cover the protectorate; he saw plainly that the job could no longer be left to a navy restricted to short visits and coastal sorties. In the end, Rose was fighting for the establishment of a permanent imperial government as the one organisation that could tackle successfully the problems of security and development.

Neither the New Guinea Company nor the Reich was interested in Rose's solutions in the early 1890s. In April 1892 the Company returned to the administration of the protectorate, with plans for retrenchment. Several smaller stations were added to the list of those which, like Finschhafen and Hatzfeldthafen, already had been abandoned. Unprofitable plantations like Jomba, behind Madang, were also closed down. The Company then turned to the north coast to develop the area's recruiting potential, and began to encourage more positively exploration of the interior.

Exploration had been part of the Company's program from the beginning. According to its 1885 instructions, the fundamental aim of scientific expeditions was to observe if conditions in New Guinea allowed Europeans to settle and work the land and 'what modifications to domestic life in housing, clothing, nourishment and other matters would be made necessary'.[18] Explorers were ordered blithely to establish the inland borders of German New Guinea and then criss-cross the intervening land in order to choose sites for a network of inland stations. In addition, they were to keep exact diaries, in dupli-cate, with daily entries on everything noticed along the way.

To those entrusted with the task, these demands were easier made than met. Inland expeditions like that of Schrader in 1886, which was ordered to report on the 'geographical, botanical, social and economic situation of New Guinea', were a failure from the start, because parties could not obtain New Guinean guides and bearers to take them inland. Because of the fragmentation of New Guinea societies, villagers feared to venture more than a kilometre or two from their homes in case of attack by traditionally hostile neighbours. Europeans who were able to find guides and bearers often found their way inland barred by coastal groups who wanted to prevent contact with tribes of the interior, for this would mean the loss of their trading monopolies in European goods from the coast inland. Other explorers were subdued by the sheer enormity of terrain and climatic difficulties: the ill-fated Otto Ehlers and his men were reduced to eating grass in their abortive attempt in 1895 to traverse New Guinea from Salamaua, in the Huon Gulf, to the Gulf of Papua. Ehlers and his German companion were finally shot by their own bearers long before they could reach civilisation.[19]

Coastal and river explorations were much more successful. In the early days von Schleinitz journeyed round the Huon Gulf, entering the mouth of the Markham for about two and a half kilometres. He was followed in late 1886 by Captain Dreger of the New Guinea Company, who also went up the Markham and into the Labu Lakes to the west of its mouth, in the process making a name for the whites as fearsome, unfriendly creatures not to be trusted because of their inclination to shoot when excited. Von Schleinitz then navigated the Sepik to a point above present-day Ambunti. In late 1896, Lauterbach travelled from Stephansort west to the Ramu River, then down the river to its mouth on the north coast, crossing a fertile, thickly-populated floodplain well suited to agriculture on a grand scale, and encountering fierce resistance near the river's headwaters from a people who manifested no know-ledge or fear of firearms.[20]

These discoveries did not, however, give the Company new heart. By 1896 the directors had decided that it was impossible to carry out

Bismarck's original idea of *Kolonialpolitik* under Chartered Rule, at least for New Guinea, and negotiations were begun for the complete and permanent transfer of political control to the Reich. The original terms proposed gave the New Guinea Company 100 000 hectares in land, a seventy-five-year monopoly over economic development in Kaiser Wilhemsland, and four million marks in compensation if the monopoly were surrendered, but domestic opposition finally reduced these to a cash compensation of four million marks and 50 000 hectares of land to be taken up by 1902. The New Guinea Company finally relinquished control in 1899.[21] To that date the Company's record, whether of profit or administration, was an unenviable one.

Economically, the firm's achievements on the mainland were confined to the planting of some 60 000 coconut trees, only a small proportion of which were bearing, and the export of a small amount of copra and inferior tobacco, 147 tonnes and thirty tonnes respectively, in the year to April 1899. Compared with the Bismarck Archipelago, which exported 3567 tonnes of copra the same year, Kaiser Wilhelmsland was a commercial flop. As Heinrich Schnee, Imperial Magistrate from 1898 to 1900 declared cynically, the Archipelago was 'the only place where the New Guinea Company got a plus', having already earned a profit of 25 000 marks on its initial investment.[22]

On the mainland, the Germans had established a small foothold on the coast, concentrated in Astrolabe Bay where plantations had risen and fallen in the last decade of the century. Except for one station on the north coast and a few on offshore islands, the Company had been driven from its other attempted settlements. Fewer than 100 Europeans were yet settled in Kaiser Wilhelmsland. Of rivers, only the mouths of the Markham, the Gogol and the Ramu had been explored, while the Sepik had been navigated but in no way 'opened up'. In 1899 the interior was still a vast unknown, and the Germans were ignorant of what lay more than one hour from most of their stations. Little or no attempt had been made to provide the prerequisites of development: there were no public roads, no health stations, no definitive maps of land or sea routes. Furthermore, European security was still an uncertain factor in areas where New Guineans had suffered massive land alienation or abuses from the Company employees. Three instances of violence, including the murder of two Lutheran missionaries, fourteen Melanesians and a white trader at Hatzfeldthafen in 1891, were still unpunished in 1899.

No doubt the climate and topography of the mainland were very real impediments to development for the New Guinea Company, as was the sparseness of the population in the areas settled. But the firm's lack of experience in Charter imperialism, its ill-judged alienation of land, particularly around Madang, its indiscriminate and erratic retaliation against New Guineans, and its refusal to establish a viable system of internal security were all larger reasons for the Company's failure.

Most of all, the Company had ignored the New Guineans themselves as a variable in the equation of profits. The Directors sitting in Berlin considered as automatic and inevitable the 'native's' conversion to the philosophy and aspirations of European capitalism, so no definable program was drawn up to encourage a permanent economic alliance by protecting the land and culture of local groups, by redressing their grievances, or by making more equitable use of New Guinean labour. It was a short-sighted policy, for in the final analysis profits depended on the continuous availability of labour and the acquiescence of mainland New Guineans in a cash economy. Between 1895 and July 1898 the Company's workforce on the mainland dropped from 2000 to 735, and the majority of these were labourers imported from South-East Asia. The number of contract labourers in the plantation district the same year was 695, only 414 of whom were New Guineans, mostly from the Bismarck Archipelago.[23] By passive and active resistance, the local inhabitants helped to foil the New Guinea Company's ambitions on the mainland.

The Missions in Kaiser Wilhelmsland

By 1899 three Christian missions were operating on the mainland. Because they provide a dramatic contrast to the Company both in their motivation and in their acceptance by New Guineans, they deserve separate treatment.

Johann Flierl arrived at Finschhafen from Australia in July 1886 to found the Lutheran Neuendettelsau Mission to the new protectorate. Mission participation in the colonisation of New Guinea was included in the Company's program at an early stage, but Flierl was the first and, for some years, the only missionary to overcome the procrastinations of the firm and gain its support for his venture. After living for two months in Finschhafen with the firm's employees, Flierl established the first mission station at Simbang, a few kilometres east of the settlement. His reception among the Yabem people in Simbang was a mixed one: while they recognised the material advantages to be gained in the way of iron and various trade goods, they had the New Guinean's inherent fear of the stranger and the outsider. Moreover, the villagers of Simbang had seen how the Finschhafen people were crowded off their land by the coming of the Company, and they regarded Flierl's arrival as an extension of that process, particularly when, out of ignorance, he neglected to enter into any agreement with the owner of the land on which he settled.[24] Only after numerous protestations, gift exchanges and a light skirmish with Simbang's leading warrior was the station able to be set up.

The mission's troubles were far from over. Because of the recurring hostility of the local inhabitants, the continued existence of the Simbang station remained in doubt for the first year, and only the close proximity of the Company saved Flierl from being driven out. The people showed a contemptuous indifference to his teachings, regarding him either as a trader or a rich philanthropist, and he suffered a great deal from thefts of his belongings. Only very slowly, as Flierl adopted a conscious policy of setting himself apart from Company employees and their actions, did he come to be regarded as a singular type of white man: Flierl went about unarmed; he would not trade for profit; he diligently learned the local language; and he offered himself as advocate in the peoples' disputes with the Company over land, labour and women. Sensitive to local mores and the fears which the villagers had of being pushed out by the white people, Flierl had early recognised that the Company's station manager at Finschhafen, Julius Winter, was a direct threat to the possibility of coexistence with the Finschhafen people, and he joined in a campaign with Fritz Rose to have Winter removed.[25] By the time the Company abandoned Finschhafen in 1891, Flierl and the three German companions who by now were with him, had gained acceptance among the people of the Finschhafen coast, though the latter had as yet manifested no desire for conversion.

Isolation after 1891 brought its own rewards. The mission's activities were no longer compromised by the presence of a commerical enterprise and the actions of men whose primary aim was profit. With a secure base on the coast, Flierl now attempted to expand into the hinterland of Finschhafen. His success was limited at first because of perennial village divisions which stopped him from obtaining bearers willing to penetrate the interior of the Huon Peninsula. In 1892 he did reach an inland plateau 610 metres above sea level and some nineteen kilometres north-west of Simbang, which had been discovered by the Schrader expedition in 1886 and named the Sattelberg. Here Flierl built his first inland station, taking care this time to build well away from the local village so as to avoid arousing its resentment. Sattelberg, too, had to withstand the ordeal of acceptance, and thefts of Flierl's belongings grew to such proportions that he was forced to construct a palisade around the station and equip himself with a rifle. The new station was particularly resented by those people living between the coast and the plateau, since it destroyed their control over the movement of European goods into the interior, and by their constant raids on Flierl's supply trains they finally forced him to seek out another, more difficult and circuitous route to Sattelberg.

On the other hand, the inhabitants of Sattelberg itself quickly reconciled themselves to the station as a regular and more profitable pipeline for the supply of iron, beads and cloth. Though Flierl knew that he was regarded as 'a good but stupid man, endlessly rich and, as a stranger, without any rights',[26] he gradually earned the respect of the villagers by insisting on reciprocity for every service he performed, and by showing himself prepared to shoot anyone who attempted to burgle the station. In his desire to establish a reputation as a man of authority and determination Flierl was prepared to use the threat of force against stealing, though in general he rejected force as an instrument of persuasion. By 1893 so considerable had his influence become among the people of Sattelberg that they were prepared to leave their weapons at home and trust in Flierl's rifle on mission trips to the coast.[27]

The mission's control, however, remained limited well into the 1900s. Its area of influence in the hinterland depended solely on local toleration of its presence, on co-operation in providing bearers and guides, and it did not succeed for some time in preventing wars and cannibalism, or in countering the fear of sorcery. By 1900 the Neuendettelsau Mission could boast of only two adult converts, but it was infiltrating villages near Sattelberg with New Guinean youths who had accepted work and limited instruction on the mission station and who were carrying the mission's message back to the village.[28] It had also advanced much further into the territory and lives of New Guineans than had the New Guinea Company to that date.

To the other Lutheran mission in Kaiser Wilhelmsland, the Rheinische Missions Gesellschaft (Rhenish Mission), New Guinea was a stumbling block for many years, and its relations with the inhabitants and with other Europeans were far from harmonious. The first missionaries, Thomas and Eich, arrived in Finschhafen in 1887 only after protracted negotiations with the New Guinea Company. Eich surveyed Hatzfeldthafen as a site for a first mission settlement, but the hostility of the villagers persuaded him to concentrate the mission's energies further south in Astrolabe Bay. In November 1887, after the New Guinea Company had refused him land on Bilibili Island, Thomas acquired six hectares in the vicinity of Bogadjim, on the coast south of Bilibili, and the first station was founded.[29] Now began a succession of tragedies which threatened to exhaust the mission's personnel, and its reserves of spirit. Missionary after missionary arrived, only to be struck down within months of beginning work. While the Neuendettelsau Mission went ahead with its program unaffected by deaths, the Rhenish Mission lost ten of the twenty missionaries sent out to Kaiser Wilhelmsland between 1887 and 1895, more than in all her other mission fields combined: one drowned before he even reached Bogadjim; another shot himself accidentally; most died from fever.

From the beginning, the Rhenish Mission was apprehensive about race relations in the Astrolabe Bay, particularly when it became the centre of European settlement after 1891. The deteriorating situation between the Company and the New Guineans soon reflected itself in local attitudes to the missionaries. In their dealings with the people, the missionaries were constantly identified less as friends of the people than as whites seeking advantage for themselves and their compatriots on the plantations: their preaching voyages to surrounding villages, for example, were seen purely as journeys for profitable barter.[30] The mission inevitably suffered from its association with the European community as the pressure on land and the competition for local products and labour increased.

Two Rhenish missionaries, Scheidt and Bösch, were murdered at Hatzfeldthafen in 1891, at least partly because they were identified with European expansion. A Company official and sixteen Company labourers had accompanied the missionaries to Hatzfeldthafen, and this stigmatised them as supporters of the plantation settlement which had been causing so much trouble to the local residents. It is also possible that Bösch had been indiscreet enough to display openly the large collection of trade goods he had brought: resentment and covetousness were a consistent formula for New Guinea attacks.

It was Flierl's private opinion that, in this case, the Rhenish Mission had been at fault in trying to expand too quickly.[31] Indeed, the missionaries had taken every opportunity to penetrate as far inland as possible. Eich and Thomas accompanied the Schrader expedition up the Sepik in 1887; the plains of the upper Ramu appear in mission reports early in the piece; and missionaries often visited the Gogol plain inland from Bogadjim. But, in the end, the loss of personnel forced the Rhenish Mission to restrict its activity to a small crescent round Astrolabe Bay and to consolidate its presence there during the Company period. Attempts to place stations in the hinterland were thwarted by sickness and by the coastal New Guineans, who refused to share their source of special wealth with inland tribes by guiding the missionaries into the interior. Thus, by 1900, the mission had four stations and four schools in a fifty-kilometre stretch between Madang and Bongu, but only 136 pupils could be attracted from surrounding villages.[32] As yet there were no converts. The people evinced no interest in the spiritual world of the whites, no sense of spiritual need. They treated the missionaries as traders or doctors or advocates, or rich men whose obligation it was to share their wealth. As Reverend Kunze reported ruefully, their attitude was summed up by a small boy who told him the missionary was there to teach strange songs and writing, and to bind wounds: it went no further than that.[33] After 1900, this indifferent and simplistic view was replaced by a more hostile attitude to the mission, as it intensified its attacks on the secret male cults and festivities of the Madang coast area.

The third mission on the mainland was Catholic, the Society of the Divine Word (SVD, or known as 'the Mission of the Holy Ghost in Kaiser Wilhelmsland') which established itself on the north coast in 1896, at Tumleo Island in Berlinhafen. After an initial struggle with the New Guinea Company over the amount of land to be sold to them, the Mission of the Holy Ghost settled also on the mainland across from Tumleo, and, in November 1899, at Potsdamhafen in Hansa Bay. By 1900 there were six priests, six brothers and four nuns on the north-east coast of the mainland, operating schools which taught over 100 pupils reading and writing in the German language. The mission baptised its first convert in March 1900.[34] At that time, the north coast was still an untamed frontier of European settlement with a mere eight traders along a 320-kilometre stretch of coastline.

All three missions had contributed more to the pacification of the mainland by the end of New Guinea Company rule than had the Company itself. The Mission of the Holy Ghost could claim with justice that the firm's recruiting attempts on the north coast would have been fruitless without the mission's civilising influence on the inhabitants. The Neuendettelsau Mission's influence on relations around Finschhafen had the same effect in encouraging recruitment; indeed the Yabem and Kai from the Huon Peninsula were the only mainland peoples to recruit regularly for the plantations of Astrolable Bay. Mission activities had established the presence of white people further inland by 1899 than any Company station had managed. Sattelberg dramatically increased the area in which European material culture—iron, cloth, beads etc.—was known and used as a medium of exchange, and through Sattelberg contact with the interior was achieved comparatively quickly in the 1900s. Even in Astrolable Bay the Rhenish Mission had tried to encourage the local people to work regularly on the plantations. More importantly, the Rhenish Mission acted as a pressure valve for New Guineans in their relations with the whites. Part of its instructions were to press the Company to provide reservations for those villagers deprived of land, and to police the treatment of indentured labourers on the plantations; while individual missionaries like Bergmann on Siar, acted as ombudsmen for the Madang people, passing on their complaints about foreign labourers to the Company.[35]

Because of the missionary's primary concern for the quality of the New Guinean's existence, there was a conflict of interests with the New Guinea Company which occasionally resulted in a breakdown in co-operation. Both Lutheran missions were at different times accused of hindering development by trying to dissuade their flocks from enlisting as plantation labourers, though in the case of the Neuendettelsau Mission, with the number of local recruits, this was patently false. The missionaries were at times angry about the abuses practised during the recruiting process and on the plantations, such as deceptions about the length of contract, the brutality of overseers and particularly the frequency of sickness and death. These were ample reason for New Guineans to refuse recruitment of their own accord. One naval report in 1896 claimed that in Stephansort workers were dying at the rate of eighty a month. By 1898 forty to fifty Yabem people had died there, a figure which represented one-twentieth of the Yabem population.[36] Missionaries were, in fact, occasionally endangered by being identified in the minds of villagers with the death of kinsfolk on the plantations. As for the villagers of Madang and the coast southward, they were simply reluctant to tie themselves to the whites by contract. Outside the increasing loss of land which embittered them, the area supplied sufficient food, and trading, for a moderate and improved standard of living without resort to wage labour.

The New Guinea Company's accusations against the missions were, in the final analysis, an unconscious tribute to the extent to which the missions had been effective in influencing and organising New Guineans. The new imperial administration, especially under Hahl, recognised that the missions provided a solid base on which to construct the model of development anticipated for New Guinea.

Race Relations on the Coastal Frontier 1900-14

Though the New Guinea Company's privilege was whittled down considerably by the 1898 treaty with the Reich, the firm remained the major force in race relations on the mainland after 1900. In effect it retained the power to exploit and monopolise, without being as fully responsible for the political consequences of its activities as had been the case in the 1880s and 1890s. Hahl's decision to concentrate on the Bismarck Archipelago in the first years of imperial rule only reinforced the Company's predominance on the mainland.

The consequences were particularly important in Astrolabe Bay, where there was little love lost between New Guineans and the Europeans. Madang and its harbour had become by 1899 almost a no-man's land for the original inhabitants; a traveller there the same year reported that most local New Guineans appeared to have been driven back away from the coast.[37] This lack of rapport continued into the new century. Only during a drought in 1902 did Madang villagers offer themselves for plantation work, and then it was always for the more remote stations. They openly rejected the enforced government labour because it meant neglecting their gardens for a four-week period. Local roadworks were continually disrupted by people absconding from the job, and then refusing to pay the fines; in 1900 and 1903, police troops had to be quartered on Siar before the villagers would comply with orders to help in road-building.[38]

Resentment of the Europeans in Astrolabe Bay reached fever pitch in 1904, and every village from Siar to Bongu had grievances about European contact. With its reversion to a private enterprise, the New Guinea Company claimed in absolute ownership all the land which it had taken up around Madang, leaving the local inhabitants no rights or privileges except by sufferance. Hahl was reluctant to dispute the firm's tenuous ownership in court, lest he thereby hinder the colony's progress and incense influential merchant circles in Berlin, so in 1904 the administration finally accepted the Company's titular right to the 5500 hectares which comprised the site of Madang, subject to the survey of native reserves.

Between 1900 and 1904, the firm's land-clearing operations were intensified: the Scheering Peninsula and Kalibob were cleared and planted, and by 1904 plantations at Madang and nearby Jomba (which had reopened in 1900-01) spread over an area of 649 hectares.[39] As clans (especially among the Bilia and Siar) lost all their land on the islands and harbour foreshores, they were forced to rent garden plots from other clans. Added to their shame and sense of deprivation was the general resentment at the enforced roadworks, the repeated punishments for transgressions of the white people's law, and the desecration of totemic objects by road-building or plantation development. The Rhenish Mission did not help its cause by condemning the secret male cults as paganistic mumbo-jumbo and a profligate waste of time. The final aggravation was the rumour that the Germans were about to regiment local villagers even further by appointing district chiefs as agents of government.[40]

The people of Siar, Kranket, Yabob and Bilibili finally determined to put a stop to the encroachments of the whites.[41] At a *meziab* clubhouse on Bilibili, in the presence of the ancestral spirits, the influential men of the four islands drew up a plan to kill the whites living around Madang. The Siar and Bilibili people were the ringleaders; the latter were the 'patricians' of Astrolabe Bay, whose potting monopoly on the Madang coast was being threatened by European expansion. The movement also included the mainland villages of Ragetta, Bogadjim and Bongu, though they were more diffident, and decided to wait on the success of the attack; in the end Bogadjim and Bongu defected.

According to local and European reports of the plan, Siar, Kranket and Bilibili Islanders were to cross over to Madang, enter the district office (*Hauspepa*) and seize the armoury of the native police before they had a chance to react. The whites would then be dispatched by a corps of former police soldiers among the rebel villagers. Not even the missionaries were to be spared, for they were guilty of collusion with the whites, but to be sure that the white man's *tibud* would not interfere, the conspirators buried a volume of the scriptures before starting out.

The plot was well organised, even to the lengths of an alternative strategy should it be discovered prematurely. In that case, each group would take refuge with the missionaries and try to convince these indulgent men of God that they were innocent. Ironically, the missionaries themselves were the first to know of the conspiracy, for news of an uprising leaked out to the Reverend Hanke at Bongu in January 1904. He gave it no credence, but, when the rumour was repeated in February, Hanke notified Wilhelm Stuckhardt, the Madang district officer. Stuckhardt did take the matter more seriously, but so well was the secret kept that he could find no confirmation of a plot, and his only action was to arm the police on duty in Madang. When the revolt did come at last, on 16 July, it took the European community completely by surprise. Eighty armed men managed to reach a small bridge near the district office without detection, and since there were only twenty-six whites in the town, very likely they would have succeeded in their object if, at the last moment, their plan had not been betrayed by Nalon of Bilia, who was houseboy to the local doctor. Stuckhardt was able to restore order very quickly: the police secured their firearms and fired on the advancing attackers, dispersing them by land and by water; one Ragetta man was shot dead in the mêlée. Even then, most whites living in Madang remained unaware of what had occurred.

Since no European had been injured, and because he had no idea of the cause of the attempted coup, Stuckhardt did not treat the incident as war, but proceeded cautiously with an investigation. The fortuitous arrival of the naval survey vessel, SMS *Moewe*, boosted his authority, and by mid-August he was in a position to negotiate the surrender of several Siar and Ragetta ringleaders, who were promptly transported to Herbertshöhe; the Bilibili people had fled *en masse* to the Rai coast. At this stage the European community was still rather dazed by the swiftness of events and took some little time to adjust to their significance. Settlers and officials living and working in the area had always been complacent about their security, believing that the Madang people were incapable of any organisation or secrecy. The sudden realisation that they had barely eluded death, and that the plot likely encompassed the coast as far south as Bongu, threw them into a panic. In mid-August, New Guinea Company officials circulated a petition, over Stuckhardt's head, urging the Governor to take sterner measures against the guilty people.[42] Since Hahl was in Micronesia, Deputy Governor Knake arrived in Madang on 16 August, and, after being subjected to further pressure from the settler community, he declared a state of martial law. The full facts were now dragged from the people, the complicity of Bongu, Bogadjim and Bilibili was established, and Knake there and then had six of the leading conspirators executed.

The sequel was particularly disconcerting to the Rhenish Mission which, with its first convert in 1903, had been optimistic that the obstacles of past years were permanently behind them. Initially, the missionaries had refused to believe that they too had been marked for the slaughter, and for a month after the attempt the Bongu and

Bogadjim villagers encouraged them in this belief. Now their peoples' treachery was revealed. The Reverend Weber on Siar learned that his boat had been drawn high up on the shore the day of the revolt in order to prevent his escaping; Hanke at Bongu and Helmich at Ragetta learned that they were to be struck down on their stations. Everyone was demoralised by the disclosures, for it was obvious that the mission had completely misjudged its position, and that the Madang coast villagers were as alien from them in their thoughts and motivations now as they ever had been. That the revolt took place in the same year as the Herero rebellion in South-West Africa, which was being blamed partly on Rhenish Mission policies, was an added cup of bitterness. In weariness and disgust, the Madang missionaries petitioned their Barmen headquarters to give up New Guinea as a thankless field of thorns.[43]

The Madang revolt revealed that the imperial government's approach to security on the mainland was based on false premises. The people were not necessarily 'docile' and 'good-natured' towards all things European, and the large plantation companies, far from guaranteeing security, had helped to undermine it through their unrelenting pressure on native resources. The government's response was to extend direct rule to Madang at the end of 1904, with the organisation of the first village groups and the appointment of *luluais*; by 1907 there were eleven in the Madang district.[44] The head tax was introduced the same year.

The Germans then focused their attention on the north coast, a thickly-populated area, where villages of 400 to 500 people promised a valuable supply of plantation labour, and where local acts of resistance had coincided with the Madang revolt. In October 1906, a full district station was established at Aitape on the west side of Berlinhafen, under Hans Rodatz, an early employee of the New Guinea Company. The coastal tribes in the immediate vicinity of the station resisted the new invasion so sternly that Hahl several times had to send Rodatz police reinforcements. Though the Aitape coast technically was subjugated by mid-1911, German control remained incomplete until the war, and Hahl was never able to introduce the head tax to the area. The Germans did secure the dividend they had been looking for in the first place: a steadily increasing number of labour recruits; by 1913, ten per cent of all new recruits in the protectorate came through the Aitape lists.[45]

But the mountain hinterland behind Aitape remained closed to the recruiters. In the constant feuding between coast and interior, where a trip to the sea could result in abuse, theft and murder, few inland inhabitants could be enticed to try the German labour lines.

Meanwhile, around Madang in the years after 1904, direct rule was proving to be an inadequate solution to questions of pacification and peaceful racial relations. Instead of beginning a new era of accommodation and co-operation, the failure of the 1904 revolt and the loss of nine men (three more Siar were executed in 1904) led to several years of passive resistance by the Madang people.

The vindictive attitude of the settlers following the affair, and the continuing failures of German land policy, kept the largely-dispersed groups bitter against the European presence. The government had been quick to realise that land was at the heart of the 1904 uprising, and the same year Hahl signed an agreement with the New Guinea Company which provided for a proper survey of the Jomba plains and the excision of reserves for the people of Madang (one hectare per head of population). Moreover, the villagers were guaranteed fishing rights, their dwelling places, and the plantations they occupied at the time of survey.[46] Unfortunately the 'time of survey' receded further and further into the future. It still had not been carried out fully by 1910, a situation which the Company in defence attributed to a dearth of surveyors with qualifications measuring up to government standards. Such 'civilised' niceties were lost on the Madang villagers, especially as they were regularly accused during these years of trespassing on Company property when they collected produce from trees planted before the Company's 'purchases', and when they used traditional clay deposits which lay in Company plantation areas.

In response, the Madang people channelled their continuing resentment into a frame of religious belief centred on one of their creation myths, and designed to rationalise the defeat of 1904 in New Guinean terms and exorcise its effects. In a subtly modernised form, the myth explained that colonial rule was the product of a stronger magic ordained by the deities. The white people had been given a superior material culture, including the firearms used to overcome the villagers in 1904, after the New Guineans themselves had rejected it in favour of their canoes and spears. However, the myth held out the hope of a better future, in which the deities would return to distribute the 'Cargo' more equitably and enable the indigenous races to fight the whites.[47] In a separate version reported by the Rhenish Mission, the deity had assured several Madang villagers that the whites had misused the guns and bullets given to them, and that retribution was certain. To have the whites disappear from their lands, the people needed only to shake their heads, or have a certain Catholic priest 'make a paper'.[48]

The common belief expressed in these Cargo myths encouraged passive resistance in the area for eight years. Until 1912, the Madang people reacted to continuing deprivations by obeying the government where necessary but obstructing it whenever they could. People in the coastal villages from Sek (north of Madang) to Bongu, and on Dampier and Bagobag islands, which were drawn into the administrative system in 1908-09, had to be forced to complete their labour on the roads even after the head tax was introduced, and 'wearying' police expeditions were always taking place to round up absconders. The government *luluais*, of which there were sixty-seven in the Madang district by late 1911, found it almost impossible to have their authority recognised or German instructions carried out, and most had to be provided with two police assistants in order to get anything done.[49]

A good example is Nalon, from Bilia, the man who in 1904 had informed the Germans of the plot against them. He had done so from an opportunist, if enterprising, motive, because the revolt had threatened to destroy the privilege he enjoyed of riding to the Rai coast on the New Guinea Company schooner to trade. But his collaboration with the Germans did nothing to solve the crisis which faced Bilia, namely the loss of all its land, nor did Nalon possess any natural leading status in his village. The Bilia made it clear that they hated the whites, and had little but contempt for Nalon as *luluai*. In the end, his impotence forced the administration to appoint another in his stead. Unlike Nalon, most of the Madang inhabitants avoided contact with the European economy, continuing to reject wage labour for the European plantations that occupied their lands. In 1906, only twenty-six of the 534 mainland recruits of the New Guinea Company came from Madang, and two years later the number had fallen to eight out of 497.[50] By that time it was an open secret that 'away with the white man' was the catch cry of New Guineans around Madang.

Included among the whites in the minds of the Madang villagers were the Lutheran missionaries, who, despite their despair in 1904, had remained to carry on their work. Yet their influence grew only slowly and their successes remained modest. The first convert did not appear until the end of 1903, and by then the mission's four schools had enticed only an additional six pupils in four years. No converts came forward in the year of the revolt. After 1904, the Rhenish Mission was hemmed in from the north as the Catholic SVD Mission occupied Alexishafen, while lack of personnel prevented it from breaking out of the coastal crescent from Bongu to Madang. By 1908, the Rhenish Mission's 63 converts compared very unfavourably with the Neuendettelsau Mission's 1300, and the 1062 of the SVD, while in 1910-11 the number of Rhenish converts actually declined from 109 to 83.[51] In 1906 there had been a dramatic turning point in villages removed from the immediate vicinity of Madang. It had started in Bongu, where the people reported to the missionaries that they had been visited by a strange 'man from heaven', who urged them to burn the images and instruments associated with the pre-contact cults and to carry the good news of peace and friendship to other villages.[52] The Bogadjim and Bilibili people, who had returned to the Astrolabe coast the same year, joined in the movement, and there were scenes of confusion as the women, traditionally barred from the cult ceremonies on pain of death, were shown the richly-decorated masks, the carved bullroarers and whistles, only to cower in anguish and run trembling to hide.

None of this, however, made any impression at the centre of Madang, where the village elders kept up a belligerent opposition to mission teaching and its attempts to reduce the influence of the male cults. Significantly, the Cargo belief had affirmed the intrinsic value of these cults by referring to a deity who claimed to have 'bought' the cults and their secrets from the New Guineans and actually to practise them himself. The missionaries and the few converts were harassed at every opportunity. At Ragetta and Siar (the centre of the most bitter antipathy), sorcery was used to try and induce the death of the leading convert, Malai. The ringleader in this campaign was Sabu, himself a former convert and *luluai*, who finally forced the Germans to remove Malai to Herbertshöhe for his own good. In 1909 Sabu tried to have the site of the village removed altogether from the vicinity of the mission station. Two years later, in 1911, the Rhenish Mission felt compelled to strike twenty-seven nominal Christians from its lists in the Madang area. Even Malai, who had been the pioneer convert in Madang and the great hope of the missionaries, failed their stern test of acceptability, and he was abandoned when caught in 'pagan' costume, taking part in a 'pagan' dance.[53]

The Madang people were astute in playing off mission and Government against each other. If services were regularly attended, it was only to maintain the friendship of the missionaries in case of a confrontation with the regime which the Madang people could not handle alone. Yet the New Guineans were quick to complain to Hahl, on his occasional visits, of mission coercion to abandon their cult festivities and of physical abuse by individual missionaries, abuses which were not always figments of the imagination. The Rhenish Mission suffered more than once from serious indiscretions by its members. The Reverend Helmich was guilty on one occasion of flogging several Ragetta villagers who were trying to undermine the mission's position, and at another time he outraged the village elders by using an old *meziab* cult instrument to chase pigs.

The worst case was that of the Reverend Weber, who was responsible for the permanent ill-will against the mission at Siar after the departure of Bergmann. Weber was young and impetuous, and a missionary whose commitment bordered on the fanatical. Suitably convinced of his mission to civilise and discipline the New Guineans, he once described himself as 'a policeman on my right side and only on the left a missionary'.[54] Weber took it upon himself to administer beatings to Siars, and he did not hesitate to chastise the German administration for its defects in front of his congregations. His behaviour was not only foolhardy but dangerous in circumstances where the inhabitants were awaiting only the right moment to reassert themselves. In fact, Weber's acts were the antithesis of most of the ideals for which the Rhenish Mission stood, and in 1909 the mission authorities intervened and dismissed him from his post.

That did not stop events from coming to a head once more in 1912. Plantation clearing had been carried on uninterruptedly since 1904, and by 1912 the Madang people were crowded on all sides by planting interests of various kinds. North of Madang, Sarang plantation had been purchased in 1910-11, and the Mission of the Holy Ghost was now solidly entrenched at Sek, with a plantation of over 1000 hectares and a workforce numbering 520.[55] The mission developed the harbour facilities, ran a sawmill, and was in the process of constructing an extensive system of roads. South of Madang, the New Guinea Company was now free to develop the Jomba Plains after escaping litigation over their ownership. Berghausen, the zealous district officer of Madang, had tried in 1910 to establish the legitimacy of the original Kubary contracts, but his challenge to the Company was thwarted by Hahl, who advised him to drop the legal investigation.[56] To Hahl, viewing this stage of Madang's development, the real question was not the legality of the Company's land acquisitions south of Madang—for the sake of the area's future, that situation had to be accepted—but the question of providing sufficient reserves for local villagers so that they could continue to subsist side by side with Germany's planting empire.

But reserves were not emerging quickly either, particularly for the inhabitants of Madang, which remained the area of fastest growth for European business. In 1911 alone, three new plantation concerns opened in the area, and preparations were being made to divide the Meiro Plains among another four in 1912.[57] Negotiations with the Bilia over the Meiro Plains, and with Siar over the purchase of 1200 hectares between Madang and Sek by Norddeutsche Lloyd, suffered from the same delays as had the survey of the Jomba Plains. Both the government surveyor and the Rhenish Mission warned the authorities that this was unsettling the people badly. The Reverend Helmich, perhaps with the trauma of 1904 in his mind, was far from sanguine about the possible consequences:

> . . . The ill feeling of local natives concerning loss of land, which is sometimes veiled and covert, and sometimes openly declared, makes it more and more clear that the resentment against the Europeans is increasing enormously and that the temper of the people is like a boiling crater. Serious consideration must be given as to whether an eruption is to be feared at an opportune moment.[58]

Nothing was ever substantiated about what next occurred, but it appears that a new, wide-ranging plot to kill the Madang Europeans began to be discussed about June of 1912. The lines of the new conspiracy resembled those of the old, with one new precaution added: this time the conspirators would wait for the night before the steamer *Koblenz* was due to depart, because they knew that the settlers would be drowsy or asleep from the effects of heavy drinking. Villagers would then attack government headquarters and seize the arms, and so be free to kill the Europeans systematically, area by area.[59]

Whether the movement ever got beyond discussion is difficult to say. After the warnings from various sides about the peoples' agitation, the district officer began to get suspicious and searched for signs of disaffection. To his mind, he found them in the unaccustomed vehemence with which the male cults were being performed and the increased interest which villagers were showing in the whereabouts of European living quarters. Extra sentries were posted on Cutter Island and Bilia, and the main watch on the administration building strengthened, all of which quietened the villagers. But the European community since 1904 had lived with the conviction that the New Guineans would try again, and the first sign of uncertainty tended to panic them. There was a false alarm on 21 August. In response, the Europeans armed themselves, the police troops were made ready, and suspects were rounded up.

From this point, German sources rely entirely on native witnesses who suddenly began to testify that there had been an anti-white plot, and that several groups were involved. Ironically enough, the ringleaders this time were supposedly the Bilia people, but the Siar, Panutibun, Ragetta and some Bilibili people were also alleged to be involved. A court was hastily convened, and a great deal of conflicting evidence was brought forward by hostile and friendly witnesses. In the end, the board of officials, which included members from the Lutheran Mission, decided that there was sufficient evidence to substantiate the allegation of a plot against the whites. Pressed on by the nervous settlers, and anxious to remove once and for all the last obstacle to European security and economic expansion, the district officer, Scholz, banished the accused groups from the area, some to the north coast behind Cape Croiselles, the others to the Rai coast, while sixteen of the suspected ringleaders were transported to Herbertshohe. This signalled the final disarray of the Madang people, and the triumph of the planting and trading community.

The Madang 'revolts' are not easy to categorise as revolts. There are a number of features which weaken the argument that the people of Madang were ready to destroy all things European and revert to their traditional existence. Firstly, the 1904 venture had been a very tentative affair. At least two villages defected at the last moment, while the would-be rebels did not even offer token resistance after being found out. Secondly, there is no evidence to prove that the 1912 'conspirators' actually were planning and organising a rebellion. The 'plot' may simply have been an extension of the Cargo myths which had sustained people since 1904, the belief that the time had come for the deities to remove the whites from New Guinea, but to retain for New Guineans the European way of life and access to its wealth. Significantly, a naval report about Madang at the time mentions that the Madang people were redistributing European roles among themselves, choosing who would be police master or magistrate in the new world, who would live in the white people's houses, and who would 'marry' the white women.[60]

On the other hand, conditions around Madang did lend themselves to violence and physical resistance by the villagers. Not only had they lost most of their land to Company plantations but, unlike the Tolai in the Gazelle, they also lacked the resources to sell to the Europeans and establish a prosperous trading exchange. Violence was more likely in a situation where the people had no prospects of advancing themselves through adaptation to the European economy.

The only exception to the racial confrontations which prevailed on mainland coasts during these years lay in the Huon Peninsula. On its coasts and in the immediate hinterland, New Guineans and the only Europeans in the area, the Neuendettelsau missionaries, had managed to cultivate a tolerant relationship based on mutual respect and reciprocal behaviour. Using two local languages, Jabêm and Kâte, the mission was able to expand from its two mainland stations and two converts in 1899, to eleven stations with 1300 baptised converts and 4000 to 5000 nominal adherents in 1908, stretched along the south coast of the Huon Peninsula to Cape Arkona (Bukaua) and Malalo (Salamaua), and deep into the Herzog Ranges. In addition, the mission followed the example of the Catholics in the north of Kaiser Wilhelmsland, and in 1908 purchased the New Guinea Company's remaining 1000 hectares of land at Finschhafen, a move as much designed to keep the Catholic SVD Mission out as to contribute to the Neuendettelsau Mission's upkeep.[61] The absence of large-scale European businesses in the Huon Peninsula after 1892 explains much of the success which the Neuendettelsau Mission enjoyed in race relations.

Its evangelical success was the result of a bold approach to conversion adopted after 1899. For many years Flierl and the Reverend Vetter had talked of organising their preaching work and the new converts in a way that was sensitive to local social structures and, more importantly, to the ideas with which contacted groups interpreted their world. The Reverend Christian Keysser, who arrived in 1899, laid the base for official policy by articulating for the first time the total social philosophy of the Kâte and Hube peoples, and laying down guidelines for working with them.[62] Keysser reasoned that seeking individual conversions was counter-productive, for native culture and social relationships were so integrally connected with the traditional religion that individual converts to Christianity would experience ostracism and social and spiritual isolation within their communities. In the end they would be unable to withstand the pressures from their fellows and must fall back into the old waysm The mission's solution was to move out into the villages and concentrate on substituting a social organisation based on the Gospel for the old social and religious life. By building Christianity into the new society, no individual should feel isolation within the group. There would be a minimum of dislocation and, the mission hoped, a more fundamental *metanoia*.

The immediate product of this approach was a mass movement around Sattelberg in 1904, when, amid scenes of the greatest drama, villagers brought cult objects and burnt them on pyres, and veteran sorcerers came forward to confess their past deeds. A severe earthquake in September 1906 rendered fortuitous assistance to the missionaries' campaign on behalf of the supernatural. Crowds of 700 to 800 attended the baptisms as the movement spread, and strong millennial expectations accompanied it.[63]

The absence of any developed business on the southern mainland (though the New Guinea Company was holding on to more than 4700 hectares of land at Lae) meant that until 1906-07 the administration did not concern itself with the area, leaving it to the peaceful ministrations of the Neuendettelsau Mission. The mission had created a secure base along the coasts and in the hinterland of the Huon Peninsula, from which it could open up the interior ranges and the vast trough-like valley of the Markham River, that disgorges itself at a furious rate into the sea at the head of the Huon Gulf. The mission's way inland had been barred continually by the predatory raids of the Wampar, or Lae Womba as they were called by the Germans, a warrior people of almost legendary ferocity whose ancestral home was on the Watut, a south-western tributary of the Markham. Late in the nineteenth century, they began pushing east towards the Markham mouth, driving groups, especially the Ahi people, before them, settling the territory north of the river, and then preying on the Lae people, who were a mixture of Kawa speakers from Bukaua and Ahi refugees from the south bank of the Markham.[64]

A government police expedition ventured up the Markham in 1905 to contact the Wampar and demonstrate the dangers of trifling with Europeans. But the Wampar got in the first blow: they attacked the party as it bivouacked overnight on the banks of the river, and the expedition was forced to retreat with three Europeans and three police soldiers seriously wounded.

Success encouraged the Wampar to intensify their raids, striking ever closer to the coast, and in three attacks on scattered Lae villages in 1907 they killed over 100 people, a result probably made easier by the loss of many young Lae men from the warrior ranks to the plantation recruiters. The Lae, scattered and dispirited from constant raiding, were finally reduced to sleeping on the beach at Cape Arkona to the east, and they refused point-blank to return to 'place belong plenty fight'. Their old settlements were scenes of desolation, with houses razed to the ground, gardens laid waste, trade boxes smashed open and their contents strewn around. Two further expeditions were organised by the Germans, but their power of retaliation was restricted by the modest size of the mainland police force and the demands being made on them by unrest in Aitape and on the north-east coast. Lack of finance ruined any idea of a permanent station in the area in 1907-08.

The Neuendettelsau Mission, whose interests in the security of the Markham Valley were the most immediate, was striving meanwhile to make peaceful contact with the Wampar. In April 1909, the Reverend Stefan Lehner, accompanied by the ethnologist Paul Neuhauss and two other missionaries, mounted a party to penetrate up the Markham into Wampar territory. For three days they made their way upstream, struggling against the current and constantly on the watch lest their guides and bearers desert in their terror at entering the enemy's lair. No Wampar were sighted but Lehner left a gift of red cloth, tobacco, a knife, an axe and a necklace of dogs' teeth on a tree branch before the party returned to the coast. Two weeks later, the Lae excitedly presented the missionaries with a wooden sword from the Wampar, who had offered to make friendship. It was the turning of the corner. Some days later, the Wampar and the Lae held a giant feast at which they exchanged 'hostages' as sureties for the peace. In June, Lehner was able to visit the area and exchange gifts with the watchful but jubilant warriors. Two years later, in 1911, the Neuendettelsau Mission founded its first station among the Wampar.[65]

Unfortunately, the new peace and goodwill did not prevail throughout the Markham Valley. Attacks on the coast had ceased, but unrest continued in the valley itself, with repeated clashes occurring between the Wampar and the Azera, a larger offshoot of the same people. In January 1911, a European Bird of Paradise hunter, Richards, was killed by Wampars in the Garagos-Wampit area west of the Markham mouth. Richards was the victim of his own mistiming. The village in which he sought overnight accommodation was in the midst of celebrating a feast to the ancestors, and, since Richards neglected to offer a friendly gift on his arrival, the villagers took him for an intruder and a harmful spirit. The logical conclusion in terms of their own culture was to cancel out his influence by killing him.[66] Two years before, on the middle Watut, people from Babwaf village who had never seen a white person, attacked Wilhelm Dammköhler, the old New Guinea hand, successful explorer and prospector who was searching for alluvial gold. Dammköhler died from arrow wounds. His companion, Rudolf Oldörp, fearfully wounded, lived to tell the story by dragging himself onto a raft and sailing down to the mouth of the Markham.

In 1909 Hahl had refused to send an expedition to avenge Dammköhler's death, since he did not have the money to intervene in places which could not yet be brought under permanent control. By 1911 this had changed: large punitive expeditions were now penetrating west of the Markham in the interests of permanent security. When war broke out in 1914, a census patrol had already been made of eighty villages in the north of the Huon Gulf.[67]

At that stage, the Huon Gulf was the only region where the Germans could boast of a limited control further than ten to fifteen kilometres inland. Most of this was the product of the Neuendettelsau Mission's peaceful labouring in the area since the 1880s, for while government expeditions impressed villagers with the power and efficiency of the Reich, it was the missionaries who inspired trust and acceptance of many of the white people's ways. The mission's policy of communal conversion brought about a veritable revolution in living patterns in some areas. By 1914 the Kâte people in the vicinity of Sattelberg had, of their own initiative, introduced new legal sanctions and procedures into their social system, and were restructuring the division of labour within the larger, regional parish community that had been formed. By 1914, also, the mission had a permanent missionary at Lae, had pushed its way to the 1000-metre-high Cromwell Mountains deep in the Huon Peninsula, and was making preparations for a mission presence among the cannibalistic Azera people, over a hundred kilometres from the Huon coasts.

As for the rest of the protectorate, one can only assess Germany's final hold over the multifarious communities of New Guineans by looking at the stages of contact region by region. From this point of view, the Bismarck Archipelago seems to fare better than Kaiser Wilhelmsland. At the outbreak of war, the Gazelle Peninsula (excluding the area beyond the Varzin and the outer Bainings) and northern New Ireland were, to all intents and purposes, areas where physical security was no longer the first consideration of settlers and administration. Large district confederations were being formed, and were concentrating on the demands of economic development—public works, education, agricultural improvement, and technological innovations like copra driers, wagons and horses. Elsewhere in the Archipelago, rather crude frontier conditions were the order of the day, conditions which meant that the Government still accepted with resignation the occasional murder of careless Europeans. The worst was over in the older areas of conflict like the Admiralties and northern Bougainville, but security of life and of property here were not yet guaranteed. Meanwhile, there were vast areas in New Britain and Bougainville which were completely uncontacted at the outbreak of war.

On the mainland, north of the Huon Peninsula, the nominal control which the Germans claimed over the entire coastline amounted to little more than a record of formal contact and a thin veneer of direct rule. The authority of the Reich was hardly acknowledged beyond the coastal enclaves of European settlement—Aitape, Potsdamhafen-Monumbo and Madang—and their immediate hinterlands.

At Madang, racial relations altered dramatically after the exile of the 1912 'conspirators'. Having achieved nothing by active or passive resistance, the Madang peoples tried a new tack towards the millennium which they believed was imminent. This time they chose limited co-operation with the new culture. Their strategy was reflected in a startling increase in recruitment for European plantations (from 619 in 1910 to 1955 in 1913) and in a more forthcoming attitude to the Lutheran Mission. Conversions were made thick and fast. The Siar-Ragetta people returned from exile in 1914, after the Australian occupation, and immediately started to fill the churches; fifty people soon reported for baptism. The number of Christians in the area of Madang (including villages inland) multiplied thirteen times in the five or six years after 1914.[68]

Conversion offered a new rallying point and created a new hope: the hope that through conversion New Guineans might gain access to the white people's material wealth and self-confidence. Conversion was also a new, more subtle form of resistance to social disintegration, and carried with it the desire to show Europeans that New Guineans were not just primitive savages. In all this there were explicit millenarian overtones, for these villagers of the Madang area conceived of the new religion as the ritual equivalent of their traditional beliefs and the long-sought-for secret to the Cargo. After 1914 this led to the development of a 'secular' political organisation with its own cult leader.[69]

Madang and the Huon Peninsula were exceptions to the general situation on the mainland. The Sepik district, with nearly one-quarter of the total population of the protectorate, was quite uncontrolled in 1914, except for the immediate vicinity of the Aitape station. Still an uncertain quantity was the north-east coast, where hostile tribes had been pushed back into the mountains as the Germans occupied the coast. Completely unknown, though suspected, were the vast populations and the sophisticated agricultural systems of the New Guinea Highlands.

The nominal peace on the coasts was regularly disrupted by the invasions of mountain tribes. One of the unforeseen effects of coastal pacification, and of the recruitment of able-bodied warriors, was increased aggression from inland or mountain tribes, which the Germans found hard to counter. The hinterland of Aitape, the territory inland from Potsdamhafen and Bogia, and the Rai coast ranges were the most troublesome. Hahl did make an effort to influence the Sepik interior by establishing a staging point for recruitment at Angoram on the lower length of the river in 1913. And on the Rai coast the regime tried to stop mountain people preying on coastal villages in a series of fiercely-fought battles in 1910, but the final effect was only to drive the offending tribes deeper into the Finisterre Range.

In all these attempts to impose a physical control over the communities of their far-flung protectorate, the Germans relied heavily on the colonial police force. If Hahl was unable to secure law and order in the German manner when and where he wanted it, part of the reason was the deficiencies of his police force. Though the largest in the Pacific empire, numbering nearly 1000 men by 1914, the New Guinea police remained too small to handle unrest throughout the protectorate, particularly when unrest occurred in different areas simultaneously.

In 1904 the Bainings massacre and its repercussions highlighted the ease with which a surprise New Guinean attack might overcome even a major centre of European settlement where a station's complement of forty or fifty police was absent on security duties in other parts. The Madang revolt the same year very nearly succeeded, in spite of the fact that the police were on active sentry duty. Again, in late 1910, when news of the Ponape insurrection reached New Guinea, most of the better-trained police were in Morobe, Madang or Aitape, or on the Anglo-German border expedition, and fewer than 100 of the newest recruits and inferior soldiers could be mustered as reinforcements for the besieged colony. The most serious deficiency was revealed in 1913, when the entire expeditionary force had to be mobilised to deal with an uprising in southern New Ireland, and many of the local police contingents were also drawn in, leaving the rest of the protectorate practically bereft of military protection.

The inadequacy of numbers was overcome in some places by recruiting local auxiliaries to assist in punitive operations. Auxiliaries played an important role in the 1893 war in the Gazelle Peninsula, in Bougainville and in various campaigns on the mainland, but their employment was always a risk since they could not be controlled effectively in the jungle, and indiscriminate killing was the occasional result. The conditions under which the police were used also impaired their effectiveness as agents of law and order. When a German district officer was opening up new country, the police were often the first people to go into an uncontacted village, thereby setting the standard for subsequent relations, and there are documented cases of intimidation, rape and pillage by native police, and of their use as press gangs to obtain labourers.[70]

This was a particular risk with the expeditionary troops, a contingent of over 100 men developed out of the existing force as an instrument to help open up new territory and lay the groundwork of 'pacification' for civilian administrations. In Hahl's 1914 three-year plan, the expeditionary troops were envisaged as an increasingly essential arm of the government, as a 'vigorous' means of bringing the vast interior within the German orbit. Though this hardly constitutes the establishment of a standing army, it is clear that Hahl's plan would have leaned ever more heavily on military pressure and forceful pacification. Only time would have told how such a program would have been received by the New Guineans, especially in the Highlands.

The problems of imposing control aside, time ran out for the Germans in 1914. At that stage, relations on the mainland remained poised on a thin line between uneasy peace and open war. The Germans had reached a stage of partial control best defined by a later military observer as:

> Where the *luluais* will respond to a summons to appear at a government station, but where it is not altogether advisable for traders and others to wander about without protection, where tax payments are made only here and there, and at irregular intervals, and where the people are prone to disregard orders received from the District Officer through their *luluais*.[71]

Where every village was a law unto itself, and few larger, regional ties existed, the Germans could not be sure of any areas except the very oldest coastal settlements occupied by the planters and missionaries. Security depended on the acquiescence of New Guineans in the presence and practices of Europeans. Even in a place like the east coast of the Gazelle Peninsula, where the Germans were most dominant, peace was less the product of superior Western technology than the voluntary realisation by the native people that they stood to gain most, with minimal discomfort, from economic co-operation with the colonial economy.

Anatomy of Pacific Island Resistance

8

Resistance
Conservatism and Innovation

To Europeans of the nineteenth century, violence and conquest were inevitable features of colonialism. As we have seen, a man like Governor Hahl could dismiss repeated collisions with New Guineans as un-avoidable in the continuing conflict between 'culture' and 'savagery'. In the Pacific, the German regimes confronted Island societies which had demonstrated emphatically their capacity to resist European interference. As a result, Samoans, Ponapeans and New Guineans were treated at various times with caution, as very real threats to the stability of the German Pacific empire. The object of the following chapter is to show that the Pacific Island answer to German rule ranged through varying degrees of accommodation and opposition, dictated by a wide variety of considerations, and only in a few isolated cases did it amount to rebellion against German hegemony.

The three Island societies with which we have been dealing were receptive to the presence of Europeans, and even to limited foreign suzerainty. Most Pacific societies found advantage and profit in the arrival of the white people, for they brought new metals, tools and skills, as well as strange and inviting ornament. Many of the earliest encounters with European explorers ended in bloodshed, but there were generally good reasons, either the pressure put upon scant area and food resources, or European ignorance of local custom.[1] Seldom was such conflict a case of simple, undefined tribal resistance, or of total and irreconcilable opposition to the whites and their ways.

Most societies made an effort to find the basis for a coexistence of mutual profit. Beach communities of resident Europeans flourished in all corners of the Pacific long before the Powers annexed their empires. Later colonists were also accepted, and, depending on their willingness to acknowledge local norms of belief and custom, an acceptable level of co-operation and exchange was usually worked out, as with the London Missionary Society in Samoa before 1900, or Ralum plantation in New Guinea before 1893.

Accommodation did not prevent the Pacific Islanders from attempting to bargain with a colonial regime, or from using limited opposition as a political tactic to get their own way. In many cases the actions which Germans interpreted as laziness, deceit or wilful obstruction, were efforts by local elites to control change, to create a balance between new demands on the socio-political order and established patterns of political life, status and social solidarity. For example, to call the movement for a Samoan co-operative in 1904 'very little other than a manipulation of the Samoan national trait to periodically rise in political upheavals every five or ten years', as one later New Zealand administrator did,[2] is a myopic political judgment bordering on wilful prejudice. The *Oloa* movement was not a blind, irrational adventure, nor was it a simple economic response to shifts in the world market. Organised by the leading chiefs and speakers in Mulinu'u, its aim was to create a power base for these chiefs against the policies of the Governor, and to reinforce the *Malo*'s traditional claims to authority; in other words, to restore the traditional system of political dynamics.

But to explain it as a conservative Samoan *response* designed to perpetuate old rights and freedoms is to see only one side of the coin. The *Oloa* was also an example of the creative realignment of institutions and behaviour patterns, of an endeavour to synthesise old values with the new. Through the *Oloa*, Samoan elites were trying to adapt the native copra industry to the vagaries of the world market. Copra production had been a critical feature of indigenous economic life for more than a decade. Throughout the entire German period Samoan plantings (covering more than fifty per cent of the planted area of the group) continued to supply the vast bulk of copra exported from Samoa; copra sales enabled the Samoans to pay head taxes and mission contributions regularly without having to resort to wage labour for Europeans. The importance of the industry explains why falling copra prices in 1903-04 should so concern many Samoans and attract them to the idea of their own co-operative. Samoans' commercial expectations may have been unrealistic, and their lack of expertise in the management of a co-operative would have been a liability at first, but neither of these impediments diminishes the imaginativeness of this attempt to update the Samoan copra industry in line with the fluctuations of a world market. In seeking to compete with modern European commerce in its own idiom, the *Cumpani* would have allowed Samoans to shape their economic life under colonial rule.

There are other, equally pertinent examples of constructive opposition in the German Pacific. One is the unrest which Nanpei engineered on Ponape in 1908, designed at once to strengthen his own position in traditional society and yet to secure for Ponapeans, or at least for some Ponapeans, a greater share of political power under the Germans through Nanpei's 'advisory council'. In New Guinea, the Tolai people provide another case. They refused to be assimilated into a planters' wage-economy but, instead, enthusiastically developed a system of cash cropping which enabled them to rationalise copra production along Western lines.

The combination of progressive and conservative aims in these various ventures demonstrates what one historian in the African context has termed the 'ambiguity towards modernisation' manifested by the peoples of developing countries.[3] The desire for European material goods, new technology and institutional improvements was balanced by distaste for many aspects of European laws, morality and living patterns. Conversion to Western values was not automatic, as many Europeans anticipated, nor was it complete. Rather, the history of colonial penetration shows that at different times, and according to their reading of the situation and the resources at their disposal, Pacific Islanders made conscious acts of selection and rejection of European culture.

Local choice becomes as important a category of explanation as European dynamism. Proto-co-operatives, advisory councils, cash cropping, payment of head taxes, even Cargo cults were all original responses to colonial rule. Yet there are as many convincing examples of the hold of tradition on societies undergoing social change: the Tolai refused to jettison shell money as a status indicator amongst themselves despite their immersion in a cash economy; the Ponapeans continued to make regular votive offerings to their High Chiefs even after the German reforms released them from the obligation and the sacrifices it entailed; all three societies refused to accept the European work ethic: only a handful of Melanesian labourers adopted wage labour as a permanent way of life during German times, and the Samoans looked on regular plantation work as fit only for serfs.

Sometimes such assertions of the right to contribute to a changing society took the form of militant discontent, even intimidation and force. But where the Germans refused to recognise Pacific Islanders, especially Pacific Island leaders, as political equals, no other course existed. There were no official organisations to express protest and opposition. Local government structures set up in each colony were designed to transmit executive orders to the people, and only incidentally operated in the opposite direction. This was logical to the Germans. The primary concern of imperial administration was to encourage the economic productivity, not the political development of colonial populations; to create a prosperous peasantry in the employment of imperial designs. Thus any movement of dissent was defined as illegitimate. Moreover, because of the assumption that a subject people would automatically resist conquest, signs of opposition on the part of Pacific Islanders tended to be interpreted as wholesale rebellion against the very idea of German rule.

These, of course, were common reactions among late nineteenth century colonial regimes. Only with the era of decolonisation did the rhetoric change: colonial opposition movements became respectable and their aspirations towards independence were accepted as reasonable. But in German times, Pacific Islanders were forced to resort to expedients like the Vaimea incident, the *mau e pule*, the 1908 campaign in Ponape to try to frighten the regime into conceding some form of compromise. Resistance or opposition in this sense was merely an extension of ordinary political processes, a calculated tactic with limited objectives.

None of this is to deny that there *were* instances of rebellion against colonial subjection, of refusal to submit to the Germans. Herbertshöhe, Madang, the Varzin Mountains and the Baining Range were all the scenes of large-scale violence against whites in German New Guinea. As well, the situation in Ponape did produce finally what can only be termed a revolt.

To generalise about these protests is difficult because of the varying stages of colonial penetration and the widely differing historical circumstances in each area. By and large, they were the product of overwhelming frustration at German pretensions: the tendency to make demands and exploit resources without reference to those affected, or without offering some form of compensation. Many New Guinean groups, for instance, were prepared to accept German sovereignty on New Guinean terms. But they refused to admit the extreme assumptions of colonialism—that the colonies existed for unrestrained profit-making at the expense of their inhabitants. Europeans made revolutionary demands on New Guineans, depriving them of their land, requisitioning their labour, proscribing certain economic, religious and sexual customs. Yet, in return, they treated the people as an untouchable caste, restricted their freedom of action, and offered them only the most trivial compensation from the white people's vast material wealth.

At first glance, then, the history of race relations in German New Guinea, and the wider Pacific, would seem to be explained best in terms of social and economic deprivation, a sense of despair caused by 'an inability to obtain what the culture has defined as the ordinary satisfactions of life'.[4] On closer analysis, however, the evidence suggests otherwise. 'Deprivation' is a relative term, depending very much on the horizon of expectations of the people concerned. In the Pacific, there is no simple correlation between the number and extent of demands made by the German administrations and the instances of rebellion. The nature of local response seems to depend on a 'cost-benefit analysis' by the leadership of each group, as well as on the compensating resources which the group possessed.

Ponape, for instance, was the severest test which the Germans had to face in the Pacific, yet the colony was not subject to the pressures of labour recruitment, excessive land alienation and a vocal white settler community which caused so much friction in other colonies. The disadvantages of the German land reforms to a chief like Henry Nanpei were far outweighed by the security he gained for his personal estates. In contrast are the repercussions which land reform had for lesser chiefs with fewer resources, especially for the chiefs of Sokehs district. They were the most vulnerable to German demands because, along with Net, they lived the closest to the seat of the German administration; therefore they had to bear the brunt of Boeder's crusade. Where the Ponapean 'commoners' stood during the successive crises is harder to evaluate, but their close links with section heads and district chiefs, plus the fact that they had everything to gain from the Germans' land changes, suggest that generally they played a passive role and followed where their chiefs led.

New Guineans experienced the hand of Germany unevenly, according to their proximity to major European settlements and the consequent ability of the regime to mobilise them in support of its demands. But even where the pattern of white settlement and administrative commands were similar, the response of the local populations varied significantly. What mattered were the alternative opportunities available to the local society. For example, the coastal Tolai of the Gazelle Peninsula and the Madang people on the mainland both suffered the loss of large scale land resources and had imposed upon them the obligations of direct German rule (corvée labour, head tax). The Tolai managed to reconcile themselves to this state of affairs after the war of 1893, for as a group they were strong and important enough

205

to be able to negotiate defined land reserves; moreover, the possession of an abundance of coconuts and good transport and marketing opportunities enabled them to enjoy an increasing cash income and a rising standard of living. For the Madang people, there were few if any compensations: most of their land had been lost in the expansion of company plantations, and they possessed too few saleable resources to provide the basis for a permanent trading economy; even wage labour gave them negligible purchasing power. It was the sort of situation, with no prospects for advancement through acceptance of the European order, which led logically to the physical resistance of 1904 and, perhaps, 1912.

This uneven effect of structural changes to economic or political life, or to social authority, is the model which prevailed in all three German colonies. The southern districts of Ponape, in contrast to Sokehs, accepted the German program of reforms voluntarily in 1909, although the traditional authority of chiefs was thereby reduced considerably and the only source of income for many chiefs through tributary labour was abolished. In Samoa, not all the chiefs affected by Solf's policy of diminishing chiefly influence and privileges followed Lauaki in his campaign to restore chiefly power. Some chose to collaborate and accept roles within Solf's new local government bureaucracy. Such men played an important part in the Lauaki crisis of 1908-09. Co-operating fully with the German government's counter-strategy, or weighing carefully the options open to them in the conflict, they gave Solf an important lever over the Samoan community and enabled the Islanders to avert civil war. New Guineans resisted the European invasion of trading monopolies which were established between coastal and inland groups and which were an important link in the static subsistence economies of both. And many reacted in a hostile manner to the depopulation of villages through recruiting, to the enforced relocation of settlements, such as at Madang and Herbertshöhe, or to the subversion of cults and social sanctions by missionaries. Yet other structural innovations, like *luluais* and the head tax, did not lead to widespread resistance, nor did recruitment and mission efforts to change the patterns of village life provoke violent clashes in all areas. This reinforces the argument that the term 'deprivation' must be used with caution in trying to explain the causes of Pacific Island opposition.

One of the self-evident causes was the overt racial arrogance of German planters, recruiters and administrators, and the abuses which sprang from it. The New Guinea Company's disciplinary ordinance of

1887-88 was quite explicit in treating the New Guinean as a brutish, almost subhuman savage, and its assumptions were not softened though the ordinance itself was 'improved' in later years. The record of continual desertions from plantations, of hostility to recruiters, and the prominence of ex-labourers in attacks on white people all testify to the resentment which the misuse of their labour aroused in New Guineans. The sense of racial and moral superiority which some missionaries wore like a badge also caused antagonism: the Baining massacre and the conspiracies against the Madang missionaries demonstrate that New Guineans would not lightly accept these pretensions either.

Ponape provides the best example of the emotions which German excesses could arouse. Boeder's constant disregard for Island sensibilities, from the time of his arrival to his murder in October 1910, points to a deliberate contempt for the Ponapeans as civilised people, which on Ponape with its troubled past and defiant record, was cause enough for violence. Yet, significantly, almost nine months elapsed between the time the new land and labour system was forced on Sokehs and the uprising in October. Resort to violence was in many cases due to the failure of the German regimes to respond to local protests against abuses and loss of resources. The Sokehs chiefs had made repeated attempts to mitigate the effects of Boeder's policy before their position became untenable. Similarly, in the case of the Varzin war in the Gazelle Peninsula, To Kilang, the 'big man', had tried avenues of non-violent protest without securing any review of his problem before taking matters into his own hands.

Beyond the external causes of Pacific Island opposition to German rule, whether physical or political, is another, less obvious, but equally important set of explanations. Often the actions which Germans interpreted as unprovoked aggression or rebellion were the result of social and political forces internal to the Island societies and largely independent of the Germans.

For example, violence against whites was occasionally the expression of traditional community sanctions. Europeans living in or near Island communities and entering into the local system of relationships were given short shrift if they violated taboos and canons of social behaviour. Several of the murders of lone traders in the New Guinea Islands before 1900 can be traced to this mistake; witness also the attack on Ralum in 1890, which followed after Europeans had repeatedly ignored the importance to the Tolai of local cult centres and fishing areas.

In New Guinea the practice of 'blood revenge' or 'pay back' was also responsible for a share of European deaths. In cases where a New Guinean descent group or residential unit considered that it had been seriously wronged by another social group with which it had no close ties, then any member of the latter group was liable to be attacked in retaliation, either physically or by sorcery. On occasions, a white was murdered if a group had suffered from the visit of an earlier European, or if the visit coincided with the death of a group member. This group solidarity also operated in the Sokehs rebellion in Ponape; in fact, it was the primary, if temporary, force which rallied the people of Sokehs behind Soumadau in the fight against Germany.

Fear of the outsider was another factor which influenced the behaviour of New Guinea village groups towards Europeans. In the days before contact, most New Guineans lived in small, highly integrated and self-sufficient residential groups, each suspicious of its neighbours and treating the intrusion of any stranger as a possible threat to the delicate balance of its existence. Attacks against advancing Europeans were usually initiated at this level rather than at the regional level, and they were often intended, however unnecessarily, as acts in defence of the residential group. The murder of Dammköhler west of the Markham in 1909, and of Richards, the Bird of Paradise hunter, in 1910 can best be explained in this way. European explorers and travellers also affronted villagers by their insensitive curiosity about peoples' living habits, and their frequent failure to observe the proper decorum in villages. Traditionally, even friends and allies not belonging to the territorial unit were objects of distrust, for New Guineans feared the sorcery and trouble which might result from non-residents learning the intimate details of their lives.

A variation on the theme of internal causes of resistance is to see opposition to the Germans as an extension of the balance of power among local groups. The relationship between various descent, residential or district units was often the key to the way Pacific Islanders handled Europeans. One of the dangers of interpreting Pacific history from European records is to see that history in terms of a simple involvement between Pacific Islanders on the one hand and Europeans on the other. In reality, the involvement frequently took the form of an encounter among several local groups pursuing their traditional purposes (whether war, alliances or exchanges), in which Europeans were only one variable in the equation, and one to be manipulated in pursuit of traditional aims. Often an event interpreted by contemporary observers as a crisis in the relationship between the colonial regime and the Island people was in fact an episode in the changing patterns of conflict and alliance among indigenous groups.

The history of Ponape under German rule makes this evident. The sequence of threat and counter-threat, of clandestine meetings and raids on chiefs' property which Georg Fritz in 1908 thought was an attempted *putsch* against his regime was a chapter in the struggle between the two chiefs of Kiti, Henry Nanpei and Sou Kiti, which carried over to their relations with the Germans. As we have seen, Nanpei skilfully managed the confusion that resulted from his deliberate provocations, with the dual intention of intimidating Fritz while enlisting his support against Sou Kiti. Regional jealousies also played an important part in the uprising of 1910: the chiefs of Sokehs suspected that the German land reforms were Nanpei's inspiration and that he had formed an alliance with the Germans against the northern districts; Fritz's approval of Nanpei's 'advisory council', as well as Boeder's general aggressiveness, seemed only to confirm their suspicions.

If we turn our attention to Samoa, the *mau e pule* immediately presents itself as an extension of the factional intrigues which had long riven Samoan politics. Alongside the restoration of *Tumua* and *Pule* to their old positions of influence, Lauaki aimed to entrench his own faction in power under the Germans, and it was Solf's recognition of this which enabled him to split the mass front Lauaki had so carefully organised during 1908. The Lauaki crisis then developed along the lines of a uniquely Samoan party struggle; the 'declaration of war' which Lauaki made in January 1909 was directed less at the Germans than at Lauaki's Samoan enemies, the chiefs of *Tumua*.[5]

New Guinea provides perhaps the most diverse set of examples of the same process, though they are seldom recognised as such in the government records of the time. To take just two cases: mission reports and later local additions make it plain that what Hahl regarded as an infringement of colonial peace and order in the Admiralties, when Pominis led his village in a retaliatory raid on his neighbours, was in reality an expression of their long-standing hostility, with no suggestion of rebellion. Two years later, the people of Valum village on Pak Island killed the three Solomon Islands labourers who had murdered their employer Schlehan and retired to Pak Island with the booty. The incident initially was considered rough justice by the regime, and the turning point in the long and bitter struggle which had been carried on since the 1880s to pacify the Admiralty Islanders. But a later patrol discovered that the 'rough justice' was not justice at all; that in fact the Valum people had killed the labourers because the neighbouring village of Mogara had given the refugees shelter, and shared in the plunder from Schlehan's trading station.[6] Too afraid of government punishment to participate in the pillage themselves, the Valum people had acted out of jealousy of their neighbours.

In spite of these local cultural explanations of Pacific Island 'resistance', a warning must be entered against rationalising away every act of violence in which Europeans and Pacific Islanders were involved. On the New Guinea frontier, at least, avarice led to many of the attacks on whites. In an area like New Ireland before 1900, where traders were isolated and left in charge of large caches of trade goods, the temptation to plunder often proved too great for villagers. The same was true of the Solomons and the Admiralties, where off-shore Islanders were particularly adept at pirating European vessels. There were always groups, even friendly to the administration, who were prepared to indulge in looting, as with Mogara village on Pak Island, or the Tolai district of Malagunan in the attack on Wolff's house in 1902.

Exasperation at the readiness of New Guineans to appropriate anything left lying around is a major theme in many accounts of colonial pioneering. The Reverend Flierl recounts how the Sattelberg people in the Huon Peninsula brazenly warned him to guard his possessions closely, for they were considered fair booty if only the villagers could get their hands on them. Flierl also claimed that the covetousness of the Simbang people could easily have led to murder at Finschhafen in the early days.[7]

The desire for European material wealth, and the violence such desires could generate were not necessarily anti-German or anti-European. With very few exceptions, and all of them in New Guinea, none of the uprisings against German rule or expressions of hostility to it can be classified as the total rejection of Europeans and their civilisation. There may have been present a longing for a simpler past, with the certainties of the old ways, but Pacific Islanders were not committed to reaction for its own sake, nor, necessarily, were their actions designed to overthrow the colonial regime. Campaigns like the Samoan *Oloa* movement, and Lauaki's *mau e pule* took the framework of colonial rule as established, and sought rather to manipulate its institutions and reduce its effects. There is no proof that Lauaki intended open rebellion when he began his fight for *Tumua* and *Pule* in 1908; indeed, Lauaki consistently denied any such purpose.[8] Perhaps to defend Lauaki as being essentially loyal throughout the affair, as did Solf's district officer in Savai'i,[9] was going too far. The movement had generated its own momentum. Schultz's action in prohibiting the demonstration on Solf's arrival frustrated Lauaki's strategy, reducing his options and virtually forcing him openly to oppose the administration or to back down. But, even after events became explosively rebellious, with *Tumua* lining up against Lauaki, there exists little evidence to prove that Lauaki sought an open break with the regime, or that he intended using violence against the whites in Samoa. The compromise which Lauaki so masterfully engineered at Vaiusu, plus the fact that he surrendered in the end to save Samoa from war, suggest that Lauaki was reluctant to cross the thin line between intimidation and physical violence.

In New Guinea, major insurrections occurred in only a few areas, and even then they were usually aimed against specific grievances and lasted a short time. For instance, considering the economic advantages which coastal Tolai gained from the growth of the plantation markets before 1893, it is doubtful whether the war of the bullet-proof ointment was intended to annihilate all Europeans living in the Gazelle Peninsula. Since peace persisted so strongly after 1893, more likely it was intended to ease pressure on Tolai land, and restore the earlier, more favourable relationship of coexistence and mutual economic benefit with the whites. The Baining massacre in 1904 was not a general anti-white movement either. Planned and executed by a small group of Baining people, it was aimed specifically against the Sacred Heart Mission and the personalities responsible for the humiliations of St Paul. In the rampage that followed the murders, the rebels left alone a white settler living in the area, who was married to a New Guinean woman.[10]

Even at Madang, where the people were twice accused of plotting to destroy the European community, there is a case for arguing that the so-called 1912 rebellion was actually an expression of the Cargo beliefs that were circulating in Madang villages, where people were discussing whether the time had come to expel the whites who were responsible for the loss of village land, but to embrace the 'white' way of life.[11]

Finally, when we turn to Ponape and the Sokehs rebellion, it is clear that even the militantly independent Ponapeans had never excluded the idea of compromise with Europeans. They met the original Spanish demands readily enough, and it is likely that all the districts would have submitted to the Germans' decrees but for the brutality of Carl Boeder. That right up to the moment of rebellion there existed a party of Sokehs leaders which opposed such a Draconian solution indicates that, almost always, someone was ready to compromise with the Germans; any determination to destroy German rule, if it existed, was only lukewarm.

The Sokehs uprising is best interpreted as an explosion of frustration against Boeder and his accomplices by the district which suffered most from his tyranny. 'We felt wretched and furious and we did not much think . . .',[12] was the judgment of Samuel, the last of the rebel chiefs to give himself up. Resistance ebbed rapidly once the German forces arrived, and the Sokehs warriors surrendered quietly. Moved by the sense of fate that predestined their destruction, Samuel conceded the struggle to the Germans 'so that our souls would be tranquil'. This is decidedly not the cloth from which fanatical liberation movements are cut.

9

The Social Dynamics of Protest
Organisation and Leadership

There are no spectacular successes in the history of Pacific Island resistance to the Germans. The only two major threats to the empire—Lauaki's *mau e pule* and the Sokehs rebellion—both ended in exile or death for their participants. In retrospect, they never could have succeeded. Aside from the fact that German officials could always appeal to the home government for help to repress opposition in an emergency, the Island communities lacked a number of organisational preconditions which were necessary for an effective attack on German sovereignty.

Firstly, there were no 'masses' in any of the three colonies, no politicised peasantry or proletariat which could be used as a lever against the German regimes. In 1914, though social changes were beginning to have visible effects, Samoa, Ponape and New Guinea still contained well-integrated, pre-industrial societies. The Samoans remained tied to their local descent groups and village organisations of production and distribution; they rejected any efforts to draw them into wage labour on a regular basis. The Ponapean reforms emancipated the ordinary Islander from the uncertainties of the feudal system without altering the traditional mode of economic life or the set of close-knit loyalties and obligations within the districts. New Guineans experienced much greater mobilisation of labour for the plantations and more radical social change, but no urban work force or permanent pool of wage labour had emerged before 1914; employment with Europeans was generally a temporary experience in those years.[1]

The explanation for this state of affairs lies partly in the weakness of the colonial economy, and its subordination to the imperial economy. The home government's failure to provide sufficient support for rapid commercial growth, and the unwillingness of *Grosskapital* interests in Germany to invest where returns were still small and uncertain, saved the Pacific colonies from large-scale economic penetration and helped to preserve local social structures. The latter, in turn, gave the colonial peoples shelter from the economic demands of the regime: the Islanders could always choose between growing crops for subsistence or for market, or they could sell their labour. The local alternative, with its greater independence, was usually preferable. This depended, of course, on the availability of land. In an area like Madang, some of those who lost land were able to find shelter and support from neighbouring groups and still avoid wage labour, while in the Gazelle Peninsula and other areas reserves provided some guarantee of a local economic alternative to plantation labour. Instead of a growing proletariat, the Germans had to deal with a moving labour frontier which receded further from the old areas of settlement as cash cropping and other forms of economic opportunity became more widely diffused.² Such a frontier was too unstable to act as the focus of mass movements.

We have seen also that colonial rule fell unevenly on social groups within the colonies. While chiefs had their powers whittled away, ordinary people in the villages remained largely untouched by foreign governments, or, as in Ponape, benefited from reforms at the expense of their chiefs. Each community or individual elite got something different from the colonial system, which made it difficult to organise a mass movement against the Germans.

If there was no mass movement of the dispossessed, neither was there any new vision of society capable of defining the enemy and unifying all the old hostile groups. The appeal to patriotism (*lotonu'u*) by the Samoan *Malo* in the *Oloa* movement may have been more widely received in a more sophisticated anti-colonial age, but the rapid disintegration of solidarity among the chiefs after the Vaimea incident shows that it had little meaning for the Samoan people in 1904-05.

In the two open resistance movements of the German Pacific—Lauaki's *mau e pule* and the Sokehs rebellion—the ideological call which marshalled support initially was not sufficient to sustain revolutionary sentiment or create a permanent wider organisation. Lauaki was unable to offer all Samoans a more stable, more prosperous life than they were already enjoying under Solf's regime. The importance of the *Ali'i Sili* question and the power of *Tumua* and *Pule*, for which Lauaki was fighting, were challenged effectively by Solf's rule. *Tumua* and *Pule* were responsible for several disruptions to peace—in 1900, 1903 and 1904—and the new Samoan administration was proving more functional and efficient in 1908-09 than the old *Malo* ever had. Lauaki's ideas were an appeal to old ways, but to old ways that were not uniformly regarded as perfect ways; Lauaki's ideas were designed to reinforce traditional divisions not to transcend them. Moreover, his view of Samoa in 1909 as the cockpit of imperialist rivalries among the Great Powers was obsolete, and offered nothing but a return to chaos.[3]

On Ponape, Soumadau en Sokehs emerges as the legitimate leader of the Sokehs uprising. It was not a crusade for Ponape's liberation, but an angry reaction against Carl Boeder's mounting persecution, and most of the districtspeople followed Soumadau in loyalty to clan and district. Only one vision moved them all: that was the negative belief that Sokehs was to be destroyed, an idea which applied to Sokehs alone, and which made the rest of Ponape hang back in fear when Germany brought in her military might.

In neither of these cases did Lauaki and Soumadau have sufficient strength of personality to make up for the absence of an indigenous proletariat or the lack of a revolutionary ideology. There is a sense in which both men can be said to have possessed 'charismatic' qualities. Lauaki, the supreme orator chief, more than any other Samoan, embodied the highest values of Samoa in his knowledge of tradition and his skill in politics. Soumadau en Sokehs, the warrior chief par excellence, had led famous charges against the Spaniards in 1898; he was the self-appointed guardian of district honour, the successful store owner and erstwhile friend of the German Governor. Both men had all the trappings of a magnetic personality, all the hallmarks of potential charisma. Yet both lacked the ability to overcome all the instabilities inherent in their movements and to commit a broad cross-section of people to their campaigns.

It is this which defines a truly charismatic movement. In the view of one sociologist, charisma is less an individual quality than a social relationship in which the message and the movement itself are more important than the greatness of the leader.[4] Firstly, true charisma exists only within the context of a social movement: until recognised by others it does not become real. Secondly, there must be a message which is relevant to the people and expresses their unsatisfied wants. The truly charismatic leader in these terms is followed because he embodies and articulates values and aspirations in which his followers have an interest; and because he offers a realisation of those values.

Lauaki's vision of the restoration of traditional politics did not capture the imagination of all, or even of most Samoans. In fact, a large group and their leaders perceived it as divisive, selfish and retrograde. Only if Solf had resorted to force against the orator chief in March 1909 would Lauaki have received the signs and martyrdom necessary to give him a genuinely charismatic role.

In a similar way, Soumadau was able to draw only his kin and districts people to him, in what was generally perceived to be a hopeless gesture. His protest, like that of Lauaki's, was by and large the protest of a political elite, with a select following; it represented a crisis for him, rather than for the whole people. The only Islanders both men could mobilise were those already susceptible to integration through traditional bonds of authority and social solidarity.

Though these acts of open resistance failed, not all opposition to German policy proved fruitless. It is clear from the histories of the three colonies that German rule in the Pacific was a process of constant compromise between relatively weak and highly personalised administrations on the one hand and the leaders of Island communities on the other. Whether in New Guinea, Ponape or Samoa, the Germans never gained absolute control over the politics of their Island populations. We have seen, for instance, that the New Guinea policy of permanent government presence through the appointment of *luluais* was constantly subject to disruption and frequently it failed to achieve even the minimal organising goals expected of it.[5] Other instruments of colonial control, like the head tax and compulsory road works, also had only a limited effect.

If, in theory, Micronesia and Polynesia contained much more penetrable societies than New Guinea, and lent themselves to manipulation through their hierarchical authority structures, in practice they proved as large an obstacle to German control as did New Guinea. Ponapeans were able to influence German administrative policy right up to Boeder's last brutal acts, since none of the four governments between 1899 and 1910 was fully aware of what was going on in the districts. The rebellion occurred after Boeder had made it clear by his actions that he spurned any idea of compromise between his regime and the Islanders. Only when the Islanders had been beaten or cowed into subjection by the sheer weight of numbers were the Germans able to do what they wanted on Ponape.

Of all three colonies, Solf's Samoa comes closest to achieving a workable system of control and the genuine bureaucratisation of Pacific Island authority. In a compact and homogeneous society such as Samoa, a great degree of direct involvement between the Island community and the colonial Governor was possible. A strong personality like Solf, having a positive conception of his role and a good knowledge of, and sympathy for, local custom, was able to influence greatly the pattern of inter-communal politics. Solf understood local aspirations and the limits to which the Samoans were prepared to be pushed. This was manifest in his refusal to bully the Samoans into serving only the European economy; in his defence of his paid native bureaucracy as a delicate balance between German and Samoan notions of sovereignty; in his sympathy for Mata'afa Josefo despite his complicity in the *Oloa*; and, most importantly, in his reliance, during the Lauaki crisis, on a political strategy right up to the brink of civil war and total bankruptcy of his administrative conception.

Yet, for all that, not even Solf gained complete control over the Samoan polity. If his administration had the appearance of a methodical progress towards a political ideal, that was because Solf was skilful at rationalising the decisions forced on him by the turn of events. In reality, the Solf period was one of experiment and of pragmatic solutions to current crises.

From the beginning, Solf had to compromise with those Samoans who wielded political power. To gain acceptance for the German regime he was forced to allow the continuation of the *Malo* style of government: a central Samoan administration controlled by the chiefs and orators of the victorious party; the dictatorship of the strong. The local government which Solf set up in 1900 also represented a delicate balance between Samoan and German power. Though it served to counteract the old power of *Tumua* and *Pule* chiefs, Solf found he was obliged to pay incumbents' salaries as a kind of indemnity for the prerogatives they surrendered when Samoa became a German colony, and to use officials who were familiar to local villagers since the people would not obey a stranger. In effect this meant that the traditional power of village elites was hardly inhibited, and the colonial government could exercise relatively little control over them, particularly as the wages paid to them were not enough to guarantee loyalty, and dismissal could alienate the villagers.[6]

This balance of interests continued to operate through to the end of German rule. Solf had to negotiate the question of the head tax with the Samoan elites before implementing it; he had to maintain the political fiction of the paramountcy long after he had succeeded in undermining the *Oloa* movement and abolishing the *Malo*; he found it necessary to allow Lauaki freedom of movement up until late 1908 despite the fact that Lauaki consistently championed campaigns to reinstate the old elites in power. Even when Solf had the upper hand in 1909 he could not afford to use a military offensive for fear of provoking a general rebellion. The final compromise lay in his solution to the *Ali'i Sili* question. All Solf's plans for Samoa had revolved around the removal of this final obstacle between government and people. But here, too, Solf was forced to meet the Samoans halfway. The old, single position of *Ali'i Sili* was now replaced by two new ones, the *Fautua*, which created an entirely new relationship between the two royal families and the administration. Furthermore, the Germans felt obliged to distribute a considerable indemnity to the chiefs to forestall their protests. In the light of these constant adjustments of purpose, it becomes clear that what one author has called Solf's 'thorough, if diplomatic absolutism',[7] was more diplomatic than thoroughly absolute.

In Pacific Island politics, therefore, the role which Islanders themselves played in shaping the character of German rule cannot be ignored. Their initiatives, counter-thrusts and general political sophistication helped to influence colonial policy even when open resistance failed. The key to their success lay with the Island leaders or elites, those people with a major influencing or decision-making capacity. Leadership is crucial in explaining any process of socio-political change. In the Pacific it has added importance, for Island elites like Nanpei, Lauaki and To Bobo not only possessed multiple roles in their societies as politicians, businessmen and church officials, but also they were the most immediately affected by the impositions of a foreign, centralised government.

As we have seen, German colonial rule rarely engaged the whole society. Those who lost their prerogatives and their freedom of manoeuvre were men like the cartel of chiefs and orators in Samoa, and the higher district chiefs in Ponape. These were the Islanders who resisted any encroachment on their powers, or schemed and intrigued in order to influence German policy. The history of Pacific Island politics under German rule is the history of elites, not mass movements, of interactions between *leaders* of different groups and different cultures. Particularly in small colonies like Samoa and Ponape, the major crises of sovereignty occurred when Island elites suddenly found themselves forced to choose between total dependence on the new regime or stubborn defence of their old ways and traditional prerogatives.[8]

Lauaki and Soumadau en Sokehs chose the latter course and, on the surface, failed. Yet they cannot be dismissed simply as unrepentant 'resisters' or 'romantic reactionaries' in contrast to the 'more deft' collaborators like Nanpei and To Bobo. These are terms which, thanks to the work of African historians, have been shown to be outdated and misleading.[9] 'Collaborators' and 'resisters' were often the same men in the Pacific. Lauaki and Soumadau, after all, did not come to grief until late in the German period, when they decided to challenge German rule head on. Until that moment they had acted as important spokesmen for their people and gained respect as effective leaders in the eyes of the Germans. Lauaki had organised the support that had allowed Mata'afa Josefo to stake a convincing claim to the paramountcy on the eve of German rule. He had been involved in the *Oloa*, an attempt to modernise the people's economy while defending the right of the old *Malo* to speak for Samoa. In switching his allegiance from Solf to the *Oloa* and then to Solf again in 1904-05, Lauaki proved himself an extremely adaptable politician, and he gained an important, if temporary, victory when he persuaded Solf not to deport him along with the other ringleaders of the movement in 1905.

As for Soumadau, if the Germans were able to establish a hold on Ponape in their early years and work through the district chiefs with a minimum of conflict, then Soumadau was one of the chiefs who made it possible. Even Carl Boeder is said to have counted Soumadau as a special friend and to have cultivated the chief's friendship in the early days of his reign.[10] Certainly Soumadau virtually led the negotiations over the district's grievances about work periods in 1910, and he was made overseer at a high rate of pay as a tribute to his influence and organising capacity.

The Germans clearly needed the co-operation of such men in their effort to assert control over the Islands. Without the collaboration of Lauaki and Soumadau in the early days of German rule, they would never have been able to make Germany's presence acceptable with so little use of force. That Solf, Hahl and Fritz—even Boeder—realised this, is implicit in the way they cultivated the friendship of these chiefs and sought their support.

In the end both Lauaki and Soumadau were committed to a traditionalist view of life, a view which led them into open resistance and removal from any further influence on their societies. Yet both have achieved a new level of influence, perhaps a new kind of charismatic appeal, posthumously. Lauaki was resurrected by nationalist Samoans of the 1920s and 1930s as the persecuted proto-nationalist of Samoa, and even today, in areas well beyond his home district, he is regarded as Samoa's model orator chief. Soumadau and the district of Sokehs had already gained admiration and respect from the other districts, even enemy districts, at the time of the rebellion, because they were prepared to make the ultimate sacrifice of their lives to uphold Ponapean self-respect in a manner honoured by the people. Soumadau, and the districtspeople with him, had proved that they were the embodiment of the Island's warrior ethos. The lesson has lost little over the years. In the final analysis, an effective, even a charismatic leader does not have to be successful: in the long-term perspective of history, adversity and failure can serve as much as success to strengthen faith in a person and that person's goals.

There were, however, other elites who, in the end, did not go the same way as Lauaki and Soumadau, elites who never threw down the gauntlet to the Germans in the way Lauaki and Soumadau felt compelled to do. Once again, to call these men simply 'collaborators' would be misleading. They were men who co-operated for a variety of reasons, not necessarily from the conviction that all things European were automatically superior. Some, like Saga and Taumei in Samoa, Henry Nanpei in Ponape, or To Bobo in New Guinea, were seeking a middle way. They never responded inflexibly to the demands of their German rulers. They made no permanent choice to serve or to resist, but moved between co-operation and opposition according to the pressures upon them and their own political and economic objectives.

Perhaps this is the measure of the most successful Islanders under German rule, for astute leadership and limited resistance often succeeded in checking European pretensions, thus enabling the leaders to consolidate their own positions and move relatively quickly into modern politics. A good example is Henry Nanpei. During German rule his position was far greater than his title suggested. He was the leading benefactor and organiser of the Protestant Church on Ponape, regarded by both Spanish and Germans as the 'commander' of the Protestant forces in the south against the Catholics in the north. In addition he was the Island's largest and most prosperous businessman and its most Westernised chief. The Germans counted him, rightly, as the key element in their control of the Islanders, at least in the south, and successive administrations courted his support and aid for their policies.

For his part, Henry Nanpei had grasped quickly the long-term meaning of European sovereignty, and he was prepared to try new forms of leadership and authority under the Germans: witness his 'advisory council' to act as consultant to the regime. And in accepting the land reform scheme, as well as influencing others to do so, Nanpei was able to fashion an alliance with the administration which assured him of German support and assistance during the remainder of German rule.

For all that, Nanpei in no way abandoned traditional values or traditional commitments. Sympathy with the direction of social change did not exclude loyalty to established patterns of political life. Nanpei's major concern remained his position within Kiti district. He had engineered the disturbances in 1908 in order to deter the Germans from penetrating too deeply his stronghold in Ronkiti, just as he had led the campaign against the Spanish in 1898; he had set out to intimidate the German regime while collaborating with it in order to guard his position and landed estates against the encroachments of Sou Kiti; during the revolt of 1910 he is said to have succoured the rebels from his own trade stores with equipment and foodstuffs.[11] The suspicions about Henry Nanpei's activities, which flourished in all quarters, among Ponapeans as well as among Germans, confirm the ambiguity of his attitude to European rule. Though, outwardly, he remained faithful to the German regime until 1914, it was probably because he was satisfied that it provided him with the best possible support for his position and influence in Kiti. The shrewdest assessment of Nanpei's priorities throughout German rule was made by Governor Hahl:

> His activities were designed constantly to assert his own claims, never those of the German regime. He certainly would have become a rebel, as in the Spanish period, if he had feared that we endangered his reputation or his possessions. In my opinion he relied [on us] with all possible caution.[12]

To Bobo in the Gazelle Peninsula is a second example of this cautious attitude to the Germans. Like Nanpei, he could see beyond the immediate crisis of the 1893 war to the permanent effects of the changes going on around his people, and he chose the government to be his future patron. As 'big man', preacher, organiser and later *luluai*, To Bobo was an important support to the German administration. But, like Henry Nanpei, he remained ambivalent to the Germans and did not support their policies under all circumstances. He fought the Germans for land reserves, and encouraged independent cash cropping by the Tolai rather than the regular wage labour for plantations which Hahl favoured. To Bobo is an example of those creative elites who recognised colonial rule as a revolutionary situation and encouraged their societies to adapt.

A third example is the Manus Islander, Pominis, the 'cannibal' catechist accused of warring on his neighbours and raiding European schooners. After selling his village's land to the mission, Pominis abandoned his ministry for the life of a secular 'big man'. His case illustrates neatly the dual strands of co-operation and resistance in emergent Pacific leaders. Pominis's training enabled him to stake a more powerful claim to leadership in his own society, but it did not inhibit him from following custom and going to war to protect his group. Again, his conversion and work for the mission did not guarantee that he would never return to the old ways and old ambitions of material power. This was a common risk which continually undermined the evangelising successes of missionaries in German New Guinea.

Such leaders were able to combine cultural conservatism with innovation, were able to exploit new avenues of power and opposition while remaining loyal to traditional values. Frequently their motives are not altogether fathomable. Some of them wished to encourage their societies to adapt to the structural changes and new patterns of development. Most of them, it must be recognised, were primarily self-interested, and possessed only a vague vision of betterment for their communities. All of them were involved in what one historian has called 'the politics of survival':[13] the need to come to terms with vastly more powerful forces which exercised the ultimate say over the future of their societies. But such a phrase, which tends to emphasise the *response* of Pacific Islanders to German rule, must not be allowed to obscure the creative side of their political activity. For Pacific Islanders, through their leaders and institutions, often took the initiative in colonial politics, while the Europeans struggled to make responses which accorded with their colonial objectives and their own image of themselves. The colonial relationship was never equal, and Pacific Islanders were seldom able to maintain their autonomy, but, given the presence of sufficiently gifted individuals in influential positions, their societies were dynamic enough to adjust of their own accord and to a level upon which they themselves had decided.

Notes

Introduction

[1] Good written accounts of Samoa's social structure can be found in E. Schultz, *Die wichtigsten Grundsatze des samoanischen Familien und Erbrechts* (Apia 1905), and his *Samoanische Familien—Immobiliar—und Erbrechts* (3rd edn, Apia, 1911); F. M. Keesing & M. M. Keesing, *Elite Communication in Samoa: A Study of Leadership* (Stanford, 1956).

[2] For descriptions of Ponapean social structure see P. Hambruch, *Ponape* (Hamburg, 1932) Vols I and II; J. L. Fischer, *The Eastern Carolines* (New Haven, 1957); W. R. Bascom, *Ponape: A Pacific Economy in Transition* (Berkeley, 1965); S. Riesenberg, *The Native Polity of Ponape* (Washington, 1968).

[3] A. Hahl, 'Mitteilungen uber Sitten und rechtliche Verhaltnisse auf Ponape', *Ethnologisches Notizblatt* 2, 2 (1901).

[4] See R. Parkinson, *Dreissig Jahre in der Sudsee* (Stuttgart, 1907); R. F. Salisbury, *Vunamami: Economic Transformation in a Traditional Society* (Berkeley, 1970); P. G. Sack, 'The Range of Traditional Tolai Remedies', in A. L. Epstein (ed.), *Contention and Dispute: Aspects of Law and Social Control in Melanesia* (Canberra, 1974).

[5] *Verhandlungen des Bundesraths des deutschen Reichs*, Session 1879, Bd.2, Denkschrift xxiv-xxvi.

[6] P. M. Kennedy, 'Bismarck's Imperialism: the Case of Samoa 1880-1890', *The Historical Journal*, XV, 2 (1972), pp. 269-77.

[7] H. H. Kraft, *Chartergesellschaften als Mittel zur Erschliessung kolonialer Gebiete* (Hamburg, 1943), p. 157.

[8] J. W. Spidle, The German Colonial Civil Service: Organization, Selection and Training (Ph.D. thesis, Stanford University, 1972), pp. 45-6.

[9] Spidle, pp. 222-71.

[10] K. Hausen, *Deutsche Kolonialherrschaft in Afrika* (Zurich, 1970), pp. 30, 118, 197.

[11] P. Leutwein, *Dreissig Jahre deutsche Kolonialpolitik* (Berlin, 1913), pp. 39-43.

[12] P. M. Kennedy, 'The Development of German Naval Operations Plans against England, 1896-1914', *The English Historical Review*, LXXXIX (January, 1974), pp. 72-3.

Chapter 1

[1] For example, in one of the earliest encounters, eleven of La Perouse's expedition of 1787 were massacred on Tutuila by Samoans visiting from Upolu.

[2] For accounts of this early period see E. Turner, *Nineteen Years in Polynesia* (London, 1861); R. E. Watters, 'The Transition to Christianity in Samoa', *Historical Studies*,

Australia and New Zealand, VIII (1959), pp. 392-9; R. P. Gilson, *Samoa, 1830-1900: The Politics of a Multi-Cultural Community* (Melbourne, 1970).

3 Solf to Colonial Dept, 15 September 1907, RKA (Reichskolonialamt Records, Potsdam), 2953.

4 Gilson, *Samoa 1830-1900,* pp. 367ff.

5 Consul Travers to Bismarck, 3 January 1887, RKA, 2546.

6 MS., 'Elf Jahre in Samoa', von Wolffersdorf in Solf Papers, File 161, Bundesarchiv, Koblenz.

7 SMS *Bussard* to Admiralty, 11 September 1894; Scheder to Admiralty, 30 October 1894, BA/MA (Bundesarchiv-Militararchiv, Freiburg), 7577.

8 Lauaki's political reputation dated back to the 1860s, to his intervention in the Laupepa-Talavou wars. His father, Namulau'ulu Atama, had been a contemporary of Malietoa Vai'inupo who accepted Christianity from John Williams. The title 'Lauaki' was presented to Atama by Taufa'ahau, later King George Tupou I of Tonga, on a trip to Samoa in 1828 or 1842. Atama's son Mamoe then inherited it. MS., 'The Mau of Pule', Tofa I'iga Pisa in Davidson Papers, Australian National University. J. W. Davidson and D. Scarr, *Pacific Islands Portraits* (Canberra, 1970) contains the best account of the early Lauaki.

9 Sibree to Newell, 20 March 1899, LMS (London Missionary Society Papers), South Seas, Box 45/3B.

10 Petition of Malietoa Fa'alogoi 1899 and Grunow to Chancellor, 21 December 1899, RKA, 3057.

11 Meyer-Delius to Colonial Dept, 29 January 1900, RKA, 3057.

12 Quoted in E. von Vietsch, *Wilhelm Solf: Botschafter zwischen den Zeiten* (Tubingen, 1961), p. 65. Solf was born into a comfortable business family in Berlin in 1862. Educated in Eastern Studies at various universities, he joined the German Foreign Office in 1888 and worked for two years in India, revelling in contacts with both the Indians and his British colleagues. In 1891 he began law studies and in 1898 took up an appointment as judge in Dar-es-Salaam, from where he was dispatched to Samoa.

13 von Bulow to Schanz, 14 November 1903, with Solf's minuting, in Solf to Colonial Dept, 4 December 1903, RKA, 2949.

14 Copy of Solf dispatch, 9 April 1900, Solf Papers, 20.

15 Governor's address to the Chiefs, 11 April 1900, Solf Papers, 20.

16 Huckett to Cousins, 11 June 1900, LMS, South Seas, 46/1.

17 Solf to Colonial Dept, 6 February 1901, RKA, 3060.

18 Colonial Dept to Solf, 31 May 1900, RKA, 3059.

19 Solf to Chancellor, 24 December 1899, RKA, 2550; Solf to Colonial Dept, 10 February 1901, RKA, 3060; *Annual Reports (Jahresberichte uber die Entwicklung der Deutschen Schutzgebiete . . .),* 1900-01, p. 101.

20 Schnee to Colonial Dept, 15 April 1901, RKA, 2767; Schlettwein to Colonial Office, 6 February 1913, RKA, 2768.

21 Solf Memo, 7 March 1904, German Administration Papers, Series 17b, Folder 3, Vol. 3, No. 39, National Archives, Wellington.

22 I am indebted to a series of lectures by R. P. Gilson (Gilson Papers, Australian National University) for the elucidation of these Samoan objections.

23 Davidson and Scarr, *Pacific Islands Portraits,* pp. 267-8.

24 Charles Taylor Memo, 27 November 1903, German Administration Papers, Folder 2, Vol. 1, No. 64.

25 S. G. Firth, German Recruitment and Employment of Labourers in the Western Pacific before the First World War, (D. Phil thesis, Oxford University, 1973), p. 246.
26 R. Deeken, *Manuia Samoa: Samoanische Skizzen und Beobachtungen* (Oldenburg, 1901).
27 *Samoanische Zeitung*, 16 May, 5 September, 12 September, 3 October 1903; G. R. Lewthwaite in J. W. Fox and K. Cumberland (eds), *Western Samoa* (Christchurch, 1962), p. 151.
28 *Kolnische Zeitung*, 7 May 1903; *Der Tag*, 20 April 1904; O. Riedel, *Der Kampf um Deutsch Samoa* (Berlin, 1938) p. 190.
29 *Taimua* and *Faipule* to Solf, 25 June 1903, RKA, 3063.
30 Firth, German Recruitment, p. 314.
31 *Samoanische Zeitung*, 18 June 1904; Trood to Solf, 8 June 1904 and Heimrod to Solf, 8 June 1904, Solf Papers, 25.
32 Deeken to Solf, 31 May 1904, enclosed in Solf to Colonial Dept, 11 June 1904, RKA, 2950.
33 *Tumua* and *Pule* to Solf, 8 June 1904, RKA, 2950.
34 Militarpolitische Bericht SMS *Condor*, 23 September 1904, DR ('A Documentary Record and History of the Lauati Rebellion in Western Samoa—1909') I: 33, National Archives, Wellington.
35 *Annual Reports*, 1902-03, p. 122; 1903-04, p. 113.
36 Nothing is known of Pullack except that he was the son of a former German Customs Officer and had received an elementary education in San Francisco. According to the *Samoanische Zeitung* (3 December 1904), the Samoans anticipated raising 12 000 marks for the project. Pullack claimed to be able to offer 16 Pf. a pound (US4c) for copra.
37 In a private letter Solf stated that European merchants not only asked exorbitant prices for trade goods, they also used false weights to measure copra. Solf to von Koenig, 30 April 1904, Solf Papers, 25. Firth, German Recruitment, p. 245 mentions that Samoans were often cheated by 30 to 50 lbs. in every 100 lbs. of copra they traded.
38 Solf to Lauaki, 25 December 1904, DR, I: 49, 46.
39 Petition of Mata'afa Josefo and *Malo*, 9 January 1905, RKA, 3063.
40 Schultz to Solf, 2 February 1905, Solf Papers, 132. In *fa'a Samoa* terms, Malaeulu had mildly insulted the Governor.
41 Mata'afa Josefo and *Malo* to Schultz, 28 January 1905, RKA, 3063.
42 To 'break into' Vaimea was not a mammoth job, since the prison consisted simply of a compound of fencing wire with a simple lock at the entrance.
43 Mata'afa Josefo to Schultz, 18 February 1905, DR, I: 73-4.
44 Militarpolitische Bericht SMS *Condor*, 23 October 1905, BA/MA, 5186.
45 Quoted in F. M. Keesing, *Modern Samoa: Its Government and Changing Life* (London, 1934), p. 89.
46 Enclosed in Solf to Colonial Dept, 4 August 1905, RKA, 3064.
47 Schultz claims that Lauaki argued in favour of negotiating for the release of the two chiefs rather than the use of force, yet the 'reliable' Chief Laufa of Safotu testified that Lauaki was one of the main instigators of the break-in. Schultz Memos, 31 January and 15 February 1905, DR, I: 60-1, 63-4.
48 Solf to Williams, 15 August 1901, German Administration Papers, Folder 10, Vol. 1, No. 22. Solf used the Samoan 'tilotilomasae' to describe Lauaki.

⁴⁹ Schultz to Solf, 2 February 1905, Solf Papers, 132.
⁵⁰ Printed in *Deutsche Zeitung*, 28 March 1905.

Chapter 2

¹ D. H. Pitt, *Tradition and Economic Progress in Samoa. A Case Study of the Role of Traditional Social Institutions in Economic Development* (Oxford, 1970), p. 22.
² Report on Schulwesen in Samoa, in Solf to Colonial Office, 15 September 1907, RKA, 2953; see also *Annual Reports* 1905-06, Anlage GIV, p. 377.
³ Only three per cent of British, seven per cent of American and sixty per cent of German claims were accepted. *Deutsche Kolonialzeitung*, 11 January 1896.
⁴ *Samoanisches Gouvernements-Blatt*, III, No. 60, p. 192.
⁵ Riedel, *Der Kampf um Deutsch Samoa*, p. 222. It seems fair to suggest that Solf was hypersensitive to criticism at times; at one stage there were pending in the courts 64 actions for libel which he had brought against opponents.
⁶ In RKA, 2953. See also his *Kolonialpolitik: Mein politisches Vermachtnis* (Berlin, 1919).
⁷ W. Solf, *Eingeborene und Ansiedler auf Samoa* (1908), pp. 28-9; *Hamburger Nachrichten*, 18 July 1911.
⁸ Lauaki to Coerper, 26 March 1909, DR, III: 360-1.
⁹ Solf to Colonial Office, 10 May 1909, and enclosures, Solf Papers, 30. Solf's very extensive report of 10 May and his draft of an article 'Der Aufstand auf Samoa' (n.d.) form the basic sources for the sequence of events which follow.
¹⁰ The phrase is Richard Williams's, district officer on Savai'i, who continued to believe Lauaki was loyal to the Germans long after the Chief had moved beyond diplomacy to action. Williams to Solf, 3 April 1909, Solf Papers, 30.
¹¹ Excerpt from speech by Taumei, 22 December 1908, DR, II: 169.
¹² Speech by Lauaki, 18 December 1908, DR, III: 23-4.
¹³ Lelei to Solf, 7 December 1908, German Administration Papers, Folder 11, Vol. 3, No. 3.
¹⁴ Davidson and Scarr, *Pacific Islands Portraits*, p. 296.
¹⁵ Speech by Solf to Upolu chiefs, December 1908, DR, II: 132.
¹⁶ Statement by Lauaki to Richard Williams, 27 February 1909, DR, II: 289.
¹⁷ Solf Memo, 4 January 1909, Gilson Papers, File 202.
¹⁸ Solf to Schnee, 3 June 1909, Solf Papers, 131.
¹⁹ Protokoll der *fono*, 25 January 1909, in Solf to Colonial Office, 10 May 1909, Solf Papers, 30.
²⁰ Note by Solf, 3 February 1909, DR, III: 331.
²¹ Newell to Dora (daughter), 2 April 1909, LMS, Personal, Box 4.
²² *Hamburgischer Correspondent*, 16 March 1909.
²³ Lauaki to Solf, 23 March 1909, and letters of colleagues, DR, III: 338-40. See also Solf's proclamation, 22 March 1909, DR, II: 207.
²⁴ Newell to Dora, 2 April 1909; also Newell diaries 32/1909 *passim*, LMS, Personal.
²⁵ *Pule* and *A'iga* to Trood, 27 March, and Trood's reply, 28 March, in Solf's report, 10 May 1909, Solf Papers, 30.
²⁶ Neil to Danks, 4 April 1909, excerpt Methodist Conference Records, Samoa, in Gilson Papers, File 26.
²⁷ MS. by Alex Hough, Samoa 1909, LMS, South Seas Odds, Box 4.

[28] Solf to Schnee, 3 June 1909, Solf Papers, 131.
[29] Militarpolitische Bericht SMS *Condor*, 21 June 1909, BA/MA, 5186; *Samoanische Zeitung*, 3 April 1909.
[30] Newell in Solf to Colonial Office, 20 September 1909, RKA, 3070.
[31] Firth, German Recruitment, pp. 265-81.
[32] The Colonial Office thought this article important enough as an expression of government policy to have it republished in the official colonial gazette, *Deutsches Kolonialblatt.*
[33] Solf to Colonial Office, 11 April 1910, RKA, 3010.
[34] Colonial Office to DSG, 9 March 1910, RKA, 3070; Dernburg to Trimborn, 31 March 1909, RKA, 3069.
[35] Protokoll der *fono*, 29 January 1909, in Solf report, 10 May 1909, Solf Papers, 30; Trood to Solf, 6 February 1909, Solf Papers, 30.
[36] Solf to Colonial Office, 12 December 1909, RKA, 3065; Solf to Colonial Office, 4 September 1910, German Administration Papers, Folder 2, Vol. 4, No. 18.
[37] Colonial Office to Solf, 15 April 1911, German Administration Papers, Folder 2, Vol. 4, No. 58.
[38] Quoted in C.G.R. McKay, *Samoana* (Wellington, 1968), p. 37.
[39] Riedel, *Der Kampf um Deutsch Samoa*, p. 161.
[40] Mata'afa Josefo to Kaiser, 5 January 1912, German Administration Papers, Folder 2, Vol. 4, No. 92.
[41] *Samoanische Zeitung*, 10 February 1912.
[42] Schultz to Colonial Office, 10 July 1913, RKA, 3067.
[43] *Annual Reports*, 1909-10 to 1912-13; G. R. Lewthwaite and K. B. Cumberland in Fox, *Western Samoa*, pp. 154-60, 243-4; Firth, German Recruitment, pp. 241-83.
[44] An unpublished diary of Solf as Colonial Secretary suggests colonial rule would have been left much more to the colonies themselves: P. Gifford and W. R. Louis (eds), *Britain and Germany in Africa* (New Haven, 1967) pp. 700-01.
[45] Schultz to Colonial Office, 11 March 1914, RKA, 3067.
[46] Schultz to Solf, 8 April 1914, Solf Papers, 132.

Chapter 3

[1] Riesenberg, *The Native Polity of Ponape*, p. 2.
[2] D. Shineberg (ed.), *The Trading Voyages of Andrew Cheyne, 1841-1844* (Canberra, 1971), pp. 10-15, 156-73 and chapters 9-10. See also A. Cheyne, *Islands in the Western Pacific Ocean* (London, 1852).
[3] G. L. Coale, A Study of Chieftainship, Missionary Contact and Culture Change on Ponape, 1852-1900 (M. A. Thesis, University of Southern California, 1951), pp. 46-83; J. L. Fischer, *The Eastern Carolines*, pp. 29-34.
[4] Spanische Missions-Chronik, 1887 (translation), KM (Kapuziner Mission Archives, Munster), File 58; J. L. Fischer, S. H. Riesenberg and M. G. Whiting (eds) *The Book of Luelen* (Canberra, 1977), chapter 66. Much material relating to the Spanish and German periods has been taken from the above two sources, which are unusually good eye-witness accounts.
[5] Fischer, *The Eastern Carolines*, p. 37.
[6] MS., Geschichte der Spanier in Ponape, written by a Ponapean, tr. P. Hambruch, 1910, enclosed in Hambruch to Oswald, 22 December 1910, RKA, 3009.

7 Spanische Missions-Chronik, 1890.

8 SMS *Falke* to Admiral, 15 December 1895, BA/MA, 7577; SMS *Arcona* to Kreuzergeschwader, 16 October 1898, BA/MA, 697.

9 F. W. Christian, *The Caroline Islands* (London, 1899), pp. 64-5.

10 Fischer, *The Eastern Carolines*, p. 44; see also Hahl to Colonial Dept, 23 August 1900, AA (Australian Archives, Canberra), Series CRS G1, Item 116.

11 'Denkschrift betreffend die Inselgruppen der Karolinen, Palau und Marianen', in *Stenographische Berichte uber die Verhandlungen des Reichstags*, 10. Legisl. 1. Session, 1898/1900, Bd. 174, No. 394.

12 *Annual Reports*, 1900-01 to 1903-04; Bascom, *Ponape*, pp. 3-4, 33, 78. Dominic Etscheit came up from the Australian goldfields and worked first for Godeffroys on Ebon, in the Marshall Islands. He settled on Ponape about 1878 and remained until 1919, when he was forced to leave by the Japanese; his son, Carlos, still runs a trading store on the island. Dominic claimed to have bought the estate of Johann Kubary, the ethnographer who lived on Ponape, which would have given him land in excess of 1500 ha. Pers. Com. Carlos Etscheit, August 1974.

13 Firth, German Recruitment, p. 292.

14 Hahl to Geheimrath, Colonial Dept, 23 June 1899, RKA, 2998. Born in 1868 in Lower Bavaria, Hahl was educated at Freising and the University of Wurzburg, where he studied law. Hahl joined the Colonial Department from the Bavarian Civil Service in 1895 and in January 1896 he arrived in New Guinea as Imperial Magistrate. As Deputy Governor, Hahl had jurisdiction over all administrators in the island sphere but the ultimate authority lay with the Governor of German New Guinea. After 1918 Hahl became a Director of the New Guinea Company and was later prominent in the Nazi *Reichskolonialbund*, though his Nazism was only nominal. See P. Biskup, 'Dr Albert Hahl—Sketch of a German Colonial Official', *Australian Journal of Politics and History* 14 (December, 1968), pp. 342-57.

15 A. Hahl, *Gouverneursjahre in Neuguinea* (Berlin, 1937), p. 108.

16 Hahl to Bennigsen, 8 May 1900, RKA, 2765; Hahl to Colonial Dept, 3 December 1899, RKA, 2999.

17 Hahl to Bennigsen, 8 September 1900, AA, CRS G1, Item 8.

18 Paradoxically, present day memories of Hahl on Ponape mark him as the best-liked administrator during the German period. According to these stories he lived with a Ponapean woman, drank the native beverage, *sakau*, and on ceremonial occasions wore the Ponapean grass skirt and allowed himself to be rubbed down with coconut oil. Pers. Com. P. M. Ehrlich, August 1974.

19 Berg to Colonial Dept, 26 January 1902, AA, CRS G1, Item 209.

20 Colonial Dept to Berg, 12 February & 26 February 1902, RKA, 3001.

21 Berg to Colonial Dept, 30 April 1905, AA, CRS G1, Item 138; *Annual Reports*, 1905-06, p. 117.

22 Berg to Colonial Dept, 17 May 1906, RKA, 3004.

23 Fischer, *The Eastern Carolines*, p. 49.

24 Spanische Missions-Chronik.

25 Report of the ABCFM Mission, Ponape 1900-01, AA, CRS G1, Item 126.

Chapter 4

1 Hahl to Fritz, 29 May 1908, AA, CRS G2, Item W21.

2 *Annual Reports*, 1907-08, p. 4.

3 Fritz to Colonial Office, 21 July 1909, AA, CRS G2, Item N16; *Missionsbote*, No. 1, 1909, p. 4.

4 G. Fritz, *Ad Majoram Dei Gloriam! Die Vorgeschichte des Aufstandes von 1910/11 in Ponape* (Leipzig, 1912), p. 59.

5 Fritz to Hahl, February 1908, RKA, 3005.

6 Fritz to Hahl, 25 January and 20 February 1909, RKA, 2766.

7 In sifting and analysing the Nanpei-Sou Kiti affair, the author's debt to documentary sources can hardly be separated from his debt to individuals in the field, especially P. M. Ehrlich.

8 Venantius to Kilian Muller, 20 June 1910, KM, File 70; Kilian Muller to Hahl, 21 December 1910, RKA, 2589. It is possible that the Capuchins believed Sou Kiti would be the next Nahnmwarki of Kiti and would thus create an opening for the conversion of the whole district. German sources argue that Sou Kiti was definitely in order of succession to the Nahnmwarki-ship, and interpret Nanpei's concern as fear that Sou Kiti would drive him from his estates once he was High Chief. But from subsequent investigations it seems that Sou Kiti's claim to succession was in German times at least, tenuous, for though in the ruling clan, he was not in the ruling sub-clan. True, it was dying out and Sou Kiti was sufficiently eminent and versatile to have seemed to the Germans a possible candidate; his section title from Enipein also stood in a special relationship to the Nahnmwarki line. For the Germans to credit Sou Kiti as important it was not necessary that he be in line to succeed, but that the Germans should *believe* he was. In typical Ponapean fashion Sou Kiti would not have denied to anyone that he was a possible successor: to keep open one's options to the end is a worthy Ponapean ideal. And in actual fact Sou Kiti did become Nahnmwarki after the death of Nahnmwarki Paul, though this did not occur until the 1920s, during the Japanese occupation. Pers. Comm. S. Riesenberg, April 1972 and P. M. Ehrlich, August 1974.

9 Fritz to Hahl, 26 August 1908, RKA, 3005.

10 This is a title reserved to children born after their father's accession to the title of Nahnmwarki or Nahnken. Riesenberg, *The Native Polity of Ponape*, p. 18.

11 Denkschrift, Crescentius, July 1908, KM, File 70.

12 Deutsche Missions-Chronik, 1908, KM, File 59; this whole incident can be followed in Fritz's report to Hahl, 21 July 1908, RKA, 3005.

13 For this dispute see KM, File 59; Fritz to Hahl, 26 August 1908, RKA, 3005; Fritz, *Ad Majoram Dei Gloriam*, pp. 43ff.

14 Hahl to Colonial Office, 7 July 1908, RKA, 3005.

15 Hahl to Colonial Office, 30 September 1908, RKA, 3005; Fritz to Hahl, 7 January 1909, RKA, 3006.

16 Berg to Colonial Dept, 26 January 1902, AA, CRS G1, Item 209.

17 Dernburg to Hahl and Fritz, 14 November and 9 December 1908, RKA, 3005.

18 Hambruch, *Ponape*, I, pp. 292-3.

19 MS., Die Ursachen des Aufstandes der Jokaschleute, P. Hambruch, KM, File 75.

20 Kilian Muller to Karlowa, 28 January 1911, RKA, 2589.

21 Report on discussions with Sokehs chiefs, 15 February 1910, and record of approval by Sokehs, 16 March 1910, Boeder Papers, RKA, 3009.

22 Hollborn to Boeder, 21 April 1910, Boeder Papers.

23 Boeder to Hahl, 15 April 1910, RKA, 2763.

[24] Note by Brauckmann, 31 May 1910, RKA, 3009. This whole incident can be followed in detail in Brauckmann's and Boeder's papers, RKA, 3009.

[25] Boeder to Colonial Office, 10 July 1910, RKA, 3006.

[26] MS., Die Ursachen des Aufstandes der Jokaschleute, Hambruch.

[27] Girschner to Colonial Office, 20 November 1910, RKA, 3009; Boeder to Hahl, 19 September 1910, RKA, 3006.

[28] Bascom, *Ponape*, p. 13; see also report by Ignatius, 27 December 1910, KM, File 76.

[29] Hambruch, *Ponape*, I, p. 300.

[30] MS., Mitteilungen uber den Aufstand auf Ponape 1910/11, Father Gebhardt, 15 February 1911, KM, File 75.

[31] P. Ehrlich, The Sokehs Rebellion 1910-11 (paper presented to ASAO Symposium, March 1975), pp. 10-11.

[32] Kammerich to Kersting, 15 May 1911, RKA, 3010.

[33] Pers. Com. P. M. Ehrlich, August 1974. There is also an eye-witness account of the events by Father Gebhardt, one of the two priests at the Sokehs mission house: Mitteilungen uber den Aufstand auf Ponape 1910/11, KM, File 75.

[34] Girschner to Colonial Office, 20 November 1910, RKA, 3009.

[35] Hahl to Colonial Department, 16 March 1904, AA, CRS G1, Item 27.

[36] Ehrlich, The Sokehs Rebellion, p. 9.

[37] Fischer, *The Eastern Carolines*, p. 55.

[38] Quoted in 'Tagebuchblatter von P. Ignatius, Ponape', *Aus den Missionen* (1911), p. 24.

[39] Girschner to Colonial Office, 20 November 1910, RKA, 3009.

[40] Oswald to Colonial Office, 26 December and 29 December 1910, RKA, 3009.

[41] Jahn to Kersting, 16 May 1911, RKA, 3010.

[42] SMS *Emden* to Admiral's Staff Office, 31 January 1911, BA/MA, 3438.

[43] Kersting to Governor, 10 June 1911, RKA, 3010.

[44] SMS *Emden* to Admiral's Staff Office, 18 February 1911, BA/MA, 3438.

[45] *Amtsblatt fur das Schutzgebiet Neuguinea*, 1 March 1911, pp. 27-8.

[46] Kersting to Governor, 10 June 1911, RKA, 3010.

[47] Oswald to Colonial Office, 29 December 1910, RKA, 3009.

[48] A full account of the trial is to be found in RKA, 3010: Gerichtsprotokoll des summarischen Verfahrens gegen die Morder von Boeder und seine Kameraden, 23 February 1911.

[49] This is the way present-day Ponapeans remember the execution and may or may not be significant. I am indebted to Nansau Ririn en Kiti, who was a lad of sixteen at the time, for a most moving account of the sequence of events. Two of the condemned rebels had already been transported to Yap with one of the early contingents of Sokehs prisoners. They were executed later.

[50] Kersting to Colonial Office, 15 November 1911, RKA, 3010. The navy's point of view is to be found in, Kpt. Lt. Gartzke, 'Der Aufstand in Ponape und seine Niederwerfung durch S. M. Schiffe, *Emden, Nurnberg, Cormoran* und *Planet*', *Marine Rundschau* (1911), Heft 6.

[51] Kersting to Hahl 13 September 1911, AA, CRS G2, Item W21. Full details of all individual land holdings in Ponape and a copy of the actual land deed issued are enclosed in this report.

[52] Bascom, *Ponape*, pp. 67, 69.

[53] Kersting to Hahl, 21 January 1912, RKA, 2763.

54 'Tuen me Nanmariki pan Kapun', Ponape, 7 April 1913. Thanks are due to Ersin Santos of Ponape for allowing me to see this rare copy of the regulations, and to J. L. Fischer, whose translation (1951) was included.

55 Venantius to Provinzial, 25 March 1911, KM, File 70.

56 MS., Organization und Ziele der Verwaltung im Inselgebiete, H. Kersting, 8 May 1912, Hamburger Weltwirtschaftsarchiv.

57 Deutsche Missions-Chronik, 1913; Kersting to Hahl, 14 November 1913, RKA, 2584.

58 Pers. Com. P. M. Ehrlich, August 1974.

59 Ehrlich, The Sokehs Rebellion.

Chapter 5

1 G. Brown, *George Brown, D.D.: Pioneer Missionary and Explorer: An Autobiography* (London, 1908), pp. 112, 130, 228.

2 'Denkschrift betreffend den Archipel von Neu Brittanien', in Stubel to Bismarck, 20 April 1884, RKA, 2791.

3 Brown, *George Brown, D.D.*, pp. 257-78.

4 H. Schnee, *Bilder aus der Sudsee* (Berlin, 1904), p. 74; R. Salisbury, *Vunamami*, pp. 24, 27.

5 Robertson and Hernsheim to Bismarck, 18 August 1884, RKA, 2791; Schnee, *Bilder*, p. 350.

6 T. S. Epstein, *Capitalism, Primitive and Modern: Some Aspects of Tolai Economic Growth* (Canberra, 1968), p. 39.

7 *Tambu* or *Diwarra*, as the Tolai currency was called, consists of small *Nassa calossa* shells strung on rattan lengths and stored by wrapping them in fathoms (equivalent to two arms' lengths) on larger bamboo coils.

8 Emma Forsayth (*nee* Coe), the daughter of an American father and a Samoan mother, came to Melanesia from Samoa with Thomas Farrell in the 1880s. A shrewd businesswoman, Emma ran the plantation under the name of E. E. Forsayth & Co. and gained the name 'Queen Emma' for the way in which she presided over the commercial and social life of the Europeans in the Gazelle Peninsula. Ralum remained the single most prosperous plantation in the entire Archipelago; it was sold to the Hamburg company, H. R. Wahlen AG, in 1909, reportedly for a sum near £1 million sterling. Emma was also sister-in-law and patron to Richard Parkinson, planter and ethnographer extraordinaire, who made the first detailed study of Tolai life and customs. See R. W. Robson, *Queen Emma* (Sydney, 1965) and a recent novel by Geoffrey Dutton, *Queen Emma of the South Seas* (Macmillan, 1976).

9 MS., Lebenserinnerungen von Eduard Hernsheim, p. 80, Familienarchiv Hernsheim, Staatsarchiv Hamburg.

10 Copy of 'indenture' between Parkinson and the 'chiefs and rulers' of Kalil and Vairiki, 10 October 1884, RKA, 2572; Stubel to Bismarck, 6 August 1883, RKA, 2787.

11 'Denkschrift betreffend die deutschen and fremden Interessen', RKA, 2791; P. Biskup (ed.), *The New Guinea Memoirs of Jean Baptiste Octave Mouton* (Canberra, 1974) p. 24.

12 See for example, W. D. Pitcairn, *Two Years Among the Savages of New Guinea* (London, 1891), p. 176 and H. Cayley-Webster, *Through New Guinea and the Cannibal Countries* (London, 1898) p. 87.

[13] Epstein, *Capitalism Primitive and Modern*, p. 37.

[14] *Nachrichten uber Kaiser Wilhelmsland und den Bismarck Archipel*, 1891, p. 14.

[15] Rickard to Schmiele, 29 March 1890, and Protocol 4 April 1890, AA, Series AA63/83, Box 39, File 6.

[16] MS., Tagebuch, R. Parkinson, Museum fur Volkerkunde Hamburg; Schmiele, 8 April 1890, RKA, 2979.

[17] *Nachrichten*, 1893, p. 24; 1894, pp. 16, 20-1.

[18] MS., Tagebuch, Vol. 1, J. Weber, MSCM (Mission du Sacre Coeur Archives, Munster).

[19] P. Biskup (ed.), *The New Guinea Memoirs of Jean Baptiste Octave Mouton* (Canberra, 1974), p. 114.

[20] Salisbury, *Vunamami*, p. 80.

[21] SMS *Sperber* to Admiral, 26 January 1894, copy in RKA, 2983.

[22] Couppe to New Guinea Company, 5 August 1894, RKA, 2571; *Nachrichten*, 1897, pp. 24, 45.

[23] For many of the details about To Bobo I am indebted to Salisbury's study of Vunamami.

[24] A. Hahl, *Gouverneursjahre in Neuguinea* (Berlin, 1937), pp. 20-1.

[25] Hahl to Company Governor, 22 July 1896 and 22 March 1897, RKA, 2276.

[26] Salisbury, *Vunamami*, p. 115.

[27] Epstein, *Capitalism Primitive and Modern*, p. 38: Table 1 and notes.

[28] *Nachrichten*, 1896, pp. 33-4; 1897, pp. 49-50.

[29] *Annual Reports*, 1899-1900, p. 185.

[30] *Annual Reports*, 1898-99, p. 168.

[31] Salisbury, *Vunamami*, p. 30.

[32] Couppe to New Guinea Company, 5 August 1894, RKA, 2571; Couppe to Hahl 12 March 1897, RKA, 2574.

[33] *Nachrichten*, 1897, pp. 66-8.

[34] New Guinea Company to Colonial Dept, 23 August 1890, RKA, 2979.

[35] Schnee to Colonial Dept, 8 April 1899, RKA, 2987.

[36] Rose to Bismarck, 29 May 1890, RKA, 2979; see also Oertzen to SMS *Albatross*, 13 February 1886, RKA, 2976.

Chapter 6

[1] *Annual Reports*, 1898-99, pp. 161-5; *Deutsches Kolonialblatt* 1899, pp. 89, 405-6; *Koloniale Monatsblatter*, I/1899, pp. 44-6.

[2] MS., Peter the Island King, Papers of W. C. Groves, 1825, in possession of Mrs D. K. Groves, Hawthorne, Victoria.

[3] Peter G. Sack, *Land between two Laws: Early European Land Acquisitions in New Guinea* (Canberra, 1973), pp. 112-13.

[4] The only extant copy of this regulation is to be found in the Parliamentary Papers of the Commonwealth of Australia, *Report to the League of Nations on the Administration of the Territory of New Guinea*, September 1914 to 30 June 1921, Appendix B, p. 40.

[5] Hahl to Colonial Dept, 30 May 1906, RKA, 2763. There were some 400 Tolai engaged on road-building projects for the administration in 1906.

Notes chap. 6

6 *Annual Reports*, 1909-10, pp. 170-3; Epstein, *Capitalism Primitive and Modern*, pp. 39, 41, 44; Salisbury, *Vunamami*, pp. 118, 242-3.

7 Firth, German Recruitment, p. 175. The figure of ten per cent is the same as the percentage of all contacted villagers in German New Guinea estimated to have worked for Europeans by 1913, which is a high overall figure (see p. 155). But considering the continuous and close contact the Tolai had always had with the European economy, their percentage contribution to the work force in 1910 was decidedly low.

8 *Annual Reports*, 1902-03, Anlage E IV.

9 Hahl to Colonial Dept, 23 January 1901, RKA, 2575; Salisbury, *Vunamami*, p. 82.

10 P. G. Irwin, 'Land Use and Tenure in the Blanche Bay District of New Britain', *The Australian Geographer*, X, 2 (1966), p. 99; R. G. Crocombe (ed.), *Land Tenure in the Pacific* (Melbourne, 1971), pp. 311, 313.

11 'Bericht betreffend die Unruhen am Varzin . . .', Assessor Wolff, 5 August 1902, RKA, 2989.

12 ibid.

13 Wolff to Colonial Dept, 20 May 1902, RKA, 2989.

14 Colonial Department Denkschrift, 27 February 1904, RKA, 2990.

15 'Bericht betreffend die Unruhen am Varzin . . .', RKA, 2989.

16 *Annual Reports*, 1902-03, pp. 94-7 and 1903-04, p. 90.

17 Report of Br L. Dorfler, 25 April 1926, Braam Collection, MSCM. These papers contain a preliminary investigation of the Bainings incident to decide whether a case existed for the canonisation of Rascher.

18 Hahl to Colonial Dept, 6 November 1904, RKA, 2577.

19 Quoted in Militarpolitische Bericht, SMS *Moewe*, 28 August 1904, BA/MA, 5186.

20 Hahl to Colonial Dept, 6 November 1904, RKA, 2577.

21 MS., Tagebuch Weber, Vol. 1, MSCM.

22 Collectanea Rascher I, Braam Collection.

23 *Annual Reports*, 1912-13, pp. 172-3.

24 Stubel to Governor, 12 April 1914, RKA, 2313.

25 Ibid.; *Annual Reports*, 1902-03, Anlage E IV.

26 Militarpolitische Bericht, SMS *Cormoran*, 23 July 1911, BA/MA, 5187; Militarpolitische Bericht, SMS *Condor*, 2 February 1910, BA/MA, 5186.

27 H. Nevermann, *Die Admiralitats Inseln. Ergebnisse der Sudsee Expedition 1908-1910* (Hamburg, 1934), pp. 18-27, 48-60.

28 Von Bennigsen to Colonial Dept, 26 February 1900, RKA, 2987.

29 Von Bennigsen to Colonial Dept, 24 August 1900, RKA, 2988.

30 *Die Katholischen Mission*, 1907-08, No. 3, p. 69.

31 'Bericht des Bezirksrichters Knabe . . .' in Hahl to Colonial Dept, June 1904, RKA, 2990.

32 Hahl to Colonial Office, 21 April 1908, RKA, 2993.

33 Colonial Office to Hahl, 5 October 1908, RKA, 2993.

34 'Bericht des Bezirksamtmann Herbertshohe . . .' 25 December 1907, RKA, 2992.

35 'Application for Restoration of Title', Roman Catholic Mission Kavieng, 10 September 1962, Land Restoration Files, TPNG Dept of District Administration.

36 ibid.

37 Firth, German Recruitment, p. 172; Militarpolitische Bericht, SMS *Cormoran*, 31 August 1911, BA/MA, 5187.

[38] *Annual Reports*, 1912-13, pp. 185-6; Firth, German Recruitment, pp. 325-6; Sack, *Land Between Two Laws*, pp. 98, 175.

[39] 'Denkschrift betreffend die hauptsachlichsten Forderungen fur die weitere Entwicklung des Schutzgebiets in den drei Rechnungsjahren 1915, 1916, 1917', AA, AA63/83, Box 138, File 2.

[40] *Annual Reports*, 1902-03, p. 95.

[41] See lists of poll tax returns in AA, AA63/83, Box 135, Files 1 and 14; 138, File 2.

[42] Hahl to Colonial Office, 24 May 1913, RKA, 3108.

[43] Stubel to Governor, 12 April 1914, RKA, 2313; Firth, German Recruitment, p. 163.

[44] Draft Ordinance on Restriction of Recruiting, Hahl, 30 April 1909, RKA, 2311.

[45] DHPG Branch Mioko to Headquarters, Apia, 7 March 1914, German Collection, Government of Western Samoa.

[46] *Amtsblatt fur das Schutzgebiet Neuguinea*, 15 April 1914.

Chapter 7

[1] See Mikloucho-Maclay, *New Guinea Diaries 1871-1883*, tr. C. L. Sentinella, (Madang, 1975); F. Greenop, *Who Travels Alone* (Sydney, 1944); P. Lawrence, *Road Belong Cargo* (Manchester, 1964).

[2] Oertzen to Bismarck, 3 December 1884, RKA, 2797; O. Finsch, *Samoafahrten. Reisen in Kaiser Wilhelmsland und Englisch Neu Guinea* (Leipzig, 1888), pp. 28-69.

[3] *Nachrichten*, 1885, II, p. 9.

[4] *Geschaftsbericht der Direktion der Neu Guinea Compagnie*, 1888, 9:2; Neu Guinea Compagnie, Instruktion fur Landeshauptmann, 1885, copy in RKA, 2408.

[5] Firth, German Recruitment, p. 88.

[6] Von Schleinitz to New Guinea Company, 27 August 1887, in RKA, 4781.

[7] *Nachrichten*, 1888, pp. 233-4.

[8] Judgment delivered by J. Phillips at Madang, 25 May 1932 . . ., Central Court of the Territory of New Guinea Records. I am indebted to Dr P. G. Sack, A.N.U., for access to this document.

[9] Quoted in Sack, *Land Between Two Laws*, p. 140.

[10] E. F. Hannemann, 'Village Life and Social Change in Madang Society', mimeographed (n.d.).

[11] E. Kriele, *Das Kreuz unter den Palmen* (Barmen, 1927) p. 64; *Berichte der Rheinischen Missionsgesellschaft*, 1893, pp. 341-3.

[12] Firth, German Recruitment, p. 108.

[13] 'Instruktion fur das Verhalten der Kommandanten der Kaiserlichen Kriegsschiffe . . .', enclosed in Foreign Office to New Guinea Company, 6 June 1887, RKA, 2657.

[14] Heusner to Admiralty, 19 December 1887, BA/MA, 7577.

[15] Twenty-six New Irelanders were killed and several marines wounded during a series of punitive raids in 1886 by SMS *Albatross*; Admiralty to Bismarck, 11 April 1886, RKA, 2976.

[16] Quoted in Rose to Bismarck, 29 May 1890, RKA, 2979.

[17] Rose to Caprivi, 9 September 1891, RKA, 2980.

[18] 'Instruktion fur wissenschaftliche Expeditionen', 1885, in RKA, 2408.

[19] 'Verlauf der Expedition', Rudiger, 13 April 1896, and Hahl to Chancellor, 1 September 1897, RKA, 2363.

[20] Lauterbach to Colonial Dept, 23 October 1896 and 12 December 1896, RKA, 2369.

[21] S. G. Firth, 'The New Guinea Company 1885-1899: a Case of Unprofitable Imperialism', *Historical Studies* (October 1972), p. 376.
[22] Schnee Papers, 22:8, Staatsarchiv Berlin-Dahlem.
[23] Firth, German Recruitment, pp. 120, 125.
[24] G. Pilhofer, *Geschichte der Neuendettelsauer Mission in Neuguinea* (Neuendettelsau, 1961) Bd.I, p. 71.
[25] Flierl to Deinzer, 23 July 1891, NH (Neuendettelsau Hauptarchiv), Flierl Letters; Rose to Caprivi, 5 October 1890, RKA, 2409.
[26] Flierl to Deinzer, 9 October 1894, Flierl Letters.
[27] Flierl to Deinzer, 3 May 1893, Flierl Letters. See also *Nachrichten*, 1896, p. 65: as 'peace people', the missionaries were exempted by local people from any blame for a smallpox epidemic which raged through the area in 1895.
[28] *Annual Reports*, 1898-99, pp. 174-6; Pilhofer, *Geschichte der Neuendettelsauer Mission*, I, p. 107.
[29] Kriele, *Das Kreuz unter den Palmen*, p. 35.
[30] Jahresbericht Ragetta 1899, RMG (Rheinische Missions-Gesellschaft Archives), Stationen.
[31] Flierl to Deinzer, 23 July 1891, Flierl Letters.
[32] Lawrence, *Road Belong Cargo*, p. 53.
[33] Conferenz January 1899, RMG, Conferenzprotokolle II.
[34] *Annual Reports*, 1899-1900, pp. 202-3; *Deutsches Kolonialblatt*, June 1900, p. 406.
[35] Kriele, *Das Kreuz unter den Palmen*, p. 64.
[36] SMS Falke to Admiral, 12 January 1896, BA/MA, 666; Firth, German Recruitment, p. 121.
[37] H. Chewings, *Amongst Tropical Seas* (Adelaide, 1900) p. 14.
[38] Jahresberichte Siar 1900 and 1903, RMG, Stationen.
[39] *Annual Reports*, 1903-04, Anlage EIII, p. 341.
[40] Vorstand to Deputation, 29 August 1904, RMG, Conferenzprotokolle II.
[41] The following account of the Madang revolt is based on an analysis of a range of European observations, including Station and Annual Reports of the Rhenish Mission; Administration Reports (Hahl and Stuckhardt, RKA, 2990 and 2992); Papers of H. E. Woodman (Notes of evidence by natives in the Jomba Plains land case), Pacific Manuscripts Bureau, Reel 602; E. F. Hannemann, 'Village Life and Social Change in Madang Society', (n.d.); Kriele, *Das Kreuz unter den Palmen*; and Lawrence, *Road Belong Cargo*.
[42] Stuckhardt to Hahl, 23 October 1906, RKA, 2992.
[43] Vorstandssitzung, 27 August 1904, and Vorstand to Deputation, 29 August 1904, RMG. Conferenzprotokolle II.
[44] *Annual Reports*, 1907-08, p. 7; Lawrence, *Road Belong Cargo*, p. 43.
[45] *Amtsblatt fur das Schutzgebiet Neuguinea*, 15 April 1914, p. 133.
[46] Judgment delivered by J. Phillips, 25 May 1932.
[47] Lawrence, *Road Belong Cargo*, pp. 69-72 explains the substance and significance of this belief which he obtained from fieldwork in the southern Madang district, 1953 to 1958.
[48] Jahresberichte Ragetta 1905 and Bongu 1905, RMG, Stationen. The use of confessional rivalry in this version is an interesting extension of the villagers' feelings of oppression.
[49] *Annual Reports*, 1907-08, p. 7, and 1910-11, p. 155.

[50] Firth, German Recruitment, p. 156.

[51] RKA Denkschrift, 'Stand der Missionen in Deutsch Neu Guinea', 10 November 1908, RKA, 2565; Annual Reports, 1910-11, p. 161, and 1911-12, p. 158.

[52] The sources referring to this movement are fragmentary. Compare: Protokoll, 17 March 1907 and Deputation to Conferenz, 12 August 1907, RMG, Conferenzprotokolle II; Berichte der Rheinischen Missionsgesellschaft, 1907, pp. 54, 90.

[53] Berichte der Rheinischen Missionsgesellschaft, 1910, p. 100; Kriele, Das Kreuz unter den Palmen, p. 126.

[54] Protocol Scholz, 18 September 1908, AA, AA63/83, Box 225.

[55] 'Stand der Missionen', 10 November 1908, RKA, 2565; R. M. Wiltgen, 'Catholic Mission Plantations in mainland New Guinea', The History of Melanesia (ed.) K. Inglis (Canberra, 1971) pp. 350-1.

[56] Judgment delivered by J. Phillips, 25 May 1932.

[57] Amtsblatt fur das Schutzgebiet Neuguinea, 15 November 1911, p. 242; Scholz to Colonial Office, 3 September 1912, RKA, 2995.

[58] Quoted in Judgment delivered by J. Phillips, 25 May 1932.

[59] Testimony of tultul Tagari, enclosed in Scholz to Colonial Office, 3 September 1912, RKA, 2995.

[60] Militarpolitische Bericht, SMS Condor, 28 September 1912, copy in RKA, 2995.

[61] J. Flierl, Forty Years in New Guinea (Wartburg, 1927) p. 93; Sack, Land Between two Laws, pp. 172-5; 'Stand der Missionen', 10 November 1908, RKA, 2565.

[62] MS., Die Seele der Papua Christen in der ersten Generation, C. Keysser, NH, Christian Keysser Papers.

[63] Pilhofer, Geschichte der Neuendettelsauer Mission, I, pp. 126, 131-9.

[64] I. Willis, Lae, Village and City (Melbourne, 1974) pp. 2-5; P. G. Sack, The Bloodthirsty Laewomba? (Canberra, 1976).

[65] K. Holzknecht, 'The Exploration of the Markham Valley', Journal of the Morobe District Historical Society (December 1973), pp. 44-5; H. Bottger, Friede auf Erden (Neuendettelsau, 1912) pp. 5-8.

[66] MS., Die Seele der Papua Christen, Part I, Ch. 2, Keysser Papers.

[67] Willis, Lae, p. 41.

[68] Kriele, Das Kreuz unter den Palmen, pp. 140, 147-8. For recruiting statistics see Firth, German Recruitment, p. 170.

[69] See Lawrence, Road Belong Cargo.

[70] See for example, R. Neuhauss, Deutsch Neu Guinea (Berlin, 1911) Vol. I; O. Manganau, 'My Grandfather's Experience with the Germans', Oral History, No. 6, 1973.

[71] Quoted in L. P. Mair, Australia in New Guinea (Melbourne, 1970) p. 34.

Chapter 8

[1] See for example, W. H. Pearson, 'The Reception of European Voyagers on Polynesian Islands 1568-1797', Journal de la Societe des Oceanistes, 26 (1970), pp. 123-50.

[2] Braisby note, DR, I, p. 37.

[3] T. O. Ranger, Revolt in Southern Rhodesia 1896-7: A Study in African Resistance (London, 1967) p. 353.

[4] B. Barber, 'Acculturation and Messianic Movements', *American Sociological Review*, 6 (1941), p. 664.

[5] See p. 60.

[6] Karlowa to Hahl, 10 March 1906, RKA, 2992.

[7] Flierl to Deinzer, 8 April 1893, Flierl Letters.

[8] See for example, statement by Lauaki, 27 February 1909, and speech at Safotulafai, 18 December 1908, DR, II: 275-323.

[9] Williams to Solf, 3 April 1909, Solf Papers, 30.

[10] Knake to Colonial Dept, 27 August 1904, RKA, 2991.

[11] See p. 189.

[12] Quoted in Kersting to Hahl, 28 February 1911, RKA, 2584.

Chapter 9

[1] See pp. 165-6.

[2] According to H. C. Brookfield and D. Hart, *Melanesia: A Geographical Interpretation of an Island World* (London, 1971), p. 264, casual wage labour was still the norm throughout Melanesia in the late 1960s and long-term contract labour was declining.

[3] See p. 63.

[4] P. Worsley, *The Trumpet Shall Sound: A Study of 'Cargo' Cults in Melanesia* (London, 1970), pp. 285-96. See also B. McLaughlin (ed.), *Studies in Social Movements: A Social Psychological Perspective* (New York, 1969) and C. J. Friedrich, 'Political Leadership and the Problem of the Charismatic Power', *Journal of Politics*, 23 (1961).

[5] See pp. 158-9.

[6] Compare D. H. Pitt, *Tradition and Economic Progress in Samoa*, pp. 114-15.

[7] F. M. Keesing, *Modern Samoa* (London, 1934), p. 81.

[8] Compare E. Stokes, 'Traditional Resistance Movements and Afro-Asian Nationalism: The Context of the 1857 Mutiny Rebellion in India', *Past and Present*, No. 48, 1970.

[9] See, for example, J. Iliffe, *Tanganyika under German Rule, 1905-1912* (Cambridge, 1969); T. O. Ranger, 'Connections between Primary Resistance Movements and Modern Mass Nationalism in East and Central Africa', *Journal of African History*, No. 12, 1968. The classical expression of the early 'resister-collaborator' idea is to be found in R. Robinson and J. Gallagher, *Africa and the Victorians: The Official Mind of Imperialism* (London, 1961).

[10] See p. 103.

[11] See p. 107.

[12] Hahl to Colonial Office, 19 December 1912, RKA, 2584.

[13] J. F. Ade Ajayi in *Emerging Themes of African History*, ed. T. O. Ranger (Dar-es-Salaam, 1965), pp. 189-200.

Abbreviations

Archival collections are described fully the first time they are cited; thereafter abbreviations only are used. For private papers the place of repository is mentioned the first time only; subsequent references are simply to the papers themselves.

AA	Australian Archives, Canberra
Annual Reports	*Jahresberichte uber die Entwicklung der Deutschen Schutzgebiete in den Jahren . . .*
BA/MA	Bundesarchiv/Militararchiv, Freiburg
DHPG	Deutsche Handels-und Plantagen-Gesellschaft der Sudsee Inseln zu Hamburg
DR	'A Documentary Record and History of the Lauati Rebellion in Western Samoa—1909'. 3 vols. Compiled by A. L. Braisby. New Zealand National Archives, Wellington.
KM	Kapuziner Mission Archives, Munster
LMS	London Missionary Society
MSCM	Mission du Sacre Coeur Archives, Munster
NH	Neuendettelsau Hauptarchiv Evangelische-Lutherische Missionsanstalt
RKA	Reichskolonialamt Records, Potsdam. Three different central authorities are represented in this series: the Foreign Office up to 1890, the Colonial Department of the Foreign Office from 1890-1907 and the Colonial Office after May 1907. For the sake of simplicity the designation RKA will be used to cover the entire set of records.
RMG	Rheinische Missions-Gesellschaft Archives, Wuppertal-Barmen

Select Bibliography

A. Manuscript Sources

Zentrales Staatsarchiv, Potsdam
Group 1: Vols 2262-2297 Ansiedlung und Auswanderung
    2:         2298-2346 Arbeitersachen
    5:         2362-2380 Expeditionen und Reisende
    8:         2393-2517 Gesellschaften und Vereine
    10:        2532-2564 Handelssachen und Schiffahrt
    11:        2566-2610 Kirchensachen
    13:        2642-2667 Marinesachen
    14:        2668-2679 Polizeisachen
    17:        2716, 2717 Reichstagssachen
    21:        2763-2777 Steuerwesen
    25:        2785-2806 Vermischtes Neuguinea
    26:        2807-2926 Vermischtes Samoa
    28:        2939-3167 Verwaltungssachen
Sudsee-Akten: 4780-5545 Rechtssachen
Bundesarchiv, Koblenz
   Papers of Wilhelm Solf
Bundesarchiv-Militararchiv, Freiburg
   Records of German Admiralitat, Reichsmarineamt, Admiralstab.
   Bundle Numbers: 623-30, 3431-2, 3438, 5069, 5117, 5122, 5186-8, 7555, 7577.
Staatsarchiv, Hamburg
   Archiv der DHPG 1878-1917
   Archiv der Jaluit Gesellschaft 1887-1914
   Familienarchiv Hernsheim
Hamburger Weltwirtschaftsarchiv
   Book Collection: MS., Organization und Ziele der Verwaltung im Inselgebiete,
     H. Kersting.
   Personenarchiv: Eduard Hernsheim
Museum fur Volkerkunde, Hamburg
   MS., Tagebuch, Richard Parkinson 1890.
Geheimes Staatsarchiv, Berlin-Dahlem
   Papers of Heinrich Schnee
Hauptarchiv Evang.-Luth. Missionsanstalt, Neuendettelsau
   Letters of Johann Flierl
   Neuguinea: Anfange der Neuguinea Mission
   Papers of Christian Keysser

Rheinische Missions-Gesellschaft, Wuppertal-Barmen
The RMG has since been merged with other Lutheran groups to form the Vereinigte Rheinische Mission.
Korrespondenz: Heimatleitung-Prases Neuguinea 1898-1920
Neuguinea: Conferenzprotokolle I-IV 1890-1922
Stationen: Bogadjim 1899-1924, Bongu 1899-1918, Ragetta 1899-1932, Siar 1900-1911
Referate Neuguinea
Herz Jesu Mission (MSC), Munster
Manuscripts and Diaries
Collection of Johannes Braam: Akten zu Baininger Martyrer
Kapuziner Mission (Rhein Westfalen), Munster
Files 58, 59, 69, 70, 75, 76, 97, 102
London Missionary Society, London
South Seas, Boxes 38-54
South Seas Personal, Boxes 1, 3
South Seas Odds, Boxes 4, 5
Personal: Papers of J. E. Newell
New Zealand National Archives, Wellington
MS., A documentary Record and History of the Lauati Rebellion in Western Samoa 1909. A collection of documents compiled by A. L. Braisby from Native Office records, Vols I-III.
German Administration Papers (Translated Typescripts, T. Newbury)
Australian Archives, Canberra
Series CRS G1 and G2
AA63/83, Boxes 38-77, 135-8, 154, 201-227
Australian National University, Dept Pacific and SE. Asian History
Papers of J. W. Davidson
Papers of R. P. Gilson
Government of Western Samoa, Prime Ministers Office
Papers relating to the German Period
Private manuscripts obtained from Ersin Santos, Ponape; S. H. Riesenberg with the permission of A.N.U. Press The M.S. of The Book of Luelen; Pacific Manuscripts Bureau, Papers of W. C. Groves (No. 611) and H. E. Woodman (No. 602); P. G. Sack, (Judgment delivered by J. Phillips at Madang 1932, and Land Titles Restoration files).

B. Printed Sources

Official and Unofficial Collections:
Amtsblatt fur das Schutzgebiet Deutsch Neuguinea, Vols 1-6.
Aus den Missionen. Jahresberichte der Kapuziner Mission, 1910-1912.
Deutsche Kolonialzeitung. Organ des deutschen Kolonialvereins, 1884-1914.
Deutsches Kolonialblatt, 1890-1914.
DKB Supplement: *Das Deutsche Schutzgebiet der Neu Guinea Kompagnie in der Sudsee,* 1892.
Jahresberichte uber die Entwicklung der Deutschen Schutzgebiete in den Jahren 1898/1899 und 1899/1900.
Jahresberichte uber die Entwicklung der Deutschen Schutzgebiete in den Jahren

Select Bibliography

1900/1901—1908/1909: *Denkschriften uber die Entwicklung der Deutschen Schutzgebiete in Afrika und in der Sudsee. Berichtsjahre 1900/1901—1908/1909,* plus *Anlagen.*
Die Deutsche Schutzgebiete in Afrika und der Sudsee. Amtliche Jahresberichte, 1909/1910—1911/1912.
Geschaftsberichte der Neu Guinea Kompagnie, 1887-1911.
Gott will es. Organ des Afrika Vereins deutscher Katholiken 1899-1914.
Nachrichten uber Kaiser Wilhelms-Land und den Bismarck Archipel. Vols 1-14, 1885-1898. Official organ of the New Guinea Company during its administration of the protectorate. The original title was *Nachrichten fur und uber Kaiser Wilhelms-Land und den Bismarck Archipel* (1885-1886).
Samoanisches Gouvernements Blatt. Apia, 1900-1913.
Samoanische Zeitung. Apia, 1901-1914.
Stenographische Berichte uber die Verhandlungen des Reichstags, 1884-1914.

Books and Articles:

Barber, B., 'Acculturation and Messianic Movements'. *American Sociological Review,* Vol. 6, 1941.
Bascom, W. R., *Ponape: A Pacific Economy in Transition. Anthropological Records,* Vol. 22 (Berkeley, 1965).
Biskup, P., 'Dr Albert Hahl—Sketch of a German Colonial Official', *Australian Journal of Politics and History,* xiv, December 1968.
—— (ed.), *The New Guinea Memoirs of Jean Baptiste Octave Mouton* (Canberra, 1974).
Bottger, H., *Friede auf Erden: Ein Friedensschluss im Markhamtale.* Neuendettelsau Missions Schriften No. 17 (Neuendettelsau, 1912), and No. 19 (Neuendettelsau, 1912).
Brenninkmeyer, L., *Funfzehn Jahre beim Bergvolk der Baininger* (Dusseldorf, 1928).
Brookes, J. I., *International Rivalry in the Pacific Islands, 1800-1875* (Berkeley, 1941).
Brookfield, H. C. with D. Hart, *Melanesia: A Geographical Interpretation of an Island World* (London, 1971).
Brown, G., *George Brown, D. D.: Pioneer Missionary and Explorer: An Autobiography* (London, 1908).
Burger, F., *Die Kusten und Bergvolker der Gazellehalbinsel* (Stuttgart, 1913).
——, *Aus Neupommerns dunklen Waldern. Erlebnisse auf einer Forschungsreise durch Neu Guinea* (Minden, 1925).
Cayley-Webster, H., *Through New Guinea and the Cannibal Countries* (London, 1898).
Chewings, H., *Amongst Tropical Islands. Notes and Observations during a Visit in 1899 to New Guinea, New Britain and the Solomon Islands* (Adelaide, 1900).
Cheyne, A., *Islands in the Western Pacific Ocean* (London, 1852).
Christian, F. W., *The Caroline Islands* (London, 1899).
Coale, G. L., A Study of Chieftainship, Missionary Contact and Culture Change on Ponape 1852-1900, M.A. thesis, University of Southern California, 1951.
Crocombe, R. G. (ed.), *Land Tenure in the Pacific* (Melbourne, 1971).
Danks, B., *In Wild New Britain. The Story of Benjamin Danks, Pioneer Missionary,* (ed.) W. Deane (Sydney, 1933).

Davidson, J. W., *Samoa mo Samoa. The Emergence of the Independent State of Western Samoa* (Oxford, 1967).

Davidson, J. W. and Scarr, D. (eds), *Pacific Islands Portraits* (Canberra, 1970).

Deeken, R., *Die Karolinen* (Berlin, n.d.)

——, *Die Auswanderung nach den deutschen Kolonien unter Berücksichtigung der wirtschaftlichen und klimatischen Verhältnisse* (Berlin, 1908).

——, *Manuia Samoa: Samoanische Skizzen und Beobachtungen* (Oldenburg, 1901).

Dutton, G., *Queen Emma of the South Seas: A Novel* (Melbourne, 1976).

Ebert, P., *Südsee Erinnerungen* (Leipzig, 1924).

Ehrlich, P., The Sokehs Rebellion 1910-1911, Paper presented to ASAO Conference, Florida, 1975.

Epstein, T. S., *Capitalism, Primitive and Modern: Some Aspects of Tolai Economic Growth* (Canberra, 1968).

Finsch, O., *Samoafahrten. Reisen in Kaiser Wilhelms Land und Englisch Neu Guinea in den Jahren 1884 und 1885 an Bord des deutschen Dampfers 'Samoa'* (Leipzig, 1888).

Firth, S. G., German Recruitment and Employment of Labourers in the Western Pacific before the First World War. D. Phil. thesis, Oxford University, 1973.

——, 'The New Guinea Company, 1885-1899: A Case of Unprofitable Imperialism', *Historical Studies*, Vol. 15, No. 59, 1972.

Fischer, D., *Unter Südseeinsulanern. Das Leben des Forschers Mikloucho Maclay* (Leipzig, 1955).

Fischer, J. L., *The Eastern Carolines* (New Haven, 1957).

Fischer, J. L., Riesenberg, S. H. and Whiting, M. G. (eds), *The Book of Luelen* (Canberra, 1977).

Flierl, J., *Gottes Wort in den Urwäldern von Neu Guinea* (Neuendettelsau 1920).

——, *Forty Years in New Guinea* (Wartburg, 1927).

——, *Observations and Experiences* (Tanunda, 1936).

——, *Unter Wilden. Missionarische Anfangsarbeit im Innern von Neuguinea* (Neuendettelsau, 1932).

Fox, J. W. and Cumberland, K. B. (eds), *Western Samoa: Land, Life and Agriculture in Tropical Polynesia* (Christchurch, 1962).

Frerichs, A. C., *Anutu Conquers in New Guinea* (Ohio, 1957).

Friedrich, C. J., 'Political Leadership and the Problem of the Charismatic Power', *Journal of Politics*, Vol. 23, 1961.

Fritz, G., *Ad Majorem Dei Gloriam! Die Vorgeschichte des Aufstandes von 1910/11 in Ponape* (Leipzig, 1912).

——, *Die Kapuziner in Ponape* (Place of publication unknown, 1913).

Gartzke, Kpt. Lt., 'Der Aufstand in Ponape und seine Niederwerfung durch S.M. Schiffe Emden, Nürnberg, Cormoran und Planet (Nach amtlichen Berichten)', *Marine Rundschau*, 1911, 6. Heft (Sonderabdruck).

Gifford, P. and Louis, W. R. (eds), *Britain and Germany in Africa. Imperial Rivalry and Colonial Rule* (New Haven, 1967).

Gilson, R. P., *Samoa, 1830-1900: The Politics of a Multi-Cultural Community* (Melbourne, 1970).

Greenop, F., *Who Travels Alone* (Sydney, 1944).

Hagen, B., *Unter den Papuas. Beobachtungen und Studien über Land und Leute, Thier und Pflanzenwelt in Kaiser Wilhelms Land* (Wiesbaden, 1899).

Select Bibliography

Hagen, M. von, *Bismarcks Kolonialpolitik* (Berlin, 1923).

Hahl, A., 'Mitteilungen über Sitten und rechtliche Verhältnisse auf Ponape' *Ethnologisches Notizblatt*, 2(2), 1901.

——, *Deutsch Neuguinea* (Berlin, 1936).

——, *Gouverneursjahre in Neuguinea* (Berlin, 1937).

——, *Deutsche Kolonien in der Südsee* (Hamburg, 1938).

Hambruch, P., *Ponape*. Ergebnisse der Südsee Expedition, 1908-1910. (Hrsg. G. Thilenius) II. Ethnographie: A. Mikronesia, Bd. 7. Part Volume I: Allgemeine Teil. Part Volume II: Gesellschaft und geistige Kultur.

Hannemann, E. F., *Village Life and Social Change in Madang Society*, mimeographed, n.d.

Hausen, K., *Deutsche Kolonialherrschaft in Afrika. Wirtschaftsinteressen und Kolonialverwaltung in Kamerun vor 1914* (Zürich, 1970).

Hernsheim, E., *Der Bismarck Archipel und seine Zukunft als deutsche Colonie* (Hamburg, 1886).

Hernsheim, F., *Südsee Erinnerungen* (Berlin, 1883).

Hertz, R., *Das Hamburger Seehandelshaus J. C. Godeffroy und Sohn, 1766-1879*. Veröffentlichungen des Vereins für hamburgische Geschichte, Bd. 4 (Hamburg, 1922).

Holzknecht, K., 'The Exploration of the Markham Valley', *Journal of The Morobe District Historical Society*, December, 1973.

Holmes, J. R., 'Aboriginal and Modern Samoa: A Study of Cultural Change based upon L.M.S. journals, 1830-1840', M.A. thesis, Wichita State University, 1967.

Hüskes, P. J., *Pionere der Südsee: Werden und Wachsen der Herz Jesu Mission von Rabaul zum goldenen Jubiläum 1882-1932* (Düsseldorf, 1932).

Iliffe, J., *Tanganyika under German Rule, 1905-1912* (Cambridge, 1969).

Irwin, P. G., 'Land Use and Tenure in the Blanche Bay District of New Britain', *The Australian Geographer*, Vol. x, No. 2, 1966.

Kade, E., *Die Anfänge der deutschen Kolonial-Zentralverwaltung* (Würzburg, 1939).

Keesing, F. M., *Modern Samoa: Its Government and Changing Life* (London, 1934).

Keesing, F. M. and Keesing, M. M., *Elite Communication in Samoa: A Study of Leadership* (Stanford, 1956).

Kennedy, P. M., 'The Partition of the Samoan Islands, 1898-1899', D. Phil thesis, Oxford University, 1970.

——, 'The Development of German Naval Operations Plans Against England 1896-1914', *The English Historical Review*, January, 1974.

——, 'Bismarck's Imperialism: The Case of Samoa, 1880-1890', *Historical Journal*, Vol. xv, No. 2, 1972.

Keysser, C., 'Vom Sattelberg zum Markham', *Zeitschrift für Ethologie*, Vol. 44, 1912.

——, *Anutu im Papualande* (Nürnberg, 1925).

——, *Gottes Weg ins Hubeland* (Neuendettelsau, 1949).

Kleintitschen, P. A., *Die Küstenbewohner der Gazellehalbinsel* (Düsseldorf, 1907).

Koschitzky, M. von, *Deutsche Colonialgeschichte*. Part II (Leipzig, 1888).

Kraft, H. H., *Chartergesellschaften als Mittel zur Erschliessung kolonialer Gebiete. Schriften des Kolonial Instituts der Hansischen Universität*, Bd. 7 (Hamburg, 1943).

Krämer, A., *Die Samoa Inseln*. 2 Vols (Stuttgart, 1902-03).

Krieger, M., *Neu Guinea*. Bibliothek der Länderkunde (Berlin, 1899).

Kriele, E., *Das Kreuz unter den Palmen. Die Rheinische Mission in Neu Guinea* (Barmen, 1927).

Kurze, G., *Samoa, Land, Leute und Mission* (Berlin, 1900).

Lawrence, P., 'Lutheran Mission Influence on Madang Societies', *Oceania*, xxvii, 1957.

——, *Road Belong Cargo. A Study of the Cargo Movement in the Southern Madang District New Guinea* (Melbourne/Manchester, 1964).

Leutwein, P., *Dreissig Jahre Deutsche Kolonialpolitik* (Berlin, 1918).

Linckens, H., *Streiflichter aus der Herz Jesu Mission* (Hiltrup, 1921).

Mair, L. P., *Australia in New Guinea* (Melbourne, 1970).

Manganau, O., 'My Grandfather's Experience with the Germans', *Oral History*, No. 6, 1973.

Mannoni, O., *Prospero and Caliban. The Psychology of Colonization.* Tr. P. Powesland (London, 1956).

McKay, C. G. R., *Samoana* (Wellington, 1968).

McLaughlin, B. (ed.), *Studies in Social Movements: A Social Psychological Perspective* (New York, 1969).

Masterman, S., *Origins of International Rivalry in Samoa, 1845-1884* (London, 1934).

Mikloucho-Maclay, *New Guinea Diaries 1871-1883*, tr. C. L. Sentinella (Madang, 1975).

Mitteilungen der Missionare vom heiligsten Herzen Jesu: Aus der deutschen Südsee. Vol. 1: *P. Matthäus Rascher M.S.C. und Baining Land und Leute* (Münster, 1909).

Moors, H. J., *With Stevenson in Samoa* (Boston, 1910).

Moses, J. A., 'The German Empire in Melanesia', *The History of Melanesia*, (ed.) K. Inglis (Canberra/Port Moresby, 1969).

——, 'The Solf Regime in Samoa—Ideal and Reality', *The New Zealand Journal of History*, Vol. 6, No. 1, 1972.

Neuhauss, R., *Deutsch Neu Guinea.* Vols. 1-3 (Berlin, 1911).

——, *Unsere Kolonie Deutsch Neu Guinea* (Weimar, 1914).

Nevermann, H., *Die Admiralitäts Inseln.* Ergebnisse der Südsee Expedition. 1908-1910. Hrsg. G. Thilenius. II. Ethnographie: A. Melanesien Bd. 3 (Hamburg, 1934).

Newbury, C., 'Resistance and Collaboration in French Polynesia: The Tahitian War: 1844-7', *The Journal of the Polynesian Society*, Vol. 82, No. 1, 1973.

Parkinson, R., *Im Bismarck Archipel. Erlebnisse und Beobachtungen auf der Insel Neu Pommern* (Leipzig, 1887).

——, *Dreissig Jahre in der Südsee. Land und Leute, Sitten und Gebräuche im Bismarckarchipel und auf den deutschen Salomoninseln.* Hrsg. B. Ankermann (Stuttgart, 1907).

Pearson, W. H., 'The Reception of European Voyagers on Polynesian Islands 1568-1797', *Journal de la Société des Océanistes*, Vol. 26, 1970.

Pilhofer, G., *Die Geschichte der Neuendettelsauer Mission*, Vols. 1-3. (Neuendettelsau, 1961-63).

Pitcairn, W. D., *Two Years Among the Savages of New Guinea* (London, 1891).

Pitt, D. H., *Tradition and Economic Progress in Samoa: A Case Study of the Role of Traditional Social Institutions in Economic Development* (Oxford, 1970).

Ranger, T. O., *Revolt in Southern Rhodesia, 1896-7: A Study in African Resistance* (London, 1967).

——, 'Connections between Primary Resistance Movements and Modern Mass Nationalism in East and Central Africa', *Journal of African History*, No. 12, 1968.

—— (ed.), *Emerging Themes of African History* (Dar-es-Salaam, 1965).

Riedel, O., *Der Kampf um Deutsch Samoa* (Berlin, 1938).

Riesenberg, S., *The Native Polity of Ponape* (Washington, 1968).

Robinson, R. and Gallagher, J. with Denny, A., *Africa and the Victorians: The Official Mind of Imperialism* (London, 1961).

Robson, R. W., *Queen Emma* (Sydney, 1965).

Rowley, C. D., *The New Guinea Villager. The Impact of Colonial Rule on Primitive Society and Economy* (New York/London, 1966).

Sack, P., 'Early Land Acquisitions in New Guinea: The Native Version', *Journal of the Papua and New Guinea Society*, Vol. 3, No. 2, 1969.

——, *Land Between Two Laws: Early European Land Acquisitions in New Guinea* (Canberra, 1973).

——, 'The Range of Traditional Tolai Remedies', in A. L. Epstein (ed.), *Contention and Dispute: Aspects of Law and Social Control in Melanesia* (Canberra, 1974).

——, *The Bloodthirsty Laewomba?* (Canberra, 1976).

Sahlins, M. D., *Social Stratification in Polynesia* (Seattle, 1958).

Salisbury, R. F., 'Early Stages of Economic Development in New Guinea', *Journal of the Polynesian Society*, Vol. 71, No. 3, 1962.

——, *Vunamami: Economic Transformation in a Traditional Society* (Berkeley/Los Angeles, 1970).

Schmack, K., *J. C. Godeffroy und Sohn: Kaufleute zu Hamburg* (Hamburg, 1938).

Schnee, H., *Bilder aus der Südsee. Unter den kannibalischen Stämmen des Bismarck Archipels* (Berlin, 1904).

——, (Hrsg.) *Deutsches Kolonial Lexikon*, 3 Vols. (Leipzig, 1920).

Schultz (-Ewerth), E., *Die wichtigsten Grundsätze des samoanischen Familien und Erbrechts*. 1st ed. (Apia, 1905).

——, *Samoanische Familien-, Immobiliar- und Erbrechts*, 3rd ed. (Apia, 1911).

——, *Erinnerungen an Samoa* (Berlin, 1926).

Shineberg, D. (ed.), *The Trading Voyages of Andrew Cheyne, 1841-1844* (Canberra, 1971).

Solf, W., *Eingeborene und Ansiedler auf Samoa* (Place of publication unknown, 1908).

——, *Kolonialpolitik. Mein politisches Vermächtnis* (Berlin, 1919).

J. W. Spidle, The German Colonial Civil Service. Organization, Selection and Training, Ph.D. thesis, Stanford University, 1972.

Stokes, E., 'Traditional Resistance Movements and Afro-Asian Nationalism: The Context of the 1857 Mutiny Rebellion in India', *Past and Present*, No. 48, 1970.

Strandmann, H. Pogge von, The Kolonialrat, its Significance and Influence on German Politics from 1890 to 1906, D.Phil. thesis, Oxford University, 1970.

Tetens, A., *Among the Savages of the South Seas. Memoirs of Micronesia, 1862-1868.* Tr. F. M. Spoehr (London, 1958).

Trood, T., *Island Reminiscences* (Sydney, 1912).

Turner, G., *Nineteen Years in Polynesia* (London, 1861).

Vietsch, E. von, *Wilhelm Solf: Botschafter zwischen den Zeiten* (Tübingen, 1961).

Washausen, H., *Hamburg und die Kolonialpolitik des deutschen Reiches, 1880-1890* (Hamburg, 1968).

Watters, R. F., 'The Transition to Christianity in Samoa', *Historical Studies. Australia and New Zealand*, viii, 1959.

Wehler, H. U., *Bismarck und der Imperialismus* (Köln, 1969).

Werner, B. von, *Ein deutsches Kriegsschiff in der Südsee* (Leipzig, 1889).

Werner, L., Geschichte des deutschen Kolonialgebietes in Melanesien, 1866-1899. Typescript in possession of Prof. H. Stoecker, Humboldt Universität, Berlin.

Wiltgen, R., 'Catholic Mission Plantations in Mainland New Guinea', *The History of Melanesia* (ed.) K. Inglis (Canberra, 1971).

Willis, I., *Lae, Village and City* (Melbourne, 1974).

Worsley, P., *The Trumpet Shall Sound: A Study of 'Cargo' Cults in Melanesia.* 2nd edition (London, 1970).

Index

Index

Index

Index

Planters: racial arrogance, 206–7; New Guinea (colonial philosophy) 160, (relations with Hahl) 160–2, (population 1914) 161; Samoa (new arrivals 1902) 38–9, (relations with Solf) 53–4, 65–6

Planters' Society, *see Pflanzerverein*

Police: New Guinea, 130, 141, 183, (under NGC) 128, 137, (deficiencies of) 149–50, 195–6, (Hahl's plans for) 158; Ponape, 81, 94–6, 102, 104, 106, 108, (role in Sokehs revolt) 109–13; *see also Fitafita*; Melanesians

Politics, *see* Traditional politics

Poll tax, *see* Head tax

Polynesia, 74, 216

Pominis, 209; manipulates Europeans, 155–7; new leader, 221–2

Ponam Island, 154

Ponape, 10, 22, 140, 195; physical description of, 9; social structure on, 10; *see also* Sections

Ponapeans: attitude (to disarmament) 84, (to Germans) 112, (to land reforms) 87, 205, 206, (to Nanpei) 78, 90, 91, 93, (to Sokehs revolt) 107, 205, 219–20, (to Spanish) 77, 211–12; reputation for resistance, 73; situation 1914, 117–18

Population, European, New Guinea: in 1900, 140; in 1914, 161

Port Hunter, 119

Port Weber, 125

Posadillo, Captain, 74, 75; *see also* Governor, eastern Carolines

Potsdamhafen, 178, 194, 195

Powers, *see* Three Powers; Western Powers

Proletariat, absence of in German Pacific, 213–14

Proselytism, religious, Ponape, conflict over, 85, 116–17

Protestant Mission, Ponape, 75, 78; *see also* Boston Missionary Society

Protestants: Ponape, conflict with Catholics, 76, 77, 81, 85, 94, 116–17, 220; Samoa, 47

Puin en lolokon, 90, 98; *see also* Advisory council

Pule, 7, 34, 38, 46–8, 55–60, 62, 209, 211, 214, 217

Pulenu'u, 36, 48, 115

Pullack, 44, 45, 49

Punitive expeditions, New Guinea, 138, 139, 141, 144; against Tolai, 122, 127–31; by navy, 170; in Huon Peninsula, 191, 193, 195; to Admiralties, 153–4

Puritanism, of Boston Mission, 74

Pweipwei, 92, 93

Queen Emma, 232; *see also* Forsayth

Quiros, Ferdinand de, 73

Ralum Point, 125

Ramandu, 137

Rambutjo Island, 152

Ramu river, 14, 177; exploration, 172, 173

Rabalankaia, 120

Rabaul, 119, 142

Race relations: key to resistance, 206–7; New Guinea (and Rhenish Mission) 177–8, (at Madang) 180–3, (in Huon Peninsula) 189–91, (in Varzin 1902) 146, (St Paul massacre) 150; Samoa, deteriorating 1914, 71

Ragetta, 181–3, 186, 187, 189, 194

Rai coast, 163, 164, 182, 185, 189, 195

Raluana, 134

Ralum, 126, 127, 131, 133, 140, 144, 201, 207; first plantation, 123; expansion, 125, 127–8, 131; causes conflict, 127–31, 133

Rascher, Matthäus, role in St Paul massacre, 147–50

Ratavul, 122, 142

Ravalien, 131

Rebellion: categorisation, 204, 210–12; explanation of, 205–7, 208; New Guinea (at Madang) 180–3, 187–90, (in Bainings) 147–50; Ponape (against Spanish) 75–9, (possibilities 1900) 79–80, (first threat of 1910) 101, (by

259

Peter Hempenstall is Lecturer in History at the University of Newcastle. He took his B.A. at the University of Queensland in 1970, graduating with first class honours. As a Rhodes Scholar, he studied for his doctorate at Magdalen College, Oxford. In 1974–75 Dr Hempenstall conducted research at The Australian National University, Canberra, where he was a Post-Doctoral Fellow. This book is based upon his doctoral thesis. It was researched in Australia and the Pacific, in Europe and the United Kingdom. Dr Hempenstall's extensive examination and analysis of hitherto inaccessible German archives make this book unique.

This book was designed by Kirsty Morrison.

Text computer photocomposed in 10 point Sabon two point leaded at Computer Graphics Corporation Pty Ltd, Adelaide and printed on 85 gsm Bulky Book Offset at Griffin Press Limited, Netley, South Australia.

160° 180° 160°

JAPAN

40°

N O R T H   P A C I F I C   O C

H A W A I I A N   I S L A N D S

BONINS I   MIDWAY

TROPI

20°   Honolulu OAHU
HAWAII

MARIANA IS

SAIPAN

GUAM

Yap   PONAPE   MARSHALL IS

CAROLINE ISLANDS

0°   GILBERT IS   CHRISTMAS I

BISMARCK ARC.   NAURU   OCEAN I   NIKUNAU

PAPUA
NEW GUINEA   BUKA SOLOMON IS   PHOENIX IS

NEW
BRITAIN   TUVALU   TOKELAU IS

MURUA

LAUGHLAN IS   NUKAPU

VANIKORO

INDISPENSABLE   TIKOPIA
REEF   WALLIS IS   SAMOA

CORAL SEA   NEW   FUTUNA   LEEWARD
HEBRIDES   FIJI VANUA LEVU   GROUP   TAHITI

VITI LEVU   SOCIETY I
Townsville   TANA   Suva   AITUTAKI
HIENGHENE   COOK IS RAROTONGA
20°   Mackay   LOYALTY IS   TONGA   ATIU
NEW
CALEDONIA Noumea   TONGATAPU

AUSTRAL IS
Maryborough

AUSTRALIA   Brisbane

NORFOLK I

KERMADEC IS

Sydney

TASMAN SEA   Auckland

40°   NEW   S O U T H

Wellington

Hobart   ZEALAND   CHATHAM IS

160° 180° 160°